A(ZX)103

**An Introduction to
the Humanities**

The Open University

The Sixties:
Mainstream Culture and Counter-culture

Block 6

This publication forms part of an Open University course A(ZX)103 *An Introduction to the Humanities*. Details of this and other Open University courses can be obtained from the Student Registration and Enquiry Service, The Open University, PO Box 197, Milton Keynes, MK7 6BJ, United Kingdom: tel.+44 (0)870 333 4340, email general-enquiries@open.ac.uk

Alternatively, you may visit the Open University website at http://www.open.ac.uk where you can learn more about the wide range of courses and packs offered at all levels by The Open University

To purchase a selection of Open University course materials visit http://www.open.ac.uk, or contact Open University Worldwide, Michael Young Building, Walton Hall, Milton Keynes MK7 6AA, United Kingdom for a brochure. tel. +44 (0)1908 858785; fax +44 (0)1908 858787; e-mail ouwenq@open.ac.uk

The Open University
Walton Hall, Milton Keynes
MK7 6AA

First published 1998. Second edition 2000. Third edition 2005.

Edited and designed by The Open University.

Typeset by The Open University.

Printed and bound in the United Kingdom by CPI, Bath.

ISBN 0 7492 9670 4

3.1

31612B/A103b6i3.1

INTRODUCTION TO BLOCK 6

In this part of the course, we have chosen to study the 1960s, seeing this as an excellent way of drawing together the various themes and issues of Blocks 1–5. Block 6 has contributions from five different disciplines (History, History of Science, Religious Studies, Music and Art History). To help you find your way through the block, the course team has produced a more extensive introduction than those for the previous five blocks. This introduction discusses the topics you will study and the methodologies employed by the different disciplines, as well as providing hints as to how to approach the block. It is worth devoting some of your study time to a close reading of it.

Why the Sixties?

Part of the argument of the block is that the Sixties were, in Arthur Marwick's words, 'a period of exceptional cultural and social change' (p.23). In particular, it was a time in which the orthodox views of the Western cultural tradition were scrutinized and challenged. Throughout the course we have been taking a critical look at what divides the 'mainstream' from the marginal. What determines boundaries, both in religion and in science, was explicitly examined in Block 4, and you have also looked at other reactions to the mainstream: Friedrich in Block 3 and *Wide Sargasso Sea* in Block 5, to name but two. So it makes sense to look at the part of recent history during which challenges to the mainstream were most prominent (hence the subtitle of the block: 'Mainstream Culture and Counter-culture').

You might think the Sixties are too close to us to be studied properly (after all, many A103 students will have lived through the period). The more recent past is, however, as legitimate an object of study as the distant past. You will see that the History units vividly illustrate that the problems that need to be overcome in writing history (periodization, selection and organization of material) apply just as much to the Sixties as to any other period. Furthermore, there are the same problems with identifying and assessing primary and secondary texts and sorting witting from unwitting testimony that you encountered in Block 3.

That the block is about the Sixties does not mean we need to think of the period as a broad, undifferentiated event. This would be wrong in at least two respects. First, it would not capture the huge variety of experiences of the Sixties. Many people who lived through the decade did not experience the world as changing in any radical manner. This may have been because they experienced incremental changes that happened in their localities, and became aware of larger changes only as relayed to them by the press or the television. That many people would have thought of the larger changes as processes that were going on elsewhere does not mean, of course, that we cannot now look back and assess the changes from a more objective standpoint. The techniques you will learn in the History units will enable you to do that. In particular, you will find that any study such as this is going to involve selecting various aspects of the period and neglecting others (see Units 25 and 26, Section 7). For example, as you read through the block, you will notice that many of the examples are drawn from the United States. This is because, in the opinion of the writers, these examples were the most interesting and significant; after all, in many areas, the United States was leading the field. The contribution of Europe (in particular, the United Kingdom) is not neglected, however, as you will see in the History and Music units.

Second, the rich diversity of examples in the block should make clear the risks involved in making broad generalizations. To take just two examples: in the Religious Studies unit, you will see that the values of the mainstream culture were rejected by some parts of the counter-culture for not being liberal and progressive enough and by others for being too liberal and progressive; in the Art History unit, you will find that Mark Rothko's work, whilst being undeniably modern and in that sense linked with the counter-culture, was seen by its creator as being part of the mainstream tradition of great Western art. How can the counter-culture be progressive and reactionary, modern and mainstream? This is something you will need to ask yourself as you read the block. Remember: when you make claims you need to support them by evidence and argument, and this will mean looking in detail at the discussions in the individual units.

What was the world out of which the Sixties emerged? Arthur Marwick gives us some idea with his brief description of mainstream culture (pp.24–5). However, he would not suggest that the Fifties were any more a monolith than the Sixties. (After all, the first seven James Bond books, which embody many Sixties characteristics, were published in the Fifties.) The past, as Marwick reminds us, is not divided naturally into periods (p.19) and characteristics of the Sixties could be found in the Fifties and the Seventies. In a period study of the Sixties of this length, it is impossible to do justice to the Fifties (that would require a further block). The question we need to ask ourselves is whether it is worthwhile studying the Sixties as a particularly interesting or important time. This is an intriguing question that deserves discussion (see p.23).

The topics you will study

Out of the wealth of cultural initiatives throughout many parts of the developed world, the authors have had to be highly selective in the particular characteristics and issues on which they have focused. The block begins with the History units (Units 25 and 26), which offer an overview of what are seen as some of the most significant cultural changes of the Sixties: increasingly liberal and permissive attitudes towards sexual relationships; growing affluence and consumerism; the enhanced status of youth culture; a proliferation of protest and confrontation; liberation in personal and social relations; and changes in popular culture and entertainment (including music). Each of these strands of cultural development is seen as 'countering' or significantly modifying what had been, prior to 1958, the 'mainstream' or dominant features of Western culture. In some cases, the modifications were so profound that they might be described as components of a 'cultural revolution'. This overview of the decade establishes, then, a summary account of the main events and developments of the time, whilst also offering an interpretative framework within which the contributions of the later units of the block can be located. You will be alerted to the categories of 'mainstream' and 'counter' culture and 'cultural revolution', against which we may judge specific developments in science, religion, music and art.

During the Sixties, there was a shift in public attitudes to science. In particular, scientists themselves became more self-conscious about the work they were doing. The History of Science unit (Unit 27) traces the routes of this to the involvement of science with the military, and explores the attitudes of scientists to the use to which scientific discoveries were being put during the Vietnam War. Within this subject area (History of Science) we are able to look at the way in which the practitioners (the scientists) viewed their own practice (science) and at the way in which counter-cultural forces challenged not only the social and political consequences of science but its claim to objectivity. The unit examines how scientists uncovered the link between a drug that was widely used as a sedative – thalidomide – and physical defects in unborn babies. The role of a woman scientist in uncovering the link leads on to a further discussion of the 'mind set' that underlies scientific practice, and an investigation of the effects of feminist arguments on primatology – the study of primates (which includes humans, apes and monkeys).

In the Religious Studies unit (Unit 28), the emphasis is on the development in the Sixties of New Religious Movements (NRMs). These movements are examined in relation to other prominent strands of Sixties counter-cultural developments, for example those associated with pluralism (the co-existence and toleration of widely diverging traditions), personal exploration, a fascination with Eastern traditions, communal living, the use of drugs and sexual liberation. NRMs sometimes negotiated an uneasy relationship with other counter-cultural trends of the Sixties, but their religious focus made them more susceptible, in many cases, to an eventual reunion with mainstream religious establishments. As with the scientific movements discussed above, however, their influence on present-day culture has been far-reaching. Many aspects of religious worship and ceremony regarded as 'alternative' or 'counter' in the Sixties are now (at the beginning of the twenty-first century) integrated into institutions and traditions that existed well before the Sixties.

The Music unit (Unit 29) looks closely at developments in taste in the Sixties in relation to what we might loosely describe as both 'classical' and 'popular' music. It was in the Sixties that classical musicians began to demonstrate a growing interest in early music, which was increasingly reflected in concert programmes. The Early Music Revival, the name used to describe this trend, was a movement characterized by a renewed interest in the music, performance styles and instruments of medieval and Renaissance music. It provided a 'counter-cultural' challenge to the mainstream classical repertoire of the period immediately prior to the Sixties. Some of the rock and pop music that developed in the Sixties is also studied in the unit, as the popular music of the decade was a commonly acknowledged medium in which to challenge, not only musical styles and traditions, but also, through lyrics and performance contexts, many mainstream ideas on society, morality and politics. In selecting pieces of music for study, however, the authors of the unit are keen to point out that much of the music of the Sixties was not counter-cultural at all, but showed continuity with some previous musical traditions in, for example, folk and jazz. This unit, like others in the block, shows how counter-cultural elements could co-exist alongside, or even became fully integrated with, mainstream culture: a thesis that is set out in Units 25 and 26.

As far as Sixties art is concerned, Rothko and Warhol have been chosen as key artists to study (Unit 30). This is partly for the purpose of connection with other parts of the course. Rothko, for example, measured his own artistic aims and achievements against those of Rembrandt, whose art you met in Block 1. It is therefore interesting to see how far our interpretation of the kind of abstract art produced by Rothko leads us to similar questions of form and meaning, of the relationship between viewer and work of art, to those raised by a Rembrandt painting. Like Rembrandt, Rothko is an artist whose reputation is now firmly established. His work is canonical – judged to be among the best by those whose opinions are the most influential – in part because it repays sustained attention and therefore stands up well to the test of 'adequacy' outlined in Unit 1.

But it is not just for reasons of comparison, quality and topicality that Rothko's works have been selected for Block 6. As argued above, they also relate clearly to the debates about 'mainstream' and 'counter' culture that run through the block as a whole. We might see Rothko's work, for example, as perpetuating a well-established tradition of abstract or even modern art. This was, in the art world, a 'mainstream' interest that allied itself with the values of high culture and attempted to distinguish itself from the popular and the commercial. It is for this reason that Warhol's work is chosen as a point of comparison with Rothko's. Much of

Rothko's work was in fact done in the Fifties, some of it squeezing into the 'long Sixties' (1958–1973) outlined in Units 25 and 26. If Rothko's work illustrates mainstream attitudes creeping from the Fifties into the Sixties, then Warhol's emphasis on commercialization, populism and mass production shows a clear counter-cultural challenge to those attitudes.

There is, however, another way of looking at this. Warhol was not at all marginalized by Sixties culture. He was admired by the rich and famous as well as by intellectuals and academics. He gained entry to the highly regarded social milieu and exhibition spaces of the Museum of Modern Art at a much earlier stage of his career than Rothko did and his works now command higher prices. Perhaps, then, Rothko's work may be seen, in some ways, as more deeply challenging to the standard self-image of the decade than Warhol's. We may well be dealing here with an example of a counter-cultural force (Warhol) that became 'mainstream' with such rapidity, within the swiftly moving scene of the Sixties, that the art it had challenged began to look more radical. It is common today for people to regard the spiritual and emotive aspects of Rothko's art as a challenge to rampant capitalism and commercialism. All of this shows how fluid our concepts of mainstream culture and counter-culture really are, and how one label may, with time, have to be replaced by another, in the constant shifts and fluxes of cultural phenomena of which the Sixties offered so many dramatic examples.

The methodologies employed by the different disciplines

You will become aware, as you read the units in this block, that the authors adopt different methods or approaches to their subject-matter. Each of these approaches signals a set of intellectual priorities or concerns. You will probably have noticed, by this stage of the course, that these changes of approach are central to academic discussion. For example, all the writers in Block 1 concentrated on formal analysis, whilst those in Block 2 added to this a concern with historical context and with interpretations of cultural texts and objects (for example, the Colosseum) that change through time. Sometimes it is a matter of matching the approach to the subject-matter. For example, historical context will not help us to decide whether or not an argument is valid. At other times the same object (a painting, for example) can be investigated either by scrutinizing its formal qualities or by looking at its historical context (or both, as we shall see below). By looking at a number of different approaches in the course (and in this block) we hope to encourage alert, critical responses to the methods used by writers. This, in turn, will encourage healthy disputes, which help to eliminate weak arguments and interpretations.

In Units 25 and 26, Arthur Marwick attempts to produce a history of the Sixties that is as 'objective' as possible. This is done by analysing a wide range of sources in the rigorous manner introduced in Block 3, to see which trends and patterns emerge clearly. To this is added a concern with periodization: a self-conscious examination of the criteria used by historians to divide up the past into manageable, and reasonably discrete, self-standing units of study. Behind Marwick's method lies a belief that, given time, sufficient evidence and the application of rigorous methods, historians may formulate an account of the past that increasingly eliminates error and approaches truth. Whilst Marwick acknowledges subjectivity and choice of interpretative theory (for example, Marxism) as forces that may shape an individual historian's account of the past, his view is that the role of these forces may be minimized by applying the methods in the study of history that he describes.

The other disciplines in the block have their own approaches, which stand in interesting relations to those described in the History units.

As Block 4 makes clear, the history of science is a history of a particular human practice: science. Unit 27 looks at the effects of a prominent event during the Sixties (the Vietnam War) and its effect on how scientists thought about themselves and what they were doing. It employs the skills taught in the History units, in particular the analysis of primary sources. It uses the findings of such enquiry to underpin claims about the wider cultural context, particularly the role of women in science. This leads to an examination of the link between the kinds of presupposition scientists make (although these may well not be consciously made) and actual scientific practice. It is important that the contributions of 1960s writers on science are analysed within their contemporary context, rather than judged according to the truth or otherwise of their claims. The emphasis is on the dynamic relationship between developments in science and the broader concerns and values of society.

Unit 28 looks at religion in the Sixties in a way that incorporates but goes beyond the methods of historical enquiry taught in the course. As a subject area, Religious Studies is interdisciplinary in nature and draws on the methods of all of the following: History, Literature, Sociology and Anthropology. The last two disciplines are traditionally taught in Faculties of Social Science rather than of Arts. If you have already studied social sciences, you will perhaps find that some of the concepts and interpretative frameworks and methods used in Unit 28 are familiar to you. The Religious Studies unit approach, like that in the History of Science unit, goes beyond the immediate object of enquiry (religion or science) to place its developments in a wider social context. Not only will you be looking at the causes of the proliferation of NRMs, but also at such matters as people's motivation for joining them, and the role the NRMs found for themselves in the broader culture.

Music and Art History are the only two disciplines in the block that were studied in Block 1. The emphasis in Block 1 was on understanding works by analysing their form: by taking them apart and seeing how they worked. Then, in Block 3 (for Art History) and Block 5 (for Music), the importance of the historical context for understanding was introduced. Both approaches are again evident in the study of these disciplines in Block 6. Unit 29 provides the opportunity for a detailed formal analysis of two pieces of music: 'Waterloo Sunset' by The Kinks and *Eight Songs for a Mad King* by Sir Peter Maxwell Davies. These analyses are then complemented by an investigation of how the works reflect the cultural changes of the Sixties, showing, by example, how the two approaches of formal analysis and contextual explanation can combine in the examination of a piece of music.

These two approaches are also evident in Unit 30 and, once again, the author has tried to strike a balance between them. The first 'formalist' approach treats works of art, their meanings and values as far as possible as 'autonomous' or independent of factors external to art itself (although there will usually be some contextual factor in such treatments). In this first approach, the meanings and values of art are used to criticize or amplify the generalizations and details offered by historians. Thus, according to this method, we can use the detailed study of the internal qualities of the work of Rothko and Warhol to challenge or expand upon any of the details or generalizations (or generalizing techniques) about the Sixties set out in Units 25 and 26. The other approach is to assume that art, its values and meanings are rooted in historical and social phenomena, and hence to try to read or interpret works of art by reference to broader historical generalizations and details, assembled in advance to provide an appropriate 'context' for interpretation. At best, these two approaches are complementary in that they offer mutual correction and amplification. In practice, they are often used side by side (as in Unit 29, and also in the Art History unit (Unit 12) in Block 3) to offer explanations of the complex relationships between art and society.

We have introduced you to these methodological perspectives so that, as you move on to higher-level study, you will be alert to their presence and impact. It is not intended, at this stage, that you should try to rank them in terms of their effectiveness. We do hope, however, that at some later stage in your undergraduate studies, you will evaluate different methodological approaches as you develop your own ideas on cause, effect and interpretation in the arts. If, on one level, Block 6 is concerned with 'what happened' in the Sixties, it is, on another level, concerned with the problems associated with *writing* the social and cultural history of such a rich and recent period.

Approaching the block

How, then, should you approach this block? The assignment will ask you a general question on the Sixties, directing you to focus on two or three different disciplines. The History units attempt to provide a broad overview of the period, which will enable you to put your discussion in context. The other disciplines draw on their own approaches, and are thus focused more narrowly. Hence, the block will not provide a comprehensive survey of the Sixties from five points of view. Because of this, when you read the block, or write your assignment, you will need to consider the details of specific examples that you use. As we have seen, examples rarely fit neatly into an overarching theme of a mainstream culture opposed by a unified counter-culture. By the time you have finished your work on this block, we hope you will have grasped some of the social changes that made the Sixties such an important historical period. Not only that; we also hope you will have a greater appreciation of the differences between disciplines, and so of the worth of the detailed use of evidence and example as opposed to unsubstantiated generalization.

UNITS 25 AND 26 INTRODUCTION TO HISTORY, PART 2: WRITING HISTORY

Written for the course team by Arthur Marwick

Contents

STUDY COMPONENTS				
Weeks of study	Texts	TV	AC	Set books
2	*Resource Book 3* *Resource Book 4*	TV25 TV26	–	–

Aims and objectives

The aims of these units are to:

1   introduce the Sixties as a suitable conclusion to the themes and issues of the course;

2   provide the historical context for the studies in the history of science, religion, music and art history which make up the rest of this block;

3   complete our study of the basic aims and methods of history, with special reference to the writing up of history.

By the end of these units you should be able to:

1   explain why historians adopt the device of 'periodization' (chopping the past up into 'periods' – for example, The Golden Age of Athens, The Renaissance, The Age of Revolutions, the Nineteenth Century, The Twenties, The Sixties) and identify the dangers in doing this; in particular you should be able to argue intelligently about whether the Sixties constitute a period, or not;

2   following our discussion in Units 8 and 9 of technical and conceptual terms, expound the significance, and the dangers, of the use of concepts and theories and the need for precision in the use of language; in particular you should be able to explain the ways in which such terms as 'counter-culture', 'alternative society', 'cultural revolution', and 'ideology' are used with reference to the Sixties;

3   explain why historians have to develop a 'structure' for any substantial piece of historical writing and to elucidate the basis on which this is done; think in a preliminary way about a possible structure for a book on the Sixties;

4   define 'comparative history' and identify its special virtues; in particular you should be able to begin to discuss what would be involved in a comparative history of the 1960s;

5   state the most basic points about how a historian tackles the problems of historical explanation; in particular you should be able

to discuss the forces and circumstances which shaped the societies of the Sixties with their (arguably) distinctive characteristics;

6   demonstrate that you understand that producing history involves selecting and sorting material in such a way as to bring out what is significant; you should also be able to discuss and debate what were the significant characteristics of the Sixties;

7   present a persuasive case for the essentiality of scholarly apparatus (footnotes and bibliography) in a serious historical work; and explain how these are set out, specifically with reference to the principles of honesty and helpfulness;

8   distinguish between the different levels of historical communication, from scholarly works to pop history, recognizing that each should be evaluated in accordance with its own set of purposes;

9   drawing upon everything in the two units, write a brief summary of the Sixties, referring both to some of the most useful primary sources, and to some of the major controversies, which would provide an adequate context for the studies in science, religion, music and art in the remainder of this block.

1   INTRODUCTION

As remarked in the Introduction to the block, in this part of the course we have chosen to study the 1960s, seeing this as an excellent way of drawing together the various themes and issues of Blocks 1–5. I have the task of introducing the way in which special characteristics of the Sixties do mark the period out as a kind of culmination of developments discussed throughout the course. I also have to establish the historical context for the studies which follow of counter-movements in science, new religion and music, and of the artists Mark Rothko and Andy Warhol. But I am also concerned to complete the study of the basic purposes and methods of history begun in Units 8 and 9, particularly with reference to the problems of writing history. Apart from the needs of this course, and apart even from the intense intrinsic interest of the period, the Sixties form a good topic for this. Practically everyone has strong views on the Sixties: extreme conservatives see the decade as a time of decadence, extreme left-wingers see it as a time of potential revolution which was somehow dissipated. Yet there is (at the time of writing) very little serious scholarly work on the period as a whole, apart from that of a few Americans who have seen the time as one of the 'unravelling' of American society, and some French and Italian academics who have tended not to separate out the Sixties from the general context of post-war economic boom. Could the systematic application of the principles of historical study we are concerned with resolve such issues about the Sixties?

Occasionally I shall make references back to the other historical topics we have studied (the 'Family' and the 'Origins, Cause, and Aftermath of the French Revolution'), but mainly I shall be concentrating on what truly is a fascinating period in recent (or contemporary) history.

You will have seen from the contents that the two units are organized as a single entity divided into ten main sections. The notional break between Units 25 and 26 comes at the end of Section 5 and you should aim to have worked through that far by the end of your first week's work.

First, I want to make it clear that when I speak of the Sixties I am confining myself to social and cultural developments in Western Europe and North America. Now, to get us started, and before I take each of the objectives in turn, I want to elaborate on what I have already said about the significance of the Sixties.

1   Challenges to Western cultural assumptions (to '"mainstream" culture') developed in the twentieth century, but reached, so to speak, a climactic state in the 1960s, when a series of movements and shifts in ideas and behaviour came into being. Grouped together, these 'movements and shifts' are often referred to as a 'counter-culture', or even as *the* 'counter-culture'.

I shall examine the term more critically later, but for the moment here is a simple list of 'movements and shifts in ideas and behaviour' which might be labelled 'counter-cultural'. Sometimes the term 'the Movement' is used for the more obviously political activities, and I have marked these with an asterisk:

(a) black civil rights*;

(b) youth culture and trend-setting by young people;

(c) student activism*;

(d) mass protests against imperialism* – focused particularly on the Vietnam War, which was perceived as American aggression against an oppressed colonial people, and was a general preoccupation;

(e) beginnings of contemporary environmentalism;

(f) criticisms of 'technocratic society', which was seen as embodying the unrestrained application of technology and the systems approach;

(g) serious appreciation of mass culture and the advent of 'cross over' (that is, the blending of élite and popular culture) in the arts;

(h) triumph of popular music based on Afro-American models;

(i) emergence of this music as a universal language;

(j) seeking of inspiration in religious and cultural matters from the East;

(k) challenges to Enlightenment rationality;

(l) new philosophies stressing the importance of language and the alleged evils of 'bourgeois society';

(m) a general audacity and frankness in books and in the media, and in ordinary behaviour;

(n) the new feminism;

(o) gay liberation;

(p) drug culture and dropping out.

2   There were other important trends which are perhaps not so readily fitted into the notion of a 'counter-culture':

(a) enormous improvements in material conditions for the majority of people in Western countries;

(b) massive changes in personal relationships and sexual behaviour (in my view affecting the mass of 'mainstream' society);

(c) the growing strength of liberal and consensual elements in positions of power, leading, for example, to relaxation of censorship, reform of abortion laws (see TV26), etc.

(d) a great outburst of individual entrepreneurial activity and private commercial enterprise – much of it, for example theatre clubs, bookshops, boutiques, apparently 'counter-cultural'.

3   Whatever the views of proponents of 'counter-cultural' ideas, the fact is that the past century has been increasingly dominated by the discoveries of science and the innovations of technology. There has also been a long-term trend of secularization (that is a move away from religious belief and practice). Some social scientists have spoken of 'modernization', the trend towards technologically based societies, the abandonment of old faiths and shibboleths, the rise of centralized government, and democratic voting systems. In the Sixties there was, in many respects, an intensification of these trends – in essence the new popular culture came about through a convergence of (a) young people as arbiters of taste with (b) technological innovation (45-rpm records, transistor radios) combined with (c) shrewd commercial exploitation of both. One of many contradictions is that those who were benefiting from technology were often those who denounced it. On the world scene, the twentieth century was marked by the rise of America as the dominant power, a rise confirmed by the Second World War. American hegemony covered popular culture, and also many aspects of high culture. Once full recovery from the Second World War had been achieved, European countries began to enjoy something like American-style affluence. Thus Sixties' societies in

many ways provided classic examples of modern, technology-based consumer economies, dominated by the American example with, however, a couple of twists: one of the most powerful 'counter-cultural' movements was that against consumerist, technological society, and what were seen as its phoney freedoms and 'repressive tolerance' (the phrase is that of the German-American neo-Marxist thinker, Herbert Marcuse); and there were strong challenges to American cultural hegemony, particularly from Britain (the Beatles, the Rolling Stones; Mary Quant, Jean Shrimpton and Twiggy in fashion; certain films and television series). The societies of the Sixties are different from societies of today, but I think you will find that much of what we take for granted in the cultural environment of today was established then.

2 PERIODIZATION

Periodization, the chopping up of the past into, as it were, chunks or periods, is practically unavoidable in the production of history, the past being so massive and complex. Many of us are probably familiar with the idea that, in speaking of the entire development of Western Europe from the Ancient Greeks to the present day, distinctions can be made between 'the Classical Period', 'the Medieval Period', and 'the Modern Period'. Today, in history departments and other institutions of history as a professional activity, such as learned journals and libraries, it is usually felt necessary to make further subdivisions into, at the very least, for example, 'The Early Modern Period' and the 'Late Modern Period'. Such very broad periodization obviously has some inherent sense to it: values, behaviour, material conditions in each 'period' are rather different; at the mundane professional level historians do have to specialize if they are to do any serious original research, and indeed if they are to teach in a knowledgeable way. This kind of broad periodization, we could say, is essentially a matter of common sense and convenience.

However, in historical work, periodization is usually much more time-specific. In Units 8 and 9 we noted that Lawrence Stone identified a particular, relatively short period of time (the 1640s) as being the one in which a critical development relating to the family took place, the emergence of what he called 'Affective Individualism'. In my account of Enlightenment France and the Revolution, I broke my discussion up into a series of 'phases'. The implication in such devices is that particular periods of time (years or months, or it could be decades or centuries) contain a certain unity, in that events, attitudes, values, social hierarchies, seem to be closely integrated with each other, and that there are identifiable points of change when different sorts of events, attitudes and structures begin to dominate. Books covering relatively long periods of time will almost always be divided up into a number of shorter periods, indicating points of change – the emergence of new attitudes, new social hierarchies, and so on – perceived by the historian. For example, Eric Hobsbawm (Marxist but anti-postmodernist – see glossary in Unit 8), in his *Age of Extremes: The Short Twentieth Century 1914–1991*, divided his 'short twentieth century' – I'll come to that in a moment – into 'The Age of Catastrophe' (1914–1945), 'The Golden Age' (1945–1973), and 'The Landslide' (1972–1991). Hobsbawm is following standard practice in giving each of his shorter periods a label (as indeed he gives a label or, rather, two labels to the entire period covered by his book); such labels are intended to pin down the key characteristics of the particular period, what makes it different from the other periods. It should, however, be admitted right away that sometimes the labels, particularly for the entire period covered by a book, have as much to do with finding a jazzy title with commercial appeal as with truly scholarly purposes (history, I repeat once more, is a human and social activity). In the earlier, less commercialized days of professional history, general textbooks (works of detailed research, of course, have to have more exactly descriptive titles) often had austere titles like *The Thirteenth Century, The Reign of George III*, or *English History, 1914–1945*, Centuries, and decades, provide a kind of ready-made periodization, subject only to the serious disadvantage that the points of change (or 'discontinuities', as some people, particularly French philosophers, say) which historians believe they can perceive and validate do not usually coincide with the ending of a century, or beginning of a decade. So historians came up with, for example, 'The Long Nineteenth Century' which allowed them to carry on to 1914 (a rather obvious natural break), and 'The Short Twentieth Century' which allowed them to begin only in 1914.

'History', let us remind ourselves once more, is not 'the past'; it is 'the knowledge about the past produced by historians'. Periodization is simply an analytical device of historians, the periods selected depending very much on the topic being studied. Periodization which makes sense if one is interested in the activities of rich and powerful men may have no relevance if one is interested in the activities of women; 'Did women have a Renaissance?' is a classic question well worth pondering. Periods, then, do not have any fundamental existence independent of the activities of historians. The past is not (as was assumed in nineteenth-century philosophy, and by today's disciples of that philosophy), in itself, divided naturally into periods (or 'epochs', as we sometimes say for very long periods, as in, say, 'the feudal epoch', 'the capitalist epoch'). But that does not mean that the historian's periodization is arbitrary: periods must be shown to have some kind of unity and distinctiveness, and there must be justification for the implication of points of change at beginning and end. So can the Sixties be termed 'a period'? Much will depend on what aspects of the past we concentrate on: for example, the Sixties might be seen as forming a distinct period in social and cultural history, but perhaps not in economic, political, diplomatic or constitutional history. And it depends on what countries we consider: perhaps the answer might be 'yes' with regard to America, Britain – though I do remember, while researching on this very topic in the United States, an American commenting, 'Say, I never knew you guys had a Sixties over there' – and Western Europe, perhaps 'no' with regard to Eastern Europe, Africa and much of Asia.

Before I fix specifically on the Sixties, I want to explore further with you the general principles of periodization.

EXERCISE

I want you to reflect on what I said about the considerations and issues lying behind periodization, then I want you to read carefully and critically the following passages with a view to answering the following questions:

1   How is periodization being handled in each passage, and what assumptions lie behind this periodization?

2   Do any passages seem particularly cautious and carefully worked out, or particularly sweeping and dogmatic?

3   Can you detect two different answers to the question of whether the Sixties form a distinct period?

This is an exercise which calls for a great deal of thought, appropriately enough, I feel, as you enter the final block of the course. Give it a good shot – but if you are really not getting anywhere, go on to my 'Specimen Answers'.

> (A)   This book traces the transformation of the world between 1789 and 1848 in so far as it was due to what is here called the 'dual revolution' – the French Revolution of 1789 and the contemporaneous (British) Industrial Revolution. It is therefore strictly neither a history of Europe nor of the world. In so far as a country felt the repercussions of the dual revolution in this period, I have attempted to refer to it, though often cursorily. In so far as the impact of the revolution on it in this period was negligible, I have omitted it. Hence the reader will find something about Egypt here, but not about Japan: more about Ireland than about Bulgaria, about Latin America than about Africa. Naturally this does not mean that the histories of the countries and peoples neglected in this volume are less interesting or important than those which are included. If its perspective is primarily European or more precisely Franco-British, it is because in this period the world – or at least a large part of it – was transformed from a European, or rather a Franco-British base. However, certain topics which might well have deserved more detailed treatment have also been left aside, not only for reasons of space, but because (like the history of the USA) they are treated at length in other volumes in this series.

> (B)   The Revolution of 1789 marked the arrival of modern bourgeois capitalist society in the history of France.

(C)   Extract A23 from your *Resource Book 2* (Matthew Anderson, Introduction to *The Ascendancy of Europe*).

(D)   ... this investigation has revealed two great discontinuities in the essential characteristics of western culture: that which inaugurated the Classical Age (towards the middle of the seventeenth century) and that which, at the beginning of the nineteenth century, marks the threshold of our modern age.

(E)   In this book the structure of the Short Twentieth Century appears like a sort of triptych or historical sandwich. An Age of Catastrophe from 1914 to the aftermath of the Second World War was followed by some twenty-five or thirty years of extraordinary economic growth and social transformation, which probably changed human society more profoundly than any other period of comparable brevity. In retrospect it can be seen as a sort of Golden Age, and was so seen immediately it had come to an end in the early 1970s. The last part of the century was a new era of decomposition, uncertainty and crisis – and indeed, for large parts of the world such as Africa, the former USSR and the formerly socialist parts of Europe, of catastrophe. As the 1980s gave way to the 1990s, the mood of those who reflected on the century's past and future was growing fin-de-siècle [end-of-century] gloom. From the vantage-point of the 1990s, the Short Twentieth Century passed through a brief Golden Age, on the way from one era of crisis to another, into an unknown and problematic but not necessarily apocalyptic future.

(F)   ... in all likelihood, as they recede in time the Sixties will ultimately be studied as one of the handful of archetypal moments in cultural history – the American Twenties, the post-war Weimar period in Germany, Vienna at the turn of the century being others – when the modern world revealed and realized its true inner logic and illogic.

SPECIMEN ANSWERS AND DISCUSSION

The three very brief pieces (B, D and F) must inevitably come over as the most sweeping: this may seem unfair to the authors, but in fact these three short statements are not elaborated in any way and are clearly all the authors felt it necessary to say. I personally am not very happy with either (B) or (D), though you may disagree, both seeming to me too much in the nineteenth-century philosophical tradition of making sweeping historical generalizations. (B) is by the very distinguished French Marxist historian, and major contributor to our detailed knowledge of the poorer classes in the Revolution, Albert Soboul. (D) is by the French philosopher Michel Foucault, whose challenging works offer much for historians to ponder. In (F), the author, Gerald Howard, is confining himself to cultural history, but is certainly making very strong claims for the Sixties as a separate period which is not just distinctive but very important – though I'd say pretentious phrases about 'true inner logic and illogic' are best avoided in historical writing. I suppose the next most sweeping passage is (E), though personally I find it cautious and carefully worked out as a one-paragraph introduction to the structure of an entire book (you may have guessed that it is from Hobsbawm's *Age of Extremes*). Obviously the author does not regard the Sixties as a separate period, but simply includes that decade within the longer 'Golden Age', as the French and Italian historians I have already referred to tend to do. In fact, for historians this is one of the crucial questions: do the Sixties form a separate period, or are they merely part of a longer period of post-war recovery?

Extract (A) is from Hobsbawm's *Age of Revolution*. It is very cautious and carefully worked out, and, in fact, particularly interesting in connection with the range of issues I have raised with regard to periodization. To some extent the period (and countries) to be covered have been imposed on the author by his publishers. However he is happy with 1789–1848 (sensible enough periodization in itself as both dates are those of 'years of revolution'), since this can be presented as a period dominated by the 'dual revolution'. He is not concerned to cover every country, but he does refer to all countries he perceives as affected by the 'dual revolution' (this neatly makes the point that 'The Age of Revolution' as a period, like all periods, does not have universal application – that is, it does not apply to Africa and Asia). On his own criteria, Hobsbawm freely admits, America should have come in – but here the consideration that this sort of history book is a commercial product to be marketed with other books in the same series, becomes critical.

(C), as befits the introduction to a standard text book, is perhaps the most cautious passage of all (though I wouldn't quarrel if you wished to give that honour to A). It is very like (A) in the period of change it is concerned to define, but it actually sees the changes as concentrated within a shorter period (ending in 1815) – so perhaps, on these grounds it could be seen as more sweeping than (A). My main reason, in fact, for giving you this extract for your work on Units 8 and 9 is that it offers a straightforward summing-up of the consequences of the French Revolution. However, there is a more profound point with regard to periodization which I would not really have expected you to make. The commission Anderson has been given is to write a book on Europe between 1815 and 1914 (the long nineteenth century!), but he finds it impossible to plunge straight in at 1815; in order to explain his own long period, he has to summarize the short period (1780s–1815) of, in his view, vital change which precedes it. There are no utterly abrupt beginnings or endings, no absolute discontinuities.

EXERCISE

So far, then, we have had one view of the Sixties as a self-contained decade, one of the Sixties as merely part of 'The Golden Age', beginning in 1945. Already I've made my bid on behalf of the Sixties being seen as a separate period, with my list of 'counter-cultural' and innovative developments (see pp.16–17). Now I want to turn to *Resource Book 4* and the 'Chronology of social, cultural and political events, 1954–75' (A1), together with A2, 'Brief pieces of statistical and social survey information', to see if this helps further to justify the notion of the Sixties as a special period in which important things happened.

There is no need to memorize this mass of information. Rather, I want you to get a general impression that:

1   some very distinctive and significant things happened during the Sixties of a sort to bring about general changes in society;

2   some important changes actually took place in the Fifties;

3   these changes intensified towards the end of the Fifties;

4   while changes continued into the early Seventies, Hobsbawm is right in suggesting that a further (and less desirable) point of change comes in the early Seventies, bringing the period of innovation and 'counter-cultural' change to an end.

Now read the material in *Resource Book 4.*   ■

My selection of information is obviously influenced by my views about the Sixties – I include the New York Black and White Ball of 1966 and Andy Warhol's attendance at it, because I think it important to bring out the close relationship that often existed between 'counter-culture' and high society. Marcuse's call for revolution, *One Dimensional Man*, it may be noted, was funded by 'mainstream' academic bodies and private foundations, and most of the innovative ventures of the Sixties – theatres, clubs, publications – were fine examples of private capitalist entrepreneurialism. But I hope that my Chronology does provide a reasonable basis for defining the Sixties as a period of exceptional cultural and social change, running from around 1958 to around 1973. You should, in addition, make use of the material contained in TV25 and 26.

3 LANGUAGE: CONCEPTS, THEORY

Culture

The phrase which forms the subtitle of this block is 'Mainstream culture and counter-culture'. 'Culture' is one of those words which has a variety of different meanings. As I've said before, it's very important to be aware of these meanings, and to be aware each time the word is used just which meaning is intended, whether by you or by someone else. To many people the word 'culture' immediately suggests opera, art, poetry. Here, however, 'culture' is being used in a wider sense to mean 'the network, or totality, of attitudes, values and practices of a particular group of human beings'. Thus one might speak of 'aristocratic culture', meaning, perhaps, life in a big house on a landed estate, freed from the need for earning a living, but involving the manipulation of investments, the collection of rent and administration of the estate, bossing around of tenants and servants, a London 'season', fine paintings and furniture, arranged marriages, dressing up differently for different parts of the day, a belief in one's automatic right to participate in government, huntin', shootin' and fishin': all that could be said to make up the 'network' or 'totality' of aristocratic culture. Similarly one might speak of 'youth culture' – and indeed the new 'youth culture', involving coffee bars, rock music, special clothes, which began to appear at the end of the Fifties was an important and powerful phenomenon of the Sixties.

Sometimes we even speak of 'Western culture', embracing 'the Western way of life': all the attitudes and values and practices, springing from the Classical tradition, modified by Christian religion, by the eighteenth-century Enlightenment, by the French Revolution, by Romanticism, by overseas conquests and colonialism, by the upheavals of the twentieth century. One 'culture', apparently, can be very big, or quite small, depending upon the context within which the concept is being used. Cultures are a bit like periods: useful concepts for analytical purposes when handled carefully, but never to be thought of as having some predetermined, eternal existence. 'Mainstream' culture and 'counter-culture' are convenient terms, quite widely used, and very useful, provided we do not try to make them bear a whole load of theoretical assumptions they are not capable of sustaining – that is why I constantly enclose both terms in inverted commas. Since 'mainstream' is a metaphor (relating to rivers), and indeed a dead metaphor, or cliché, I'd prefer to avoid it, but since the phrase 'mainstream culture' is convenient, and *clear*, I'll stick with it. The phrase 'mainstream' culture, then, can be used to group together the attitudes, values and practices widely prevalent in Britain, and other Western countries, in the years after the Second World War. Including key elements from what I have just referred to as 'Western culture', but, focusing in on the period immediately prior to the Sixties, we might see 'mainstream' culture as including:

1   Rigid social hierarchy – clearly identifiable upper class, range of middle classes, and working class in each country.

2   Subordination of women to men, and children to parents.

3   Stuffy and repressed attitudes to sex, fostered particularly by both Protestant denominations and the Catholic church – very obvious in 'the suburbs', in the European 'provinces' and in the American 'Middle West'.

4   Respect for authority, in the family, education, government, religion, and for the nation state, the national flag, national anthem, etc.

5   The prevalence of racism, seen most evidently in the segregation still practised in the American South.

6   Universal, if often uncomprehending, obeisance to canonized art and respect for the 'giants' of science – Darwin, Einstein, etc.

7   Complacency over technological advance and the growth of affluence and consumerism (though conditions remained primitive in certain areas of all Western countries).

8   A strict formalism with regard to social relations, etiquette, dress codes, etc.

I have already suggested (pp.16–17) what sorts of thing are implied in the term 'counter-culture', and have raised questions as to whether political movements should be included within that term. My biggest difficulties arise when 'counter-culture' is presented as being in dialectical opposition to 'mainstream' culture. However, you do not have to accept my view, *you* may finally decide that there *was* a coherent integrated 'counter-culture' diametrically opposed to 'mainstream culture'. For me, and I shall henceforth be presenting *my* views, there were not really two alternative and opposite cultures. There was just one society, one culture. So-called (and, as I say, it is convenient to call it this) 'counter-culture' in fact arose within one, integrated Western culture. Boutiques, experimental theatre clubs, 'alternative' bookshops *were* part of what we are agreeing to call 'counter-culture' but they very definitely employed

FIGURE 25/26.1 *A hippie group on Sugar Loaf Mountain, Boulder, Colorado, United States, 13 June 1968. The group were predicting the end of the world on 15 June, following collision with the asteroid Icarus. They believed that this mountain area might be saved. (Photograph: Popperfoto)*

the private enterprise, commercial techniques of 'mainstream' culture. So most assuredly did the new pop music. In my view it is quite wrong to represent 'counter-culture' as being diametrically opposed to the existing structure of society, its economic organizations, distribution of power, and broad acceptance (with some qualifications) of market economics, commercialism, and the profit motive, and as tending, consciously or unconsciously towards its overthrow. All of the different movements, forms of protest and expression, which made up 'counter-culture' were opposed to something, or several things, in 'mainstream' culture; but they also had roots in, or connections with, established culture (through commercial sales, or educational institutions, or social occasions – such as the Black and White Ball, or experimental theatre productions patronized by the rich), or were so remote from any effective political stance (as with drop-out hippie culture) as not to form any threat at all to 'mainstream' culture; 'counter-culture' formed no consistent, coherent, opposition or alternative force.

EXERCISE

Many of those who saw themselves as part of the 'counter-culture', and probably most of those who felt they belonged to 'the Movement' *believed* that they were bringing about the collapse of 'mainstream' culture, or, as they usually put it, 'bourgeois society', and its replacement by the 'alternative society'. In relation to this belief, I would now like you to read a primary source in *Resource Book 4*, which comes from the first book to put forward the notion of a Sixties 'counter-culture' (A22).

1   What components make up Roszak's 'counter-culture'?

2   What, according to Roszak, is the historical context of the values which characterize it?

3   What great historical achievement does Roszak believe the counter-culture will bring about?

4   How effectively does Roszak argue on behalf of the existence of one coherent counter-culture?

DISCUSSION

1   First of all, it is based on the 'college-age and adolescent young' and 'their adult mentors'. The influences are: 'the psychology of alienation, oriental mysticism, psychedelic drugs and communitarian experiments' ('communitarian' is yet another of those words which have several meanings – what Roszak is basically referring to here, I think, is the setting up of hippie communes).

2   The counter-culture is not just opposed to values and assumptions dominating the Fifties and Sixties, but the ones which 'have been in

the mainstream of our society at least since the Scientific Revolution of the seventeenth century'.

3   The overthrow of what Roszak sees as the present 'disoriented civilisation' which is already well on the way to 'technocratic totalitarianism'.

4   Well he certainly makes all kinds of reservations and qualifications. The counter-culture only includes a minority; lots of elements are not included; it's quite difficult to identify anyway, and is 'dressed in a garish motley' ('motley' means the 'multi-coloured costume of a clown' but what exactly Roszak means is far from clear to me); it's not nearly 'mature' enough yet; and it won't actually produce any results for several generations. Roszak, I think, makes all these concessions in order to convince us of what an honest chap he is, and thus persuade us to accept his theory. I am afraid all his qualifications, together with his fancy rhetoric, simply persuade me to reject his view that there is one coherent counter-culture. This is *my* interpretation. If you reached different conclusions, think about mine. But if you find Roszak persuasive, that is fine by me. It is fair to note that many people at the time did find Roszak persuasive – they did feel they belonged to a unified counter-culture.

It follows that if you are unconvinced by Roszak's view that there was a coherent counter-culture, then it is unlikely that it could achieve the revolutionary overthrow of 'technocratic civilization' that he foresees. My view is that the 'counter-culture' embodied original and challenging ideas and values which permeated and transformed 'mainstream' society but which had no hope of overthrowing it.

Ideology

'Culture' is an all-embracing word, taking in practices and products, as well as attitudes and values; 'ideology' is more limited in meaning, being confined to the realm of the mind (ideas, attitudes, values) and not extending to practices and products. Ideology is the cluster of ideas, values and attitudes which affects the actions we take, and colours what we produce (conversations, speeches, poems, paintings, and so on), but is not the actions or products themselves. Thus, in the context of the Sixties, one might talk of 'racist ideology', leading significant numbers of white Americans to give violent support to segregation, not excluding murder, the setting of dogs on peaceful demonstrators, the bombing of churches and burning to death of children. Or one might speak of 'liberal ideology', leading Presidents Kennedy and Johnson to support moderate civil rights and anti-poverty programmes, and a Labour government to support the legalization of abortion, free contraceptives, and homosexual acts. Or again, of 'Catholic ideology', leading to determined opposition to the legalization of divorce and of abortion (the central topic of TV26).

For Marxists, and those who derive some of their fundamental ideas from Marxism, the signification of 'ideology' goes beyond that to a precise technical meaning, directly allied to the Marxist conception of class. Ideology, then, is 'the ideas, values and attitudes of a particular class, through which that class maintains its own interests as against those of the rival class or classes'. So, just as we have the very wide concept of 'bourgeois culture', we have the related, but more limited, concept of 'bourgeois ideology' – the ideas and values of the bourgeoisie designed to maintain the dominance of that bourgeoisie. According to Marxist theory, the working class should have its own ideology which will be in opposition to that of the bourgeoisie, save that, such are the workings of ideology, large sections of the working class will be led into accepting the dominant ideology, the ideology of the bourgeoisie, and will thus not recognize their own true interests. This technical conception of ideology is central to one particular interpretation of what happened in the Sixties. There was, everyone has to recognize, no revolution, no triumph of counter-culture or alternative society, no overthrow of the bourgeoisie. *But*, this failure could then be attributed to the strength of 'bourgeois ideology'.

I do not myself find these arguments persuasive. As I see it 'counter-culture' did not amount to a coherent alternative society and was, in one way or another, implicated in the mechanisms of 'mainstream' society. I do believe that, in conjunction with forces emanating directly from 'mainstream' society, 'counter-cultural' ideas and practices effected a transformation in life-styles, interpersonal relationships, and attitudes and values. Which brings me to my next conceptual term.

Cultural revolution

I have been among a number of writers to apply this term to the 1960s. Perhaps it is not a terribly good term. One problem is that the phrase 'cultural revolution' already exists to describe the policies initiated in China by Mao Tse-tung in 1965. These policies were the most wholesale ever yet seen in pursuit of the Marxist theory of ideology I have just been describing. With the intention of totally destroying bourgeois ideology, Mao forced intellectuals and other bourgeois figures to go out and work as peasants in the fields, or as navvies and construction workers. The brutality was immense, but being in service of the proposition that you could only have complete revolution if you not only removed the bourgeoisie from power, but also destroyed all vestiges of bourgeois ideology, this 'cultural revolution' was widely praised by left-wing intellectuals in the West.

Historians such as myself have had a very different kind of 'cultural revolution' in mind. It was very obvious that in the Sixties in the West nothing had taken place that theorists of revolution would recognize as revolution (many of them had placed high hopes in the student activism and widespread strikes of 1968, but in the end these had fizzled out, with existing governments generally being confirmed in power). There was no political revolution, no economic revolution. It is my own view that most people are not greatly interested in political and economic revolutions, though they are greatly interested in the conditions of their everyday life – and it was here, in my view, that 'revolution' genuinely did take place (transformations in material conditions, in sexual behaviour, in family and race relationships, in attitudes to authority, in ideas and values – matters briefly indicated in the 'Chronology' and 'Statistical and social survey information', *Resource Book 4*, A1 and A2). There was no political revolution, no economic revolution – thus the phrase '*cultural* revolution' seems appropriate.

But if one takes the view that 'cultural revolution' must mean the Mao Tse-tung type of revolution, then it would certainly be inappropriate to apply the same phrase to the cultural and social transformations (as I see them) of the Sixties. So we are back to the fundamental point that we can't really lay down rigid rules about how particular conceptual terms must be used. The usage of historians like myself is simply a kind of shorthand: the validity, or otherwise, of the phrase depends on the persuasiveness of the explanation of how and why the phrase is being used. Given the great problems we all have in wrestling with language, and the difficulties in finding telling shorthand phrases, I am on the whole inclined to think that, while far from perfect, the phrase can still be useful provided one drives home the point that it is being used to bring out that one is accepting that, while there were other, on the whole, desirable changes, there certainly was no political or economic revolution.

4 STRUCTURE IN HISTORICAL WRITING

In Units 8 and 9 we saw how historians, assisted by the secondary sources written by other historians, analyse the primary sources in order to winnow out the many different kinds of information they require. What precisely the individual historian is looking for will depend upon the particular topic or question being addressed and on the degree of specialization intended (there will be differences, for instance, between a very detailed study of a very short period, and a more general study of a long period). But in general one can say that historians are usually interested in trying to establish:

1   what actually happened;

2   why it happened;

3   the significance or consequences of what happened.

Some historians will be interested only in, say, a purely political study, but generally there will be a range of aspects, or topics to be covered, sometimes conventionally, and perhaps rather inadequately, defined as 'political', 'economic', and 'social'. When historians come to writing up the results of their researches, a vital, and agonizing, part of their activities (research, on the other hand, can often be fun), they will usually find that it is not possible to write simultaneously about political developments (who was in power, what laws were passed, and so on) and about the state of the economy (fluctuations in prices, and so on). It will not be possible to write simultaneously about the causes of certain events, and about their significance and consequences. More than this: while historians have to give a clear sense of the sequence of developments and events, that is to say, the order in which they happened (*narrative*) they also have to provide *description* of, say, what Paris was like during the time of the Revolution, or of what exactly a commonplace book was, and, most important, they have to provide *analysis* – what exactly made the crisis from 1786 on so serious, why the French peasants behaved in a particular way, and so on. Once again, it is not usually possible to fulfil all of these functions simultaneously.

Now, by this time in your studies, you will have experienced something of these problems yourself in writing essays (in all the Arts subjects) for your TMAs. You can't make all the points you want to make at once, so you have to plan, or organize your essay. Writers of history share in these general problems of writing, but there are also problems which arise from the specific tasks of the historian (as will be explained in a moment, I am thinking of scale – historians write monographs rather than essays – problems of periodization and change through time, problems of integrating the social, cultural, political and economic dimensions). Much of the most up-to-date historical research is communicated in the form of scholarly articles, each perhaps ten times the length of one of your TMAs, and, of course, based on masses of original research in the primary sources. But, on the whole, successful historians are expected to produce book-length monographs: the kinds of subject serious historians engage with tend to need the full extent of a book if justice is to be done to the subject. You have already read my outline study of the French Revolution, but for study, say, of just Nantes in the French Revolution, or the Parisian political clubs in the Revolution, or the peasantry in the Revolution, a book would be needed if any kind of satisfying account were to be provided. If, to come back to the subject of this block, a historian were to undertake a serious and convincing study of the Sixties, then, for communicating his or her results, at least one large book would be absolutely essential. Planning and organizing a book dealing with a rich and complex subject is not easy.

When we are talking about a work of this sort of scale we can scarcely avoid one of the primary preoccupations of historians, which I have already discussed, periodization. A book covering the history of the family would certainly have to be broken down into different periods – so here is another complication: it would be hard to deal simultaneously with the economic aspects of the family in the seventeenth century, and the economic aspects of the family in the twentieth century. We have already noted how Eric Hobsbawm, in covering 'the short twentieth century' had to divide his book into three separate periods. One couldn't really make sense of the French Revolution without dividing it up into separate 'phases', or 'sub-periods'. So what about 'the Sixties'? Even extending 'the Sixties' to the fifteen years I have suggested, is there really any need to break them down into further sub-periods? Couldn't one just write a series of chapters taking in turn: economic conditions; youth culture; the police; student protests; film and television; pop music; feminism? Well, we'll leave that an open question for the moment, though I'll make the important point that before making any plan one would have to do a good deal of at least preliminary research, and then, as one started writing up, see how things actually worked out.

The point I'm making is that any substantial piece of historical writing will have to have – more than just organization or a plan – a 'structure'.

This, I would maintain, is not simply imposed arbitrarily by the historian in order to find some way of resolving all the problems I have mentioned, or to give some beautiful harmony or symmetry to the work. The historian, as a result of his or her researches, and of long reflection on these researches, will begin to perceive a logical order, a series of connections and inter-relationships (a 'structure' in short) which will be as true to the actual past itself as it is possible for a historian producing knowledge about that past to make it. That is a colossal assertion, which for the moment you can only take on trust (or not!).

Before coming back to the question of the Sixties, what I want to do is to examine the structure of Eric Hobsbawm's *Age of Extremes*. I should perhaps stress that a work of this scope could not possibly be one consisting entirely, or even mainly, of fundamental primary research. Hobsbawm brings his own brilliant and original mind to bear on an enormous mass of secondary books by other historians: he also incorporates some fascinating primary research of his own. His book is genuinely a pioneering work – he is not simply following in the well-worn paths of others – thus he did have all the problems of developing a structure. Hobsbawm's table of contents is printed overleaf.

Although there is a broad periodization into three, Hobsbawm does not actually, in his table of contents, attach exact dates to the different periods, though if you go back to Section 2 you will see that I did indicate dates there when I first introduced *The Age of Extremes.*

EXERCISE

Can you pick out a couple of places where Hobsbawm clearly breaks through this periodization (for example, strays outside of what he himself has given as the dates for 'The Golden Age'); and can you suggest any reasons as to why he might have felt it necessary to break through his own periodization in this way?

DISCUSSION

Chapter 10 actually extends from the beginning of period two, practically through to the end of period three. Quite simply, being true to his perception of how developments actually happened, Hobsbawm felt that the 'social revolution', which he saw as beginning in the immediate aftermath of the Second World War, continued uninterrupted, despite the other significant, and regrettable, changes which he saw as coming about around 1973, the beginning of this third period.

Chapter 17, on the contrary, while placed in period three, actually begins quite far back in period two. Obviously, again Hobsbawm felt he had a continuing theme, with developments in the arts not being subject to the kinds of change which led him to adopt his periodization in the first place.

Hobsbawm's chapter titles, though brief, give a pretty clear idea of the main topic for each chapter. I am going to attempt an explanation of why, in Part One, Hobsbawm has ordered the individual topics in the way he has: in other words, I shall try to explain the structure of Part One chapter by chapter.

1   Clearly Hobsbawm felt that the two wars of 1914–1918 and 1939–1945 were the dominating events in his 'Age of Catastrophe' and so therefore this is the topic he starts off with.

2   But almost equally important is the Communist Revolution set off at the end of the First World War, with repercussions across the world.

3   Then, of course, practically the whole of the inter-war years were dominated by the massive economic depression. I hope you can see the logical sequence, massive events and circumstances: war, revolution, economic collapse.

4   Hobsbawm now turns to ideological (in the non-Marxist sense) aspects: liberalism was essentially a nineteenth-century set of beliefs and values, which could scarcely survive the shattering blows of war, revolution, and economic collapse (again, now that I have spelled it out, I hope you can see the logical development).

5   The title here may seem puzzling, and perhaps suggestive of some repetition, for the 'common enemy' is indeed Nazism and Fascism. However, what Hobsbawm has done, and this is very typical of the kind of analytical distinctions historians have to make, is to separate out war as a general phenomenon (involving killing, cost, destruction, etc.), and the specific, and again ideological, topic of the alien ideas of Nazism and Fascism, and how they were combated.

6   One of Hobsbawm's great strengths is the way in which he integrates discussion of the arts into discussion of other historical developments,

but obviously it makes sense to have one concentrated chapter in which the arts can be analysed in some detail.

7   Now, as it were, the wheel has come full circle: we began with essentially political and event-based topics (war and revolution); now we come back to the third great series of world-shaking events (partly induced by the wars, so this chapter must come at the end, not at the beginning), the fall of the great European empires.

EXERCISE

Now that I have given you an example of what I am getting at, try to explain why in Parts Two and Three Hobsbawm has ordered his topics as he has. Given what you have to go on, this is not easy, but I am anxious to get you thinking about how historians integrate all the things they have to deal with into a structure which is as true as possible to the actual past. Exercises are as much about forcing yourself to think, as about getting 'correct' answers.

DISCUSSION

PART TWO

8   Again we start with the dominating international political circumstances.

9   But immediately we have to come to the question of economic recovery, affluence, and material prosperity which very much determine developments, at least in the Western countries.

10 I have already referred to this chapter. Essentially, Hobsbawm is working out the consequences for ordinary people of the economic circumstances he has described in the previous chapter.

11 He then, in a further example of a logical sequence, takes this further by looking at the sorts of thing I have already been talking about, changes in human relationships, sexual behaviour, and so on.

12 Most of what he has been talking about so far basically refers to the industrialized world. Therefore, it is logical now to take a concentrated look at the Third World.

13 The other parts of the world which need special attention are those which have fallen under Communist regimes: Russia of course, but now also China.

PART THREE

14 Hobsbawm has to justify his description of this third period as 'the landslide', so he naturally starts off by identifying the new events which have destroyed his 'Golden Age'. They start with the international oil crisis of 1973, and continue with the severe troubles faced by all of

the Western economies, particularly in the face of 'globalization' and the challenge of the newly developed Asian countries.

15   Again the theme of the Third World is picked up: this is the area in which revolution is continuing.

16   Now we come to another set of crucial events characterizing this third period – however, since they only become apparent from 1989 onwards they could not have been dealt with earlier: the collapse of the Russian and the East European Communist regimes.

17   Now a switch away from politics to deal, as I have already said, with rather more long-lasting trends.

18   Another of Hobsbawm's great strengths is his ability to discuss the sciences and the technologies, and again to integrate them into other developments. Clearly a separate chapter is needed in order to give them their due weight.

19   This is essentially a summing-up chapter.

Let me try to make sure that you understand what I was doing there. I was not trying to give you a kind of instant history of the twentieth century, but just trying to show the kind of thought, determined by the author's actual reading and research, which goes into working out a persuasive structure for a massive book of this sort. What I want you to get is a sense of logical sequence, of the analytical separation out into different topics (not muddling up together matters that need to be separated out) and of how a balance is stuck between topics and periodization.

Now let us focus on the Sixties. The information I have provided you with so far is pretty scrappy, consisting of:

1   Two lists of 'counter-cultural' shifts and other trends defining what I take to be distinctive about the Sixties (pp.16–17).

2   A list of eight points defining 'mainstream' culture as it was in the Fifties (pp.24–5).

3   A Chronology of events and movements and protests, etc. (in *Resource Book 4*, A1).

4   A few bits of statistical and social survey information, mainly about developing economic prosperity, and about changing sexual attitudes and behaviour (also in *Resource Book 4*, A2).

5   You also have (though so far I've referred you to only one of them) some extracts from pre-selected primary sources relating to aspects of developments in the Sixties (*Resource Book 4*, A3–23).

I want you now to concentrate on the Chronology (*Resource Book 4*, A1).

EXERCISE

Obviously, from the point of view of providing you with anything like a complete history of the Sixties, this Chronology has very grave defects. Bearing in mind the points I have been making in this section, try to summarize what these main defects are.

DISCUSSION

Relating to some of the main points I have been making in this section, I would list the weaknesses as follows:

1   Analysis.

There is no sense at all of *how* the different events, publications, etc. are related to each other, of what lay behind any individual one, of what effects it had, etc. Specifically:

(a) Causes, explanation.

We get some sense of the sorts of thing that were happening in the Sixties, but absolutely no sense of what caused such things to happen, no explanation as to *why* the Sixties were as they were.

(b) Significance, consequences.

There is no real sense of the significance of the individual items, or of their significance relative to each other; no sense of the consequences of all these happenings.

2   Narrative.

Although the items are arranged by year, and sometimes by month, there is no real sense of the precise sequence in which they occurred.

3   Description.

There is no description of what the Shadows, or the Beatles, or SDS did, or of what was in *Lady Chatterley's Lover* or *The Affluent Society*.

4   Periodization.

Although the Chronology provides basic evidence that this was a definite period in which distinctive things happened, it doesn't give any very clear indication as to when the period began and when it ended. Nor have we any secure basis for deciding whether it should be treated as one integrated period, or whether it should be divided into phases or sub-periods.

Later I'll discuss to some of the positive uses we can make of the Chronology.

A possible structure for the study of the Sixties

At the time of writing these units (January 1997) I am structuring my book *The Sixties: Cultural Revolution in Britain, France, Italy and the United States, c.1958–c.1974,* and here I am going to give you the broad framework. I decided that if I were to explain clearly the way in which the different developments of the Sixties took place, I would need to divide the main period up into three sub-periods. For the years from roughly the beginning of 1958 to roughly the end of 1963 I felt one could reasonably speak of 'The First Stirrings of a Cultural Revolution'. I felt it was then legitimate to describe the years 1964–1969 as 'The High Sixties'. There was then a kind of culmination and perhaps period of excess, from around 1969 to around 1973, though also a period in which less developed regions caught up with the swinging cities: this I have titled 'Everything Goes; and Catching Up'. In addition, obviously, I needed an Introduction, which, in particular, would try to explain the conjunction of forces and circumstances which brought about the unique era of the Sixties, and a Conclusion which would explain the long-term consequences of Sixties' developments – 'setting the cultural agenda for the rest of the century' as I put it.

FIGURE 25/26.2 *(Left) The Beatles in 1963. (Right) John Lennon and George Harrison in the rock-and-roll circus in 1968. (Photograph: © Hulton Getty)*

5 COMPARATIVE HISTORY

Already in my discussions of the Sixties, I have been introducing a kind of comparative history. Certainly I have been approaching the Sixties in a markedly different way from the way in which, in Units 8 and 9 respectively, I introduced 'The History of the British Family' and 'The French Revolution'. Focus on the words 'British' and 'French' and I think you will begin to see how my Sixties treatment is comparative in a way that these single-country treatments could not be.

EXERCISE

How has my introduction to the Sixties been *comparative* in a way in which my approaches to 'The British Family' and 'The French Revolution' were not? If possible, add a few words explaining the term 'comparative history'.

DISCUSSION

The topic I picked in Unit 8, the 'Family', was confined to Britain; the topic in Unit 9 was confined to France. In giving you examples of developments in the Sixties I have included material from Britain, three other European countries, and North America; in identifying key developments in the Sixties, I have been suggesting that these developments occurred in several countries; they were not simply confined to one. Even from the information in the Chronology you can see that while developments in the different countries were similar, they were certainly not identical: there was no equivalent in the European countries of the centrally important civil rights movement in America; divorce and abortion reform came rather later in France and Italy than in Britain; there were serious disturbances in French and Italian secondary schools in the early and middle Sixties and on into the Seventies which had no real analogue in Britain; arguably, religious influences, usually of a highly conservative type, were stronger in France, Italy and parts of the United States, than in Britain, and created strong resistance to counter-cultural ideas, or diverted them into different channels. Comparative history, then, is history which covers similar topics over several different countries, thus bringing out comparisons and contrasts between the different countries, and showing which developments were part of the common movement, and which peculiar to individual countries.

It is quite probable that, in the past, you have studied history confined to one country – perhaps 'English history' – even if called 'British history' there was quite probably precious little treatment of Scotland or Wales, though 'the Irish question' may have figured prominently. In the preparatory material for this course (which many of you will have studied) reference was made to the very live controversies over what should go into a national history curriculum. There is much to be said for the view that children should first learn the history of their own country. If you don't have some grounding in the history of your own country, it may be difficult to plunge into the histories of other countries. Comparative history, by definition, is certainly more complex, and almost certainly covers a wider range of information, than single-country history. It may not be suitable for children. However, in the Open University History department we have laid quite a heavy emphasis on comparative history. Looking at several countries together gives a clearer sense of wider historical movements, changes in economic organization, changes in class and power structures, the influences of scientific discovery and technological innovation, the changing role and status of women, and so on. To go back to the topic discussed in Unit 8, we would obviously have a much more thorough sense of the way in which the family has developed and changed if we took several countries together, rather than just Britain. More than this, studying other countries than one's own actually helps to illuminate specific features of one's own country which one might otherwise miss: in a very real sense British youth culture, and the music and fashions associated with it, did set standards for the rest of the world during the Sixties; yet, looking at youth radio programmes and magazines in France, and, above all, the activism in the French secondary schools, one can see how conformist and unsophisticated in many respects British young people were by comparison.

6 HISTORICAL EXPLANATION

Say that I am broadly correct in what I have already suggested about movements and developments in the main Western countries between 1958 and 1973 ('the long Sixties'), that these were particularly exciting, that they involved challenges to established authorities and conventions, and that they resulted in transforming the lives of ordinary people. Say that this is a correct analysis of what was actually happening in the Sixties, an accurate description of the most significant developments of the period. We would still be left with the big question of *why* such movements and developments took place, and *why* they took place within this relatively short period of time. Such questions take us into the realm of causation (what 'caused' the Sixties?) or, to use a more precise and less crude term, *explanation* (how do we 'explain' how the Sixties came about?).

Historical explanation is one of the most complicated and difficult aspects of historical study, and we shall not go into it very deeply here. If you have ever studied any history before, you may have been introduced to the notion of historical explanation (or causation) through preparing for exam questions on such topics as the 'causes' of the Reformation, the 'causes' of the Industrial Revolution, the 'causes' of the Revolt of the American Colonists, or the 'causes' of the First World War. You may indeed have memorized lists of such 'causes'. The first warning to issue with respect to university-level historical study is that a mere list will not suffice. You will need to give some sense of the relationship between the different causes, which are more important, which less. At the very least you will be expected to make the obvious distinction between, on the one hand 'long-term causes' (or, 'situational causes', as Sir Geoffrey Elton, the famous historian of both Tudor England and of the Reformation in Europe, put it) and, on the other hand, 'immediate' or 'direct' causes. Such a scheme might be applied in expounding the origins of the French Revolution.

EXERCISE

Without wasting any time going back over Unit 9, can you suggest, *briefly* and *in the most general terms*, one or two examples of 'long-term' or 'situational' causes, and one or two examples of 'immediate' or 'direct' causes of the French Revolution? I just want an answer indicating an understanding of the basic principle at issue here, not any kind of full summary of the causes of the French Revolution.

DISCUSSION

If you said that long-term, or situational, causes were things like the chronic inefficiency of the monarchical government in raising the revenues it needed, the criticisms of existing government being mounted by the *philosophes* and diffused through the enormous expansion in publishing, and the hardships and grievances endured by the many for so long, that would have been excellent. Equally excellent, if you had said that immediate or direct causes were matters like the actual bankruptcy of the monarchical government in 1786, the dismissal of the popular minister Necker, the refusal of the Assembly of Notables and of the parliaments to cooperate in bringing in the necessary reform programme, the famine of 1787 and 1788, the summoning of the Estates General for May 1789. Something like that, indicating that you understand that long-term or situational causes are causes which have been there over a considerable period of time and which helped (in this particular case) to make the Revolution likely, without in themselves provoking the actual outbreak. It is the immediate or direct causes which determine that the Revolution actually broke out in 1789. That's fine for the question I asked.

However, moving on now to the slightly unsatisfactory nature of this simple division into two types of causes, one might note that what is set out above only takes us as far as the early summer of 1789 and the beginnings of what looked like a constitutional revolution which retained the monarchy. If we want to explain the Revolution as a complex series of interrelating events, spreading over several years, getting ever more extreme, and involving more and more people, then we have to look at the way in which the Revolution, as it were, became self-fuelling, at how some of the consequences of the early causes, in themselves became causes of further developments and change. Such events as the storming of the Bastille and the 'Great Fear' are both events of the early Revolution itself, and the causes of further developments.

All this is simply by way of showing that in history we can't have simple, mechanistic cause-and-effect models. You can't put all the causes on one side of an equation (even if you do divide them up into the two types) and say that they equal a certain consequence on the other side of the equation. The past is constantly in flux: we are constantly getting what might be crudely described as 'knock-on effects', as well as 'feedback', 'cross-currents', and reactions stimulating further action. That is the confusing reality of which historians have to provide a clear and well-structured account. The situational/direct causes model can be perfectly satisfactory for writing a student essay, but usually won't be adequate for a historian's extended study. For myself, I wouldn't talk about long-term *causes* at all. I prefer to talk of *circumstances*, indicating that in any pre-existing situation there will be forces making for change, but there will also be forces inhibiting, or setting limits on, change. I would define three broad types of circumstance, all of which may be creating a potential for change, but all of which, equally, may be setting limits on change: *structural* (basic 'material' circumstance – demography, economic conditions, levels of technology); *ideological* (theories, values, ideas, policies, beliefs); and *institutional* (the nature of a monarchical system, of the organization of the Church, and so on). The inadequacies of the main monarchical institutions of France made a revolutionary situation always strongly possible, and also ensured that there was no mechanism ready to hand (such as the British parliament) to enable change to take place smoothly and without revolutionary upheaval. If you go on to study history at third level, you will look more thoroughly at the conceptual framework of structural, ideological, and institutional circumstances that establish the parameters within which historical outcomes (for example a war, a revolution, a period of extensive change such as the Sixties) are determined. Having established the parameters, adequate historical explanation needs to show how the precise nature and timing of the outcomes are the consequence of certain more direct circumstances, including political action, accident and the particular convergence of different elements. Here I just want you to grasp the point that in a fully rounded historical account, explanation will be required, and that the kind of explanation required is far too complicated to be contained within a simple cause-and-effect model.

You may recall from Unit 9 that there used to be another way of explaining the French Revolution. This was that by the late eighteenth century in France the monarchical/aristocratic/feudal system could no longer contain the increasingly successful capitalist bourgeoisie, and that in order to pave the way for modern capitalist bourgeois society, it was necessary for the bourgeoisie to overthrow the aristocracy; that, according to the theory, being what happened in the French Revolution. Explanations of this sort are really appealing to certain alleged 'Laws of History' (said to be analogous to the 'Laws of Science'). Most working historians never had any faith in the existence of such laws; and the faithful today are very few and far between, and usually to be found only among those who are not serious professional students of history.

There are, then, three major points about historical explanation which I am seeking to put before you.

1   To provide an explanation it is not sufficient simply to compile a mixed list of 'causes' of varying character and varying importance.

2   For the sorts of relatively complex issues historians are interested in – leaving aside very limited, single, time-specific events, such as why Margaret Thatcher resigned as Prime Minister in November 1990; why President Abraham Lincoln was assassinated – historical explanation does not conform to a simple, mechanistic, cause-and-effect model.

3   Historians do not find the invocation of some general historical law a satisfactory way of providing explanation.

4   It is not that 'everything is accidental', but that, along with longer-term trends and forces, events (sudden deaths, famines, wars) play their part in bringing about particular outcomes; above all we have to look at the way in which particular circumstances *accumulate*, or *converge* (that is to say all come together at once) – actual outcomes can often best be explained by the particular way in which events and circumstances accumulate and converge (I personally see this as central in explaining the Sixties).

Historians, as I remarked at the beginning of TV9, almost always concentrate on specific and firmly defined topics: they do not go in for offering general explanations of the human condition, or of how the past becomes the present, and the present becomes the future. From this there follows a fifth observation.

5   Historians can only offer an explanation when what they are trying to explain has been clearly and explicitly defined.

Now, some time back, I raised the question of explaining how it came about that there was a period, roughly 1958–1973, in which changes of a distinctive and significant type took place. If, however, the Sixties which I have described never really happened, then there would be no point in trying to establish that explanation. If the Sixties were really rather different, then a different explanation would be called for. And if the

Sixties turned out to be a rather boring time, in which nothing very much happened, save that the existing power structure continued, existing inequalities were reinforced, then there really wouldn't be much to explain.

History, as soon as you get away from simplistic political history, monarchs and presidents and prime ministers, and into a richer social and cultural history, is like that. You don't have a series of undisputed 'effects' for which you then simply have to find 'causes'. Earlier in this course there have been discussions of 'Classicism' and 'Romanticism'. These are legitimate labels to describe networks of attitudes, values, practices, artefacts, and so on; but pinning them down in exact and simple formulas is not easy. Thus *explaining* Classicism or *explaining* Romanticism is not easy either. That's history.

So back once more to the Sixties. For the purposes of this block I think we can produce a sufficiently agreed outline version of the Sixties to make that outline an outcome *for* which one can start looking for an explanation. So we are trying to explain why it was a time, basically, of innovation, of 'counter-culture', whether it was a time of real revolutionary potential and a time of promise betrayed, or as I personally am inclined to think, a time in which genuine change did permeate most of society.

But let us be absolutely clear as to the nature and dimensions of what we have to explain. We are not concerned just with one country but with the countries mentioned in my Chronology. We are not concerned much with the formal political complexion of governments: one can't say, for instance, that everywhere the left came into power in the Sixties. Until 1969 France was ruled by the ultra-conservative General Charles de Gaulle, and from 1969 by his personal favourite, Pompidou. In Italy, it is true, governments were shifting more and more to the centre-left, with a small reversal at the end of the decade. In the United States the governments, of Kennedy, and then Johnson, were 'progressive' as these things go in that country, but by the end of the decade the conservative Nixon was in power. In Germany, the conservative Christian Democrats ruled until 1966, with the Social Democrats being in power thereafter. In Britain, Labour was in power from 1964 to 1970; but in that year, when the social and cultural trends of the decade were continuing at accelerating pace, the Conservatives under Ted Heath were returned to power. So, we are looking for an explanation of a period of social and cultural change across several countries, irrespective of whether they had conservative or 'progressive' governments in power.

I would like to be able to set out for you my explanation of the Sixties in schematic fashion (remember in Unit 9 my series of concentric circles to show how different things were happening at the same time during the French Revolution and *converging* with each other), but explaining the Sixties is just too complex. I want, above all, to stress the notions of accumulation and convergence. Then, while I believe it is important analytically to sort out structural forces and constraints, ideological forces and constraints, and institutional forces and constraints, it is necessary at the same time to recognize the longer-term social and cultural implications of the Second World War, and also the influence of the Cold War and the nuclear stalemate (or threat of mutual destruction, if you like to look at it that way) – just as, when we are actually in the Sixties, we are forced to consider the implications of the Vietnam War. However, having recognized the untidiness of historical processes as they actually happen, one can, I believe, offer a three-stage explanation, as follows.

1   Structural, ideological, and institutional forces and constraints (taking account of the effects of the Second World War and of the Cold War and nuclear stalemate). In the elaboration which follows, I leave out institutional circumstances, since they (systems of government, religious bodies, and so on) generally acted as constraints on change.

2   Accumulation and convergence: build-up and release of frustrations; beginning of formation of 'counter-cultural' and protest movements, which expand and interact with each other; tendency towards more and more 'extremism' in absence of traditional checks and balances.

3   Specific features during the Sixties: (a) continuing economic expansion; (b) strength of liberal and consensual politics; (c) reactionary forces (particularly police forces and religious bodies). Thawing of the Cold War. The Vietnam War.

Let me elaborate, retaining the three-part structure, though in a normal piece of historical writing one would not be employing numbers in this schematic way.

1   Affluence came to America during the Second World War, and (though there were still many pockets of severe poverty) continued thereafter; economic recovery began in Europe from 1948 onwards. Slowly the economic basis was established for the production, consumption, and international exchange, of new consumer goods. Between the mid-fifties and the mid-sixties there was a great increase in the number of multinational companies. New purchasers appeared in the market place: particularly young married couples, the working class in general, racial and ethnic minorities, those in the regions and provinces, asserting themselves for the first time against metropolitan dominance, and women and girls. Economic change combined with demography, specifically the 'baby boom' at the end of the Second World War, producing by the beginning of the Sixties an unprecedentedly large, and unprecedentedly well-off, teenage presence in the market place (and young people could operate as producers as well as consumers). Major technological developments of importance are those in television (including Telstar), 45-rpm records and transistor radios, in electronic synthesizers, and in advanced consumer products, refrigerators, washing machines, and

so on, and in the development of the contraceptive pill. Ideologically, conservative forces were strong, reinforced by the frigid influences of the Cold War, and hysteria in the United States about 'un-American' activities. Affluence and consumerism were taken as validating the perfections of existing society. However, new critiques of society were appearing in the Fifties, and formed the basis for the much more rapid and extended circulation of critical ideas in the Sixties: neo-Marxism (Marcuse), the beginnings of structuralism, the 'New Left', the establishment of sociology departments, particularly in the European universities, and the first limited circulation of the notions of the American Beats. Old racial boundaries were crossed in a much more comprehensive way than ever before as young whites adopted and adapted black rhythm 'n blues.

2   The Second World War, particularly through the dimensions of its being a heroic resistance to the evils of Nazism, and a war in which everyone – workers, women, black people – participated, raised great hopes, and indeed promises, of substantial social change, in regard, for instance, to such issues as civil rights for black Americans, or better conditions for Italian peasants. In the years of struggle for economic recovery (in Europe) and of dominance by the imperatives of the Cold War, very many of these hopes had been frustrated, but they began to emerge again at the end of the Fifties. In fact, a really critical factor in creating the movements we associate with the Sixties, was the breaking out of the frustrations which had been dammed up since the early post-war years. Generally, the conservative and unchanging nature of institutions added to these frustrations. Conservatism was probably most deeply rooted in Britain, and the art colleges as they had developed during the Fifties were to be particularly potent centres of change. Generally, educational institutions were very out-of-touch in America and the other European countries. The important centres of change at the end of the Fifties were: youth (including the music variously referred to as 'beat' or 'rock') and new uninhibited fashions; the arts and entertainments – happenings, pop, experimental theatre, sexually explicit novels and films; the earliest civil rights protests; campaigns for nuclear disarmament; campaigns, including older people, for the preservation of the environment; protests over women's conventional role in society (*Sex and the Single Girl*, 1962; *The Feminine Mystique*, 1963). These young people, these protesters, mostly had an unprecedented economic security, which, as it were, underwrote their daring. These different areas of change expanded and interacted, affecting more and more of society. In a time of affluence, and (on the whole) economic security, nothing succeeded like excess. Extreme positions led to yet more extreme ones. Daring films ratified daring behaviour. Though the pill was not in fact in wide use, sexual activity became a matter for discussion, and thus a matter legitimated beyond the traditional constraints. Society seemed to offer

greater possibilities than ever before for self-fulfilment, yet poverty, inequality, authoritarianism remained: hence the critiques in society got stronger and stronger. Signs of thaw in the Cold War stimulated relaxation of the more rigid nationalistic and authoritarian attitudes; the end of the Algerian War had similar effects in France.

3   The firm base for accelerating and expanding Sixties developments was continuing affluence and rising incomes. Two contrasting features of the High Sixties are the permeation of society by new ideas, and extremely violent confrontations. The basic explanation for this lies in the emergence of a triangle of contrasting forces, ideological and institutional: (1) the new protest, innovative, and 'counter-cultural' movements; (2) the liberal and consensual elements (in some areas at least, even if they had blind spots and conservative or nationalistic attitudes in others) occupying some important positions of power (Presidents Kennedy and Johnson, and, more important, their advisers and functionaries; figures believing that they had to respond to a changing society in the judiciary, broadcasting, censorship, education; Keynesians – those of progressive economic outlook – in the civil service); (3) utterly unreformed reactionary elements, particularly in the various police forces.

The Vietnam War – blind spot for many American liberals, though also opposed by many other American liberals – served to focus and crystallize general anti-imperialist, anti-establishment, sentiment, greatly intensifying it, and giving it a violent edge.

What, given my insistence throughout Units 8 and 9 that all historical accounts must be firmly based on the sources, is that account based on? Well, in so far as much of it refers to forces and circumstances developing prior to the Sixties, that part is almost entirely based on secondary sources; I have done some primary research on the Second World War which has led me to take the view of the significance of that war expressed here. My main research in primary sources has been confined to certain aspects of society and culture in the Sixties: conclusions about the Sixties themselves are based on both primary sources and secondary sources – though general histories are rare, there are many specialist works on civil rights, popular culture, student protests, and so on. All I have done here is give you an outline sketch of one way of going about explaining the Sixties. In the next section we will go on to things in more detail and look at some primary sources. For the moment, I don't want you to do more than reflect on what I have been saying, certainly not as something to be memorized, more as a model of one way of providing historical explanation. Try to sift out in your own mind how far you find my account satisfactory, how far you have questions to raise, or perhaps disagreements to express.

7 SELECTING AND SORTING IN BRINGING OUT WHAT IS HISTORICALLY SIGNIFICANT

Again we touch on a point you will have encountered in your own TMAs, in whatever subject. You can't just bung everything down, and you can't just bung it down any old how. This (leaving aside for the moment the more complex problem of developing a structure to integrate periodization, narrative, analysis, explanation and description) is certainly true in the writing of a piece of history. One has to select significant bits of information and reject the insignificant. One has to group like bits of information together so that a clear point is made, rather than have bits and pieces dispersed ineffectually throughout the essay or book. I'm not going to retread the ground of Units 8 and 9 in discussing how objective historians can be in making their selections. My position is the simple one that a historian who is an expert in the particular period or topic will have a much more secure sense of what is significant and what is not than a non-expert. Of course, even among experts there may well be disagreements, particularly, as I remarked at the beginning of TV9, if we've got a really big topic; and also if we're dealing with particularly controversial topics like censorship or abortion. My brief study of the French Revolution in Unit 9 was basically a selection of what, based on my reading of various experts, I took to be significant (particularly, of course, with respect to the immediate teaching task of providing a context for Rousseau, David and Friedrich). The two extracts I provided above from different books by Hobsbawm are excellent summaries of what Hobsbawm considered significant in two different periods ('Age of Revolutions' and 'Age of Extremes'); the same goes for Matthew Anderson on the period prior to 1815.

Coming back to the Sixties, you may well have felt that the Chronology contained more information than you could readily cope with, but of course that was only a selection from all the things I might have put in; it was *my* selection based on my work in the secondary sources and in the primary sources, and a lot of reflection on that work.

Let us concentrate for the moment on the issue of selecting *and grouping* material, and let us, from the bits and pieces we've encountered so far, select six or seven areas of significant *social* development in the Sixties – that is to say, let us leave out politics, art, literature and classical music, film and philosophy, television programmes. (TV25 does show how television programmes in Britain present evidence of the social change taking place, and were themselves changing in style and content; television was important in other countries as well – bringing the Vietnam War into American homes, for instance – though it is generally accepted that British television was the most innovative.) All of these can be related to social history, but for the purposes of the exercise, let's leave them out. When selecting 'areas', or 'headings', it is usually best, without stretching things beyond their limits, to go for inclusive headings rather than very limited ones. For example: relaxation of censorship, publication of sexy books and films, and liberation in sexual behaviour could all be included under the heading 'Permissiveness and Sexual Liberation'; civil rights demonstrations and legislation, and all other matters relating to race, could be included under a general heading of 'Changing Race Relationships'. I commend these two examples to you in attempting this exercise.

EXERCISE

Following the guidance given above, and using the material in both the 'Chronology' and the 'Statistical and social survey information' (*Resource Book 4*, A1 and A2) as a basis, select six or seven areas (not more than seven) of significant *social* development in the Sixties. You may also find the two lists of points on pages 16–17 useful.

FIGURE 25/26.3 *Carnaby Street, London, 23 May 1964. (Photograph: Popperfoto/PPP)*

DISCUSSION

1 and 2 If you took my advice, you'd have got two right away: 'Permissiveness and Sexual Liberation' and 'Changing Race Relationships'.

3   After that I went for the whole business of rising wages, rising consumer expenditure, arrival of bathrooms and electricity in remote places, and so on, to which it would be usual to apply the heading '(Changing) Material Conditions' – but such labels as 'Rising Living Standards', or 'Consumerism', or 'Affluence' would all be reasonable.

4   I felt we could hardly leave out youth in all its aspects and ramifications, well-expressed in the term 'Youth Culture'. This just about allows us to bring in all the references to the new beat/rock/ pop music, though if you preferred to put that as a separate heading, I wouldn't fault you. The new youthful fashions could also be squeezed in here, though again also could be a separate heading (though extravagant when we are limited to seven, and almost certainly entailing the leaving out of something rather important – the point of 'selecting and sorting' is to make sure we get all the significant developments).

5   Clearly the Sixties was very much a time of violent protest, or violent suppression of protest and, perhaps, revolutionary activity. Now you may have felt this was ruled out as part of 'Politics', or that important aspects had already been covered by 'Race'. Difficult choices, perhaps: but I think I'd have to say that to miss out protests and demonstrations and violent confrontations would be to leave out a very vital component of life, even if not life as lived by the majority of people in the Sixties. So my heading is 'Protest and Confrontation'. You could, I think, include the 'underground' here, though that could be fitted in under other headings ('Permissiveness' for example), or on its own.

6   Possibly the new feminism could be included under 'Protest and Confrontation', but to me it makes more sense to take all the developments affecting relationships between individuals and groups, between women and men, between children and adults, between social classes, developments in regard to gay rights, and in regard to divorce and abortion under one heading, perhaps 'Liberation in Personal and Social Relations'.

7   So what's left? Quite a lot really. The most important topic, in my view, is 'Social Welfare'.

If we hadn't agreed to leave out films and television programmes we would have needed a heading like 'Changing Popular Culture'. I think all the other things left out could be squeezed into one or other of our other seven headings. The most notable are: sport, the environment, and the liquor laws. I think we could put the abolition of the feudal rules governing professional football in Britain in with 'Liberation in Personal and Social Relations'. Environmental concerns I'd put with 'Protest', and relaxation in liquor laws with 'Liberation in Personal and Social Relations', or perhaps with 'Material Conditions'.

Does all this arguing and hesitating over how to compile a list of six or seven significant social developments in the Sixties astonish you? Perhaps you have been used to a teacher who reads out one cut-and-dried list. Now you can see that the lists which appear in our schools and our textbooks start with the researches, and the reflections, and the debates of the historical experts. History is not eternal truth; it is produced by human beings – called historians.

Let us now try to enrich our understanding of what was significant about the Sixties by looking at some primary sources, which have, of course, had to be preselected by me.

EXERCISE

I want you to start by turning to sources A3, A4 and A5, looking first at what *types* of source they are and their dates, and then reading them. They are primary sources for the Sixties, but perhaps particularly *dubious*, or shall I say *peculiar*, ones.

1   As sources for the Sixties, these all have one thing in common: say what that is, then discuss their weaknesses and strengths for helping us to understand what was significant about the Sixties.

2   Each source does express a clear view about the significance of the Sixties. In each case summarize that view even if you feel the source is particularly unreliable, prejudiced, or weak.

DISCUSSION

1   They are all written between ten and twenty years after the end of the Sixties; they are reminiscences of people who had lived through the Sixties – this being what makes them *primary* sources – but *looking back* on the Sixties. With such sources there is always the potential weakness of memory failure, romanticization, bringing in of hindsight; on the other hand, knowledge of what happened, or what didn't happen, later, do give these sources an additional strength in assessing what was significant about the Sixties.

A3 is by someone who was very active in several counter-cultural movements: to the extent that he was personally very deeply and emotionally involved he will be a strong and authentic witness, but also a prejudiced one.

The author of A4 was also involved in the events of the Sixties, though in almost an opposite situation, being one of the upholders of the university establishment against the student protesters at Cornell University in the state of New York. He comes with strong personal memories, but he is also very prejudiced.

Written by two sisters, who, in the Sixties, were ordinary lower-middle-class teenage school girls in Liverpool, A5 provides, as close as we can ever get, the voice of ordinary people. No doubt as teenagers from Liverpool they have their biases in favour of that city – we would need to check that their account is a representative one, repeated in other sources.

2   A3 is saying that, despite the enormously high hopes of the time, the Sixties really had very little long-term significance. The world wasn't changed; at most, those who participated with Haynes in counter-cultural activities perhaps changed a little as individuals. The consequences for people who had had high hopes were depression and cynicism. Haynes does speak of the fun and experimentation of

FIGURE 25/26.4 *British fashion, 2 March 1967. (Photograph: © Hulton Getty)*

the time, but his summing up of long-term significance is definitely a negative one.

A4, concentrating on universities, sees the Sixties as highly significant, but entirely for the bad. The effect of the Sixties on education and freedom of thought is likened to the impact of Nazism in 1930s Germany.

A5 echoes Haynes in recognizing the naivety of the Sixties, but comes over very strongly in support of the idea that the long-term significance of the Sixties was that it encouraged individual expression, tolerance for new ideas, and the removal of prejudices.

Do these summaries cancel each other out, or is it possible that there are elements of truth in each of them? For myself (as will already be apparent) I believe the assessment in extract A5 is nearest to being the right one (and the other contributions in the collection of women's reminiscences from which it is taken – *Very Heaven: Looking Back at the 1960s*, edited by Sara Maitland – broadly support this view). I believe that Haynes was too caught up in his own counter-cultural scene to appreciate the wider changes which people like the two sisters could feel directly. Bloom, as an ultra-conservative, it seems to me, fails to take account of what was so stultifying in universities before the Sixties, and what was so positive and liberating in what happened during the Sixties. But you should keep all of these points of view in mind as we move towards trying to sum up the significance of the Sixties.

Now, if you feel you have the time, I would like you to work on some or all of the other Sixties primary sources, A6–A23. Although I am very strongly against reducing extracts from primary sources to little more than mere sound bites, I have made a special effort to keep these ones really short so that, though, as always, they should be read carefully and critically, each one does relate clearly to one, or perhaps two, of the areas of significant social development in the Sixties we have just identified. What the sources tell us about these areas can only be arrived at when you have analysed them critically, evaluating their strengths and weaknesses, paying attention to what they are (extracts from letters, polemical books, newspapers, and so on) and to their dates (remember what you learned in Unit 9).

OPTIONAL EXERCISE

(When I say 'optional', I do mean optional. In any case you should find my Discussion useful.)

For each document from A6 onwards note down what major areas it is concerned with (using the list of seven on p.49) – and any other brief comments you feel you'd like to make.

DISCUSSION

A6 Youth culture (rock music) (when you have time to read this carefully, you might note that the document brings out both the popularity of Presley and the hostility to him of 'respectable' American society, as represented by the newspaper). That kind of hostility was largely to disappear during the Sixties when Presley became an all-American hero. My comment: nothing very counter-cultural about the adoption of Presley as an all-American iconic symbol.

A7 Permissiveness and sexual liberation; youth culture. My comment: but from two very hostile, prejudiced, and frankly absurdly untrustworthy points of view.

A8 Permissiveness and sexual liberation. My comment: we have here an establishment figure, admittedly a very liberal one, supporting teenage sexual experimentation.

A9 Changing race relationships. My comment: this is an example of what I described as a 'triangle of contrasting forces' (p.46); pressures for change interact with repression and lead to violence – including King's assassination.

A10 Liberation in personal and social relationships. My comment: this is a very early, and very moderate, feminist statement.

A11 Youth culture; 'beat' music. My comment: a careful reading will bring out the sense of a very special quality attaching to the Beatles, and the fact that their popularity already extended beyond teenagers.

A12 Protest and confrontation – university students. My comment: the Berkeley Free Speech movement and a sympathetic appraisal of it by certain Berkeley academics.

A13 Permissiveness and sexual liberation; youth culture.

A14 Youth culture and permissiveness; the use of LSD; 'dropping out'. My comment: striking that so many people took such claims seriously at the time.

A15 and A16 Changing race relationships; protest and confrontation, riots. My comment: A16 shows the reactionary and violent nature of the police.

A17 Youth culture; fashion. My comment: shows that youthful fashions have now conquered the market – though this particular middle-aged American lady is not pleased.

A18 Protest and confrontation; students. My comment: evidence of police brutality against Paris students in May 1968.

FIGURE 25/26.5 *French riot police face demonstrators in Paris, 14 May 1968.* (*Photograph: © Hulton Getty*)

A19 Material conditions – among Italian peasants. (My earlier claims about bathrooms and electricity are based on surveys like this, integrated with hard statistical information on houses with inside bathrooms, purchases of electrical goods, and so on.)

A20 Liberation in personal and social relations; permissiveness; material conditions. My comment: an example of one of the new New York singles bars.

A21 Liberation in personal and social relations; women's rights.

A22 Youth culture.

A23 Liberation in personal and social relations; women's rights; the issue of abortion.

That was a rather elementary exercise, still on the theme of selecting the significant developments of the Sixties; it was not a thorough-going exercise on primary sources since, as you know, it is quite wrong to think that each individual primary source makes a single transparent statement – before confirming these conclusions we would need to analyse the sources much more carefully.

EXERCISE

I am now going to give, on one side of the page, my own summing up of what I take to be the significant characteristics of the Sixties. On the other side of the page I want you to note critical comments that might be made by those who see things differently – feel free to make every kind of critical comment which occurs to you.

My summary of the significant features of the Sixties, which, as I see it, set the social and cultural agenda for the rest of the century	Criticism that could be made of the points
1 Unprecedented international cultural interchange. Britain, particularly with respect to pop music and fashion, film and television, played an unusually distinctive role; other examples include coffee machines from Italy, discos from France, theatrical innovation from America.	
2 Major transformations in material life, defined through such clichés as 'consumerism' and 'mod cons', which, in certain areas, involved also the arrival, for the first time, of electricity and inside lavatories.	
3 Upheavals in class, race, and family relationships.	
4 The rise of new consumer groups with new needs and tastes: teenagers, of course, but just as important as *general* trend-setters were young, and youngish, married couples.	
5 A great outburst of initiative, enterprise, individualism, doing your own thing, in fashion, photography, popular art, and so on. Sometimes these initiatives were supported by state subsidy (as with some experimental theatre) but in essence they were uninhibited examples of private enterprise and in no way socialistic – boutiques, modelling agencies, restaurants, art galleries, pornographic magazines.	

6 'Permissiveness' – that is to say, a general sexual liberation, entailing striking changes in public and private morals and a new frankness, openness, indeed honesty, in personal relations and modes of expression.

7 New concerns for civil and personal rights, including: the first resistance to a century-old (though recently accelerating) destruction of the environment; high levels of participation; protests against consumer society and militaristic imperialism; the events of 1968–1969; the new feminism, and the first stirrings of gay liberation; associated with many of these developments, bouts of extreme violence, involving deaths and massive destruction of property, these being provoked by extremism on both sides, but most often by the police.

8 Original and striking developments in élite thought and culture – some rather absurd in their claims about structures of language determining human thoughts and actions, about 'the death of the author', about the 'repressive tolerance' of 'bourgeois moderates', and about the underclass as the revolutionary class, with students as their leaders. (This, indeed, is the era of Barthes, Foucault, and Eco, and of Warhol, Pop Art, conceptual art, concrete poetry, 'chance' in literature, art, and music.) New academic approaches to the analysis of the arts, literature and other cultural practices in the past.

9 A participatory and uninhibited popular culture, whose central component was rock music.

DISCUSSION

My summary of the significant features of the Sixties, which, as I see it, set the social and cultural agenda for the rest of the century	Criticism that could be made of the points
1 Unprecedented international cultural interchange. Britain, particularly with respect to pop music and fashion, film and television, played an unusually distinctive role; other examples include coffee machines from Italy, discos from France, theatrical innovation from America.	(a) These are really extremely trivial matters. What do coffee machines and discos matter compared with the distribution of power, the oppression of the poor, and so on? (b) The reference to Britain is jingoistic and over-stated: really America was the originator of the key developments in popular culture. (c) All that these developments show is the power of commercialism. (d) Even if what is said here is true, these products were all depraved and culturally of a low standard – everywhere in the 1960s life was standardized and reduced in quality.
2 Major transformations in material life, defined through such clichés as 'consumerism' and 'mod cons', which, in certain areas, involved also the arrival, for the first time, of electricity and inside lavatories.	(a) The long cycle of increasing prosperity ('The Golden Age') began at the end of the Second World War, so that these developments cannot properly be seen as specific to the 1960s. (b) Consumerism and 'mod cons' merely blind people to their condition of oppression; in any case areas of deep poverty remained.
3 Upheavals in class, race, and family relationships.	(a) The basic class structure was the same in the 1970s as it had been in the 1950s, with the same ruling class in power. (b) Discrimination and prejudice against black people, and North Africans (in France) continued in the 1970s and afterwards. (c) Patriarchy remained in power. (d) Alas, what is said here is all too true: traditional respect for authority was fatally destroyed in the 1960s

4 The rise of new consumer groups with new needs and tastes: teenagers, of course, but just as important as *general* trend-setters were young, and youngish, married couples.	(a) The existence of what can be conveniently described as 'consumerism' is not in doubt, but there is nothing admirable about a materialistic consumer society in which, indeed, people are blinded to their true interests and the way in which they are being exploited. (b) Trends were not set by teenagers or married couples – the trends were really set by the commercial interests which profited from them. (c) Unfortunately, these new trends were utterly deplorable, reducing cultural standards throughout the Western world.
5 A great outburst of initiative, enterprise, individualism, doing your own thing, in fashion, photography, popular art, and so on. Sometimes these initiatives were supported by state subsidy (as with some experimental theatre) but in essence they were uninhibited examples of private enterprise and in no way socialistic – boutiques, modelling agencies, restaurants, art galleries, pornographic magazines.	(a) These seem particularly trivial topics. (b) Anyway, fashion is always changing – there was nothing special about the 1960s. (c) Proper standards of dress and decorum were destroyed, with disastrous consequences for the future.
6 'Permissiveness' – that is to say, a general sexual liberation, entailing striking changes in public and private morals and a new frankness, openness, indeed honesty, in personal relations and modes of expression.	(a) This is really rather a trivial matter. (b) Anyway, changes in sexual behaviour had been taking place over a long period of time – there was nothing special about the 1960s. (c) This was a fatal relaxation of morals, which has had disastrous consequences ever since.

7 New concerns for civil and personal rights, including: the first resistance to a century-old (though recently accelerating) destruction of the environment; high levels of participation; protests against consumer society and militaristic imperialism; the events of 1968–1969; the new feminism, and the first stirrings of gay liberation; associated with many of these developments, bouts of extreme violence, involving deaths and massive destruction of property, these being provoked by extremism on both sides, but most often by the police.	(a) This is not expressed nearly strongly enough – in fact there was a genuine revolutionary situation which was not properly exploited, or which was frustrated by bourgeois cunning. (b) The inclusion of bourgeois environmentalism along with the other more serious issues is absurd. (c) There were no 'extremists' on the 'counter-cultural' side – only people who saw the true nature of society clearly and ruthlessly. (d) These movements were undisciplined, utterly misguided, and lacking in proper respect for authority: their legacy has been disastrous.
8 Original and striking developments in élite thought and culture – some rather absurd in their claims about structures of language determining human thoughts and actions, about 'the death of the author', about the 'repressive tolerance' of 'bourgeois moderates', and about the underclass as the revolutionary class, with students as their leaders. (This, indeed, is the era of Barthes, Foucault, and Eco, and of Warhol, Pop Art, conceptual art, concrete poetry, 'chance' in literature, art, and music.) New academic approaches to the analysis of the arts, literature and other cultural practices in the past.	(a) The use of the word 'absurd' is offensive. The figures mentioned here, and others, were responsible for laying the basis of the way we look at the world, and at the nature of knowledge, today. (b) The developments in the arts were in themselves revolutionary. (c) The developments in the arts were mostly quite trivial. (d) There was nothing original and striking about these thinkers: what they produced was not just absurd, but subversive nonsense – it has had a disastrous effect on the world of education and the intellect ever since. (e) The developments in the arts were meaningless, decadent, and simply a con trick perpetrated on the public.
9 A participatory and uninhibited popular culture, whose central component was rock music.	(a) Not really so participatory and uninhibited – really, in fact, controlled by commercial interests. (b) In so far as rock pop music had good qualities, it represented a rip-off from black Americans. (c) An entirely decadent popular culture which, with the other developments, certainly did play a central part in the general lowering of cultural standards.

As you will have seen, the criticisms I have filled in the right-hand side column are of two rather opposite kinds. In the following section we will return to this exercise and the evidence on which my views are based.

8 SCHOLARLY APPARATUS

By scholarly apparatus, I mean the footnotes and the bibliography, which you will find in scholarly historical works – if you can possibly get to a library please do get out some scholarly books and look at examples for yourself.

EXERCISE

What do you think are the functions of footnotes and bibliographies?

DISCUSSION

It has been said by critics of history that both, and particularly footnotes, are simply there for show; they are merely a pedantic convention through which historians make a claim that their work is scholarly and reliable, though in fact this is no more than empty window-dressing.

I hope you don't feel like that. I hope you have said something along the lines that footnotes are there to demonstrate the sources upon which particular statements, interpretations, conclusions, expressed in the main text of the historical work, are based. And bibliographies are there to demonstrate the whole range of primary and secondary sources upon which the entire book is based. (Historical *articles* have footnotes, but do not have, and do not need, bibliographies.)

As I have said before, arguments over the status of history, very much depend upon one's basic assumptions. If you *assume* that historians operate in good faith and with integrity, and are not bourgeois stooges, or unwitting victims of their cultural context, and, accordingly, that it is worthwhile reading what they write if you want to find out about the past, then you will accept this view that it is through scholarly apparatus that the historian invites the reader to share in the evidence upon which the historian's account is based; if you don't share in that assumption, you will take a view different from that presented in these units.

I talked about the historian 'sharing' with the reader. Throughout these history units I have always stressed that you must be cautious and critical in your reading, suggesting that even the best of historians may only get things about eighty per cent right. Historical communication, in my view, should always involve a dialogue between reader and historian. In their minds, readers should always be raising comments like the following: 'That's interesting – where did he/she get that from?'; 'Come on now, I don't believe *that*: what on earth are the sources?'; 'Interesting idea, but I bet there's no hard evidence for it'. Readers of history should be sceptical, doubts at the ready. Doubts are most quickly resolved, or confirmed, by looking at the appropriate footnote. The footnote should be as helpful as possible, but of course it offers information in a highly condensed form. A fellow professional, a really serious doubter, may want to go back beyond the footnote to the original source in the relevant library or archive. It is important that the footnotes should provide all the necessary information for that operation to be carried out as quickly and economically as possible.

The bibliography provides an overview. The first part will be concerned with primary sources, and will indicate the range of archives consulted (and also of course, negatively, will show if some really important archive has been ignored); it will also demonstrate the variety of primary sources consulted, including the printed ones such as newspapers and conduct books. The second part of the bibliography will consist of secondary sources, enabling the reader to check if the historian has taken into account the views of historians who have pioneered this subject area, or who have presented different or contrary interpretations to the historian's own.

EXERCISE

The 'questions' and 'answers' I posed in the little two-column exercise I set at the end of the previous section was, of course, very authoritarian (though I trust you exercised *your* rights to the full). I gave *my* views, together with *my* interpretation of contrary views. In a fully written-up version, I would have to provide notes, on the one side exclusively to secondary sources, on the other side mainly to primary sources.

Which side calls for secondary sources to be identified, which side mainly for primary sources? Explain your answer.

DISCUSSION

Where, in the right-hand column, I am claiming to give the views of other writers and historians, I would have to say who they are, and where and in what books or articles, they put forward the views I am citing. These would almost exclusively be secondary sources. However, in presenting my own views in the left-hand column, based on my researches, I would have to give full references to the primary sources I have analysed and extracted information from.

Let us look at some of these primary sources, or at least at the brief extracts from a few of them that I have selected for you.

I would like you to have in front of you document A11. Reams were written about the Beatles at the time. Their importance in the Sixties has almost become a cliché. They are usually seen as being central to the themes of:

1   the new pop/rock music as a universal language;

2   the new youth culture;

3   working-class and lower-middle-class input into that culture;

4   British cultural hegemony;

5   the amazing elaboration of popular music, and cross-over with contemporary classical music later in the decade;

6   their own extraordinary popularity and emergence as symbols of the age.

EXERCISE

Do we need this document? Is there anything special about it? Does it add anything to knowledge?

DISCUSSION

I hope you said something about its direct personal and enthusiastic quality, about its being a private letter, so that one can take it as sincere and not part of any organized support for the Beatles.

Actually, it really is quite striking how many references to the Beatles keep cropping up in the letters, diaries, and memoirs of all sorts of people in the Sixties. In another private collection, for instance, I found one distinguished American intellectual writing to a friend, in a very serious kind of joke, that he was planning to write in the names of the four Beatles as a joint presidential candidate – that, of course, was after the Beatles had toured America in 1964. A striking point about the letter here is that it was written just when the Beatles were having their first series of hit records in Britain – *before* they had become international figures. There are lots and lots of indirect statements about the impact of the Beatles: this is a particularly good direct, and as I say, private, statement. I don't think the actual name of the writer, beyond the fact that at the time he was a very young academic who had just been researching in America (and is now an Oxbridge professor), is important, and I have preferred to keep it concealed (not just here, but in my book – you have to be careful with contemporary figures).

EXERCISE

Now I want you to turn to documents A15 and A16. Take A16 first. In the contextual information, always essential before any primary source can be intelligently made use of, it is made clear that this is a particularly unreliable document, since, in particular, it presents the police view of the existence of snipers, when we now know that there were no snipers. Yet, I suggest that this very bias makes the unwitting testimony of the document all the more significant. What is the point here?

DISCUSSION

Though he is trying to defend the police, Locke shows how incredibly casual the police were about the use of fire-power. The fire-power is quite unbelievably excessive in the case of the little girl who was killed. With regard to the killing of William Dalton, the first version reveals what was widely believed about police behaviour, and what certainly did happen in many authenticated incidents. Even if the second version is the correct one, it still reveals the appalling readiness of the police to shoot to kill. Everything is made even worse by our knowledge that there were in fact no snipers.

EXERCISE

How accurate an account does A15 provide of the Newark riot?

DISCUSSION

The contextual information should help you here. Certainly there were black leaders who shared the speaker's views about organized black rebellion, and there was that element within the Newark riot; but we know that, for the most part, the riot was much more spontaneous than that, with blacks (and some whites) seizing the opportunity for looting, and wanton violence.

Should such sources be used in a serious book about the Sixties, and if so, what information should go into the relevant footnotes? The answer to the first question is that even document A16 can be used, provided the full context is given in the text, and it is clearly explained what point is being derived from the document. What would be quite wrong would be to quote the document as if it could be taken as reliable, and leaving the explanation of its unreliability to the footnote. Everything that it is important to say should be said in the actual text: the footnote should only be used for making absolutely clear what the document is and, most important, where it can be found. Document A15 is important as expressing a genuine black viewpoint, even if it is far from accurate as a summary of the riot. It would have to be made clear in the text of the book that this is a report of an interview given to journalists by LeRoi Jones, this being the version of that interview printed in a leading black newspaper.

FIGURE 25/26.6 *Martin Luther King addressing a civil rights march at the Lincoln Memorial in Washington DC, United States on 28 August 1963. This was the occasion when King made his 'I have a dream' speech. (Photograph: © Hulton Getty)*

The version given by Locke appears in the form of a published book which is available in really good libraries, particularly copyright libraries (as explained in TV8). All that is needed, then, in the footnote, is the full title of the book, and the page reference. There is a simple, but vital code which historians use to distinguish between published items like this one, and unpublished items like document A15. The title of a published book is always underlined or italicized; an unpublished item should never be underlined or italicized. Simple, but very effective.

This version of the statement by LeRoi Jones was actually published in the *Washington Free Press*, on 4 August 1967. This is the vital information that needs to be contained in the footnote: an interested scholar could find the document by going to a major international newspaper library. However, the fact is that in this case I did not go to the original newspaper – it would simply not have been rational for me, researching in four countries and covering a period of fifteen years, to work through hundreds of different newspapers. In this case, I found the quotation in an excellent secondary source, Thomas Powers, *The War at Home:*

Vietnam and the American People, 1964–1967 (p. 218). Honesty, and the academic convention of giving credit where it is due to other scholars, would compel me to include that information as well in the footnote.

In an overwhelming number of cases where I have quoted from newspapers, I have found them in the form of cuttings in the various archives. The cutting about Elvis Presley (document A6), for instance, was among the Van Dyke papers in the Mississippi Valley Collection in Memphis. In this, and similar cases, it would actually be easier for other researchers, or readers wanting to check up on me, to go direct to a copy of the newspaper in a newspaper library. In this particular case, I do actually make a point in my text of stating that this cutting came with a Van Dyke letter since that in itself is historically illuminating (the son had deliberately cut out the article to send to his parents). But, in general, provided I had not actually lifted the quotation from someone else's book, I would simply give the newspaper reference, covering myself with a general statement in the bibliography (this is the major component of scholarly apparatus, remember, which sets out the complete conspectus of the research work done by the historian) that most of my newspaper items came from cuttings, rather than from whole newspapers.

The two key words for scholarly apparatus are *honesty* and *helpfulness*. Let me remark, though my main purpose here is to explain how historians go, or should go, about their work, that the same basic principles apply to you in doing your TMAs. Understanding the principles of scholarly apparatus will help you sort out more reliable books from less reliable ones, and also the different types of historical communication, the topic to which I now turn.

9 TYPES OF HISTORICAL COMMUNICATION

Back in Unit 8 I pointed out that there were different types of secondary source, from very highly specialized, totally research-based works, to general text books. In addition there are a variety of popular works, and also television programmes, some of which are authoritative, but many of which don't merit the title 'secondary source' at all.

I am now going to list the different types of historical communication, from the very narrowest and most exclusively based on primary sources, through the most important and exciting kinds of works historians produce, to text books and popular history.

1 The thesis or dissertation

Usually written by a postgraduate student for the Doctor of Philosophy (PhD; DPhil at Oxford University) degree, and based almost exclusively on primary sources. Now usually word-processed, though generations of theses, still being consulted by specialist researchers, were typed. These are then specially bound, usually in not more than three or four copies, with one copy being available for consultation by other researchers in the university where the degree was taken. Because a dissertation is not published, its title will not be underlined or italicized when being cited in scholarly apparatus.

2 The learned article

The learned article is usually the minute examination of one very limited problem or topic, like the PhD based almost exclusively on primary sources, though usually scrutinizing (and often criticizing!) any secondary sources in which other historians may have dealt with the topic, and printed and published in one of the learned journals – for example, *The English Historical Review, Past and Present, History,* or *Contemporary European History.* Usually twenty to thirty pages in length (10,000–15,000 words), this is the most characteristic product of the ordinary working historian, and the one in which the historian's activities most obviously resemble those of the scientist, at the same time strikingly demonstrating the point that historians are generally concerned with limited, precise topics, not with the grand problems of human existence. Four times a year as a professional historian and member of the Historical Association, I receive the scholarly journal, *History.* Let us consider the three articles published in the issue for February 1993:

‘The Domesday Survey: context and purpose’

‘The problems of literacy in early modern England’

‘The pests of human society: stockbrokers, jobbers and speculation in mid-eighteenth-century Britain’

The author of the first article, noting (as I did in Unit 8) the enormous use made of the Domesday Book as a source for social life in early medieval England, and the extensive application of computer-based techniques, stresses the vital importance of knowing why, and in what circumstances, the Survey was set up in the first place: it is to these limited objectives that the article addresses itself.

In Section 6, I raised questions about change, and how one explains it. Without question one of the most important agents of change in the development of societies has been the spread of literacy. The nature and extent of literacy in early modern England (roughly the sixteenth and seventeenth centuries) are very hard to establish. The second article concentrates on these very precise issues.

The third article starts off by referring to 'present-day concerns' about regulating the City of London, going on to say how particularly great that problem was in the mid-eighteenth century, a discussion of which is the specific and limited topic of the article.

When citing a learned article, the title of the published journal will be italicized, with, of course, volume number, date, and page references. The actual title of the article will not be italicized but will be put in quotation marks, as I have done above.

3   The scholarly monograph

Sometimes this is practically the same as the PhD thesis, served up as a published book; but generally a published monograph should have a subject of greater scope and importance than the average PhD thesis; it is based mainly on primary sources.

4, 5 and 6   From scholarly monograph to scholarly synthesis to partially research-based text book

It is within this range of partially overlapping types that we find the most important and distinguished work produced by historians (a tiny number of which may be reviewed in the posh newspapers, or even featured on television – but we should always be very careful to avoid generalizing about what historians do on the basis of the proportionately almost infinitesimal number of works which receive widespread attention). Of the books which have cropped up one way or another throughout the History units I would suggest that those by Peter Laslett and Lawrence Stone relating to the Family, and perhaps my own work in progress on the Sixties, come near the beginning of the range of overlapping types contained in my heading, while Eric Hobsbawm on the Twentieth Century, William Doyle on the French Revolution, and Rosemary O'Day on the Family come somewhere in the middle, perhaps tending towards the end of it. By 'scholarly synthesis' I mean a book which both has a substantial amount of original research in the primary sources, and synthesizes and interprets the monographs and other secondary works of other historians relevant to what will be a wide-ranging subject. But not all that wide-ranging. Even in their most important books historians remain *specialists*, dealing with carefully delimited topics within which they can claim to have a unique expertise. If we return to the same issue of *History*, and move to the book review pages, divided – remember our study of periodization – into 'Ancient and Medieval', 'Early Modern' and 'Late Modern', we find that the overwhelming majority of the books reviewed are also very limited and specific in context, not the sort to be reviewed in the posh Sunday newspapers. Here are some characteristic titles:

Lordship, Knighthood and Locality: A Study in English Society, c.1180–c.1280

Science and the Sciences in the Thirteenth Century

The Culture of English Anti-Slavery, 1780–1860

Rhineland Radicals: The Democratic Movement and the Revolution of 1848–1849

7 The text book

Naturally text books can be written for a variety of different age groups and audiences. On the whole, it would be true to say that the more elementary the text book the more dependent it will be on the books of others, that is secondary sources. But writing a high-level text book on a complex subject, drawing entirely on the vast amount of relevant secondary sources, including dissertations and learned articles, can be a very difficult task, calling upon very thorough professional skills. At whatever level, the basic task of the text book is to provide clear, comprehensible coverage of some period or topic, in accordance with the best existing knowledge.

Additionally, there is a type of text book devoted to the provision of extracts selected from primary sources (known as a 'source book'), or excerpts from a range of secondary sources (known as a 'collection of readings').

8 Pop history

History written for a wide audience is perfectly respectable, provided it is written honestly, and provided it is accepted for what it is. Nowadays professional academic historians, as well as journalists, participate in the writing of pop history. Television, presented with the honest intention to educate or inform, and with an awareness of the nature of historical sources, has provided the opportunity for a still more up-to-date form of pop history.

But do be very clearly aware that works which are essentially works of creative imagination, of fiction, or of entertainment, such as historical novels, or the ordinary commercial feature film, are *primary* sources, primary sources for the period in which they were produced, though, in so far as they contain reflections on a period within the memory of the producers, they may have some use as primary sources for that period as well. A good case in point is Oliver Stone's film made in the early 1990s, *JFK*. The subject matter of this film is an aspect of the Sixties: President Kennedy and his assassination. It employs, obviously, actors, and invented dialogue, which immediately rule it out as a secondary source. It is not, in any case, historically accurate. It presents a romanticized (though I personally would say, *symbolically* not utterly erroneous) view of Kennedy as a force for progress, and the widespread conspiracy to which, controversially, it attributes the assassination, as representing the powerful forces of reaction which Kennedy had battled against. For students of the Sixties then, this film *could* be used as a primary source for images and myths surrounding Kennedy. In TV25 you will see examples of television programmes which, produced within the Sixties, are really very good sources for that decade.

10 CONCLUSION: THE SIXTIES – A CONTEXT FOR COUNTER-MOVEMENTS IN SCIENCE, RELIGION, MUSIC AND ART

First, I want you in this concluding section of my second pair of units introducing history, to reflect on the different kinds of source which exist for the study of the Sixties. The selections of extracts from A3 to A23 reintroduced you to a small range of types of source. The Chronology mainly listed events, and events are certainly not sources, but the Chronology also listed items which survive today as authentic sources, that is, books, paintings, films and so on. You might find it worthwhile to read again through the two lists of points on pages 16–17, and the double-column exercise on pages 57–9.

What I hope you have learned is to be careful in your generalizations about the Sixties (or any other period), and cautious with terms like 'counter-culture'. The next unit discusses 'Counter-movements in Science' – to what extent were they 'counter-cultural' and to what extent were they part of 'mainstream' culture? Could the same questions be asked about the 'New Religious Movements' discussed in Unit 28? Moving to Unit 29, 'Change and Continuity: Music in the 1960s': were changes in taste among the relatively small audience for classical music ('The Early Music Revival') 'counter-cultural'? Is a pop singer, or a pop artist, who shrewdly exploits his/her commercial potential challenging 'mainstream' culture? Warhol looks pretty 'counter-cultural', though he clearly loved being lionized by high society. How about Rothko? All worthwhile questions. The answer: be wary of envisaging society as dividing too neatly, and too comprehensively, into two dialectically opposed entities, 'mainstream' culture and 'counter-culture'.

REFERENCES

FOUCAULT, M. (1963) *Naissance de la clinique: une archeologie du regard medical*, Paris, Presses Universitaries de France.

HOBSBAWM, E.J. (1962) *The Age of Revolution: Europe 1789–1848*, London, Weidenfeld and Nicholson.

HOBSBAWM, E.J. (1994) *Age of Extremes: The Short Twentieth Century 1914–1991*, London, Michael Joseph.

HOWARD, G. (ed.) (1982) *The Sixties: The Art, Attitudes, Politics and Media of Our Most Explosive Decade*, New York, Washington Square Books.

MAITLAND, S. (ed.) (1988) *Very Heaven: Looking Back at the 1960s*, London, Virago.

MARCUSE, H. (1964) *One Dimensional Man: Studies in the Ideology of Advanced Industrial Society*, London, Routledge and Kegan Paul.

MARWICK, A. (1998) *The Sixties: Cultural Revolution in Britain, France, Italy and the United States, c.1958–c.1974*, Oxford, Oxford University Press.

POWERS, T. (1973) *The War at Home: Vietnam and the American People, 1964–1967*, New York, Grossman.

SOBOUL, A. (1989) *The French Revolution, 1787–1799*, London, Unwin Hyman.

UNIT 27 COUNTER-MOVEMENTS IN SCIENCE

Written for the course team by John Krige
Kranzberg Professor, Georgia Institute of Technology

Contents

STUDY COMPONENTS				
Weeks of study	Texts	TV	AC	Set books
1	Resource Book 4	TV27	–	–

Aims and objectives

The aims of this unit are to:

1   describe the historical background to the rise of the counter-movement in science in the 1960s, notably in the United States of America;

2   explore the grounds for the counter-movement's opposition to the military-industrial-academic complex and to the position of women in science, including as case studies the research done at the Massachusetts Institute of Technology, the thalidomide tragedy and primatology;

3   describe the arguments for the opposition that emerged from within the scientific community itself;

4   situate the counter-movement in science in the broader context of the counter-culture of the 1960s.

By the end of this unit you should be able to:

1   describe the main features of the military-industrial-academic complex in the United States of America as it evolved after World War II;

2   identify and distinguish between the main objections to that complex made from within the scientific community in the 1960s;

3   relate the objections made by the critics of science (and their opponents) to different perceptions of the role of science and the responsibility of scientists in the Vietnam War;

4   describe the objections made by women scientists in the 1960s, and relate them to general features of the counter-culture;

5   explain what a 'mind-set' is and illustrate its importance with examples.

1 INTRODUCTION

'Science, Technology. We declare its use a sham. And subject all who use it ill to the witches' damn.'

These are the words of a 'hex', or curse, cast on the members of the American Association for the Advancement of Science (AAAS) who were meeting at a convention centre in Chicago in December 1970. The hex was pronounced by a group calling themselves the Women's International Terrorist Conspiracy from Hell (the WITCHES). They were one of a number of radical groups who sought to turn the attention of the delegates towards the need for what they called a 'science for the people'. Edward Teller, a brilliant physicist who had strongly promoted the US nuclear weapons programme, came to the convention with two bodyguards. He was heckled as a 'war criminal' while he addressed the symposium. Radicals presented him afterwards with a 'Dr Strangelove Award' for his outstanding contribution to 'science in the service of warmakers'. Furious, Teller replied that the aggression against him reminded him of the attacks he had received as a Jew in the 'witch cauldron' of Nazi Germany before World War II. Glenn T. Seaborg, Chairman of the United States Atomic Energy Commission and the president-elect of the AAAS, was similarly harassed. He fled from a meeting room before making his presentation for fear of being 'indicted' by young radicals. Immediately after he left the room the 'charges' against him were read to the assembled crowd, including television cameramen and journalists. The radicals charged that Seaborg, through his various institutional affiliations, had used science for the benefit of 'corporate America' and that he would continue to do so as president of AAAS, which they labelled 'AAA$'. They described the Association, which had a broad-based membership of about 130,000 people from many different fields of science, as 'America's primary public-relations agency of the military, industrial, government, big science, university complex'. The meeting was dissolved in confusion.

These events, reported as such in the journal *Science*, which is published by the AAAS, provide us with a point of entry to this unit and to some of the key issues that it will address. We are going to discuss the opposition to science and the scientific world-view that emerged at the end of the 1960s and early 1970s. This opposition was particularly virulent in the USA, where it was centred on the universities. Like much of the counter-culture, it spread to other advanced industrialized countries in Europe, although it never reached the intensity there that it had assumed in America. This is why anyone studying Sixties counter-culture has sooner or later to focus on the USA, which generated so much of the movement, and where the questioning of science was particularly trenchant. Hence too the largely American content of this unit.

The approach that I have chosen to follow takes the title, 'Counter-movements *in* Science', at its word. It looks at the opposition to science that emerged from *within* the scientific community itself. That community is defined as including researchers, university teachers and students. Of course, the opposition to science (and technology) was more broadly based than that, and the criticisms that were made took many different forms in the more general 'counter-culture' of the 1960s. Restricting the groups that we are going to study to those that opposed science from within has one great advantage for the historian, however. There is a fine and accessible collection of primary sources. After all, the conflict was played out between members of an educated, influential elite, who expressed themselves in writing, and whose views were often printed and reported verbatim in journals, magazines and newspapers that are still readily available. This means that we have at hand a good deal of the primary source material we need for a study like this. I must confess that I also have a personal interest in this conflict. I was never directly involved in it, but the arguments that inspired and informed it affected me deeply. I was originally trained as a scientist, and in the early 1970s I found myself being drawn ineluctably into a nuclear weapons programme. I decided not simply to leave the institution where I was working, but also to leave my field, and my country of birth, and to retrain myself in the history and philosophy of science.

As we are going to be dealing mostly with debates among scientists, some of you may fear that a professional training in science, or at least a certain level of scientific knowledge, is needed to understand this unit. Let me reassure you at once that this is not so. Technical material has been kept to a minimum and, on the few occasions where it is used, it is explained. Of course, people trained in science may be expected to react differently to the unit from those who are not scientists. Since it is *their* value-system that is under the microscope scientists may be surprised or distressed, stimulated or angered — or perhaps just amused — by some of the accusations that were made. So much the better! We are going to touch on some profoundly held beliefs in this unit, beliefs that were subjected to a sustained and violent attack by a radical science movement, and which mobilized members of both faculty and students at some of the most prestigious universities in the USA and, later, in the UK and other countries in Europe. Although some of the arguments we are going to discuss are 'dated' and were very much children of a specific time and place, others are still disturbingly valid, I think. Let's see at the end of this unit whether you agree or not!

2 ANTI-SCIENCE AND THE MILITARY-INDUSTRIAL-ACADEMIC COMPLEX

One of the major accusations levelled against science by its critics in the late 1960s was that it had become heavily militarized and that it was dedicated to the development of weapons of mass destruction rather than to improving the lot of humankind. It was not only radical critics of science who expressed this concern. Indeed, as early as 1961 similar worries were voiced by the US President and five-star General, Dwight D. Eisenhower. On 17 January 1961 'Ike' made a famous farewell address on radio and television to the American people (John F. Kennedy was soon to move into the White House). He took the opportunity to express his alarm at the economic, political and spiritual dangers posed to American society by the growth of what he called 'a military-industrial complex' and by the increase in power and influence of a 'scientific-technological elite'. Together, he implied, they posed a threat to the most sacred values of democracy. The next day he was asked by a journalist to elaborate. Eisenhower explained:

> When you see almost every one of your magazines no matter what they are advertising, has a picture of the Titan missile or the Atlas [missile] ... there is ... almost an insidious penetration of our own minds that the only thing this country is engaged in is weaponry and missiles. And, I'll tell you we just can't afford to do that. The reason we have them is to protect the great values in which we believe, and they [those values] are far deeper even than our lives and our own property, as I see it.

> (*Public Papers of the Presidents of the United States, Dwight D. Eisenhower, 1960–61*, 1961, pp.1045–6)

Eisenhower's concerns resonated with those of many of his countrymen, including some senior members of the opposition Democratic Party. Indeed, his phrase 'military-industrial complex' was soon extended by Democratic Senator J. William Fulbright into 'military-industrial-*academic* complex'. Fulbright was referring to the integration of university researchers into the development of new weapons systems, which had become a characteristic feature of the worlds of research and academia in the USA in the 1950s and 1960s.

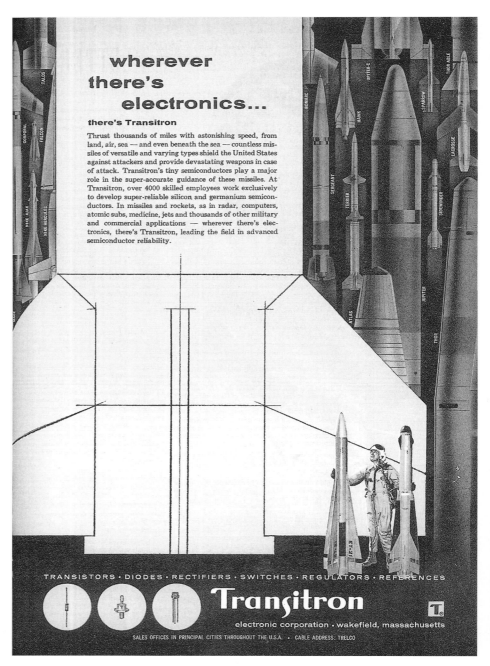

FIGURE 27.1 Advertisement for Transitron, Scientific American, March 1960. This is a typical advertisement placed by an electronics company in the popular science magazine Scientific American. Note the omnipresence of the missiles and rockets that so distressed Eisenhower. Note too the explicit appeal to the defence of the USA. To work for Transitron, it was suggested, was to make a political commitment to fight communism

In the first part of the unit we will try to get some idea of what this meant. For that purpose I shall describe the way in which an extremely prestigious US academic research centre in the Boston area, the Massachusetts Institute of Technology (MIT), worked along with the armed forces and with business to research and develop new weapons. With that basic information behind us, we shall then consider various kinds of criticism of the alliance between science, technology and the military that emerged in the USA in the first two decades after World War II.

An example of the military-industrial-academic complex: MIT

This section will investigate what lay behind Eisenhower's concerns and the extended concept, the military-industrial-academic complex. To do this it is essential to consider the historical evolution of the way research was organized at an institution like MIT. I have chosen MIT because it is a prime example of what was on Eisenhower's mind, and because of its immense international prestige based on the quality of its research schools. What is more, because of just these characteristics, MIT has been the subject of intense study by historians of science and technology. We thus have at our disposal a fine body of literature on which to base our investigation. We also know that the primary sources needed for such studies are available to anyone who would like not only to confirm these findings for themselves, but also to look again at such institutions from a new and perhaps different perspective.[1]

The changes that took place in the way scientific research was organized at MIT began before World War II, but they were accelerated and consolidated during the 1939–45 conflict. Before the war the US government invested about $48 million annually in scientific research and development. During the war this figure shot up by a factor of ten, to about $500 million annually, most of it for the military. Two huge projects were major beneficiaries of this investment. One was the Manhattan project, which led to the development of the atomic bombs that devastated Hiroshima and Nagasaki in the summer of 1945. The other was the development of radar. Radar was used to detect submarines and aircraft long before they reached their targets. It was arguably a far more important advance than the atomic bomb, even though it has received much less publicity. In fact, those who developed the technology used to say that radar won the war, whereas the bomb simply ended it.

Radar was developed as a joint British–American effort in the so-called 'RadLab' at MIT. From small beginnings this 'laboratory' exploded in three years into a huge, sprawling complex of buildings. By 1945 the

---

[1] The account that follows is from Leslie (1993). See also Leslie (1990).

number of staff had grown to almost 4000 people. About 1000 of these were academics, about half of them physicists. Here the organizational seeds were sown for the postwar development of the military-industrial-academic complex.

Even before the war was over Julius Stratton, who worked in the laboratory and was to become president of MIT, was planning for the postwar period. In the past, once war had ended, a university and its staff would cut its ties with the military and would go back to civilian life, doing fundamental research and teaching. (What is called 'fundamental research' lies at the core of science: it is research done above all to advance the frontiers of knowledge. It is not directly shaped by a concern to produce a technological application or a commercial product.) But times were changing. As Stratton wrote in a letter to a colleague in October 1944:

> Twenty-five years ago [i.e. 1919] everyone talked about the end of the war; today we talk about World War III and the Navy and Air Force, at least, are making serious plans to prepare for it. Inevitably, this national spirit will react upon the policies of our educational and research institutions. It always has, and we might just as well face it ... We shall have to deal with the Army and the Navy and make certain concessions in order to meet their needs.
>
> *(Leslie, 1993, p.24)*

What concessions did Stratton have in mind? He was surely referring to the threats to the hallowed principle of academic freedom that working with the military entailed. This had two dimensions. First, research became 'mission oriented' or 'applied'. Researchers were no longer free to do fundamental research without considering whether it was useful or not. They had to work on projects with distinct military interest. Secondly, and more importantly, the work could or would be classified as secret. The researcher was not allowed to disclose the contents of what was done without military permission. This flew in the face of academic freedom, which encourages open discussion and the publication of research results in professional journals. How could researchers discuss their work with colleagues, or publish their results in the open literature, if they were classified 'secret' by the military?

With the war over, and the dismantling of the RadLab on the horizon, the MIT group turned to industry for support. They approached electronics giants like Radio Corporation of America (RCA), who they thought could benefit from the knowledge in the field that had been built up in the laboratory during the war. These industries were not uninterested, but they were only willing to support the venture with fellowships for graduate students. This would not pay for the maintenance of the buildings nor, of course, for the costly equipment needed to do the research.

MOTOROLA *Military Electronics Division*

FIGURE 27.2 *Advertisement for Motorola,* Scientific American, *March 1960. This advertisement and the one shown in Figure 27.3 have been included to give you an idea of the defence contractors' demand for highly qualified scientists and engineers. Both are taken from the same number of* Scientific American. *Note that Motorola stresses that it is 'exclusively engaged in electronics for defense' in a wide variety of applications, that it already employs 'recognized leaders in many fields of science' who work on 'complex' problems, and that its workforce comprises 850 motivated 'top scientists and engineers'*

The military saw matters differently. They realized what an invaluable resource the laboratory had been during the war and some of them believed that the time was already ripe to prepare for World War III. They offered to continue to finance the division dealing with fundamental research for six months after the official demobilization of the laboratory itself. They also agreed to transfer $1 million worth of government-surplus equipment to it. With this support a new laboratory opened its doors in January 1946. It was called the Research Laboratory of Electronics (RLE). It began life with 17 faculty members from MIT's physics and engineering departments and 27 other former staff members, plus a few graduate students. Within a month a new contract had been negotiated with the Armed Services. It amounted to $600,000 a year for the first two years, with promises of more to come. Indeed, for the first

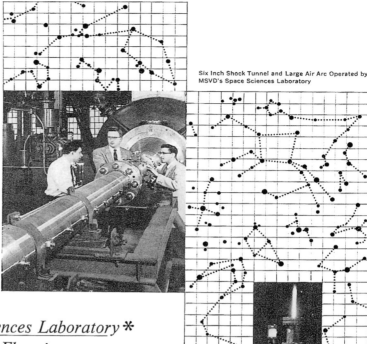

Six Inch Shock Tunnel and Large Air Arc Operated by MSVD's Space Sciences Laboratory

*
The Space Sciences Laboratory will be part of the New MSVD $14,000,000 Space Research Center now under construction. This new facility is located on a 132 acre site near Valley Forge Park, 17 miles from Philadelphia.

<u>The Space Sciences Laboratory</u> * <u>of the General Electric</u> <u>Missile & Space Vehicle Department</u> *in Philadelphia is interested in hearing from scientists who wish to pursue research in these areas:*

Theoretical Gas Dynamics A Physicist with PhD degree or equivalent experience in aerodynamics, gas dynamics, or the physics of fluids in high temperature and high altitude regimes is required. Candidate will perform theoretical investigations of the following areas of gas dynamics: magneto-gas dynamics, non-equilibrium effects in gas dynamics at high altitudes, mass transfer and heat transfer, boundary layer theory and flow field analysis.

Theoretical Plasma Investigations Opening for scientist with PhD degree or equivalent experience in physics or any of the related fields of electro-magnetic phenomena or gaseous electronics. He will perform theoretical investigations associated with the generation and diagnosis of plasmas. And, he will be offered the opportunity to study the interactions of plasmas with magnetic fields and microwave radiation and many-body and collective phenomena in plasmas.

Interplanetary and Lunar Trajectory Research A number of opportunities exist at the PhD level of Mathematics, Astronomy and Applied Mechanics to conduct analytical and computer studies in the following areas: applied mechanics, applied mathematics, celestial dynamics, analytical dynamics.

Advanced Structural Research Research in the fields of dynamic buckling, radiation shielding, high speed particle impact, etc. A doctoral degree in engineering, applied mechanics or applied mathematics is required.

Advanced Communications To work primarily on problems of interaction of electro-magnetic waves with partially ionized high-temperature gases. A PhD degree with general physics background and special competence in electro-magnetic theory is essential. An appreciation for the techniques, problems and results of aerodynamics and thermodynamics is also desirable.

Scientists and Engineers interested in these and numerous other openings are requested to send their resumes in strict confidence to Mr. T. H. Sebring, Box 59MC

Missile and Space Vehicle Department

GENERAL  ELECTRIC

3198 CHESTNUT ST., PHILADELPHIA 4, PENNSYLVANIA

FIGURE 27.3 Advertisement for General Electric Missile and Space Vehicle Department, Scientific American, March 1960. The advertisement for a firm we commonly associate with domestic appliances gives you some idea of the esoteric fields of research that were of interest to defence contractors. Note too that, from industry's point of view, the distinction between a civilian space programme and weapons development was irrelevant. The fundamental scientific knowledge and the technology were common to both

few years after the war the RLE concentrated on basic work for the military in the areas of electronics, secure communications and guided-missile homing systems (i.e. systems to direct missiles to their targets).

The RLE called for an entirely new way of organizing research. Traditionally, universities were divided by disciplines: physics, chemistry, electrical engineering, mechanical engineering, history, English literature, and so on. Each discipline had its own department, with its specialized teachers. Communication between disciplines, even in neighbouring areas, was often restricted or non-existent. The RLE broke with this tradition and was to become the model for a number of similar science and engineering laboratories at MIT. This is how Stratton described the change:

> The founding of the new electronics laboratory in 1946 represented a major new departure in the organization of academic research at M.I.T. and was destined to influence the development of interdepartmental centers at the Institute over the next two decades. These centers have been designed to supplement rather than to replace the traditional departmental structure. They take account of the fact that the newly emerging fields of science commonly cut across the conventional disciplinary boundaries. And they afford a common meeting ground for science and engineering, for the pure and applied aspects of basic research, to the advantage of both. Perhaps more than any other development in recent years they have contributed to the special intellectual character and environment of M.I.T.
>
> *(Leslie, 1993, p.16)*

The RLE at MIT thus dissolved the disciplinary and departmental boundaries that had previously existed in the university. It put together under one roof, and working side by side, scientists and engineers. It thereby ensured a continuing cross-fertilization between pure and applied research. This was necessary because innovation in newly emerging fields of science, such as electronics, called for the combined skills of people like physicists, mathematicians, materials scientists and electrical engineers collaborating within the framework of a single project, for example the development of a missile guidance system.

In June 1950 the North Korean army crossed the 38th parallel (line of latitude) separating North from South Korea, and captured Seoul. The Korean War was under way. It was to last for three years and would engage the USA heavily. Military expenditure for scientific research and development soared to new heights. These new levels were later sustained by an injection of funds for research that followed the launch of *Sputnik*, the first Soviet satellite, in October 1957, and by the increasing intensity of the Vietnam War in the 1960s. The RLE was one of the beneficiaries of the military's continuing interest in science. The laboratory took on three new, big contracts. It worked on electronic defence for the Air Force, improved radar for the Navy and combat-communications systems for the Army.

RLE was not the only laboratory of this kind on the MIT campus. In December 1950, with the Korean War getting into its stride, the Air Force asked MIT to create a new laboratory for classified work on air-defence research. This led to the creation of the Lincoln Laboratory in 1951, which was eventually situated in an off-campus site in nearby Lexington. Its staff mushroomed almost overnight to 2000 people and its annual budget quickly reached $20 million. This is how Lincoln's activities were described and justified in the early 1960s by one of its directors:

> It can provide entirely new opportunities to advanced students who wish to work in the complex fields at today's technological frontier ... It is now becoming apparent that graduate education in many of today's crucial problems requires the resources of research centers larger than M.I.T.'s laboratories in Cambridge [i.e. on campus]. In radar and in space surveillance, in radio physics and astronomy, in information processing and communications, major physical facilities are available at Lincoln Laboratory. There is a growing recognition among educators that these facilities are not regrettable manifestations of mid-century complexity, but are the environment in which tomorrow's scientists and engineers must live and work.
>
> *(Leslie, 1993, p.37)*

Lincoln was just the first of many interdisciplinary laboratories set up after RLE had blazed the trail. A special Laboratory for Nuclear Science and Engineering was created. A Center for Materials Science and Engineering was established. And so on. Indeed, in 1962 one leading scientific statesman quipped that it was becoming increasingly hard 'to tell whether the Massachusetts Institute of Technology is a university with many government research laboratories appended to it, or a cluster of government research laboratories with a very good educational institution attached to it'.

Not everyone welcomed these changes; many simply capitulated to them. One elderly MIT physicist and engineer, Arthur von Hippel, whose wife was Jewish and who had fled Europe in 1936, put it thus fifteen months after the launch of *Sputnik*:

> What has happened to the old ivory tower! Telephones ring incessantly; visitors swarm in droves through the laboratories; meetings crowd meetings; an ocean of papers blots out the horizon; and the wise men, once quietly guided by the star of Bethlehem, now frantically count time by the star of Moscow. Yet this turmoil is of our own doing. Universities showed that research pays, and huge laboratories sprang up for profit; universities devised new weapons, and the countries bristle with laboratories for defense. What an outcome for a search for understanding of nature and for peace in our times!
>
> *(Leslie, 1993, p.211)*

Von Hippel was anticipating the criticisms of some of the new, younger generation of scientists just entering those laboratories as he was writing, and who were to spearhead the counter-movement in science ten years later.

The 'anti-science' movement: some general statements

Now that we have some idea of the new relationships built up between science and society in postwar America, we are in a position to deal with the criticisms made of these trends. We shall begin with the substantial objections made by three very different people. The first is President Eisenhower. Eisenhower was anything but a member of the anti-science movement. However, on leaving office in 1961 after eight years in the White House, he voiced anxiety about the rise of the military-industrial complex. His concerns were uncannily similar to those expressed ten years later by radical critics of the place of science in society.

The second objection is in a text by Theodore Roszak. Roszak was an academic who tried to explain and defend the many complexities of the counter-culture. You have already encountered him in this course (*Resource Book 4*, A22). If you look again at that extract you will find echoes of Eisenhower's concerns about the new power of a scientific-technological elite. Roszak puts it in more florid language: he speaks of 'technocratic totalitarianism'. Now we will look at other extracts from his book, which associate him directly with the counter-movement in science.

The third objection is in a text written by Edward Shils. He was the founding editor of a middle-of-the-road professional journal called *Minerva*, named after the classical goddess of wisdom. Established in the early 1960s, one of the prime aims of the journal was to foster the development of science in a democratic society. In particular, it aimed to encourage a rational debate about the kinds of policy for science that might best lead to the strengthening of democratic societies, not only militarily, but also economically and ideologically. The journal informed its readers in detail of the turmoil in universities in the late 1960s. In the text we will consider Shils encouraged his audience to see both the strengths and the dangers of the anti-science movement in the USA.

EXERCISE

Please read the extracts from Eisenhower's Farewell Address to the American people and Roszak's *The Making of a Counter Culture* (*Resource Book 4*, B1 and B2).

1   What changes in the practice of science did Eisenhower associate with the changes in the military-industrial posture of the USA in the 1950s?

2   What two dangers did he see as resulting from this?

3   What did Roszak mean by the term 'technocracy'?

4   Why did Roszak equate technocracy with totalitarianism?

5   What, according to Roszak, was the basis of the authority of science, and the consequent power of experts?

6   What had to be done to root out the distorting assumptions that had led so many to make their peace with technocracy?

7   What basic similarities do you find in the arguments put forward in these extracts by Eisenhower and by Roszak?

DISCUSSION

1   The President remarked that the conventional image of the scientist as a lone, amateur inventor tinkering in his workshop no longer had any meaning. Instead, as a result of the technological revolution, scientific research had become far more organized and costly. It was increasingly undertaken by, for or at the request of the (Federal) government. Universities had not escaped this process. Traditionally, the researcher had been driven by the need to know, without being concerned with the practical applications of his or her research. Ideally, at least, research in universities was curiosity-driven, not mission-oriented. That intellectual freedom was no longer possible, since so much research was being done under government contract. Such external funding was needed because the research was costly, but it imposed constraints on what researchers could do, and it demanded that they justify their research in terms of its usefulness.

2   The President envisaged first that, attracted by the power of money, researchers would betray their traditional calling, lose their intellectual freedom and simply become government employees working on government-inspired and financed projects. (This would include military projects, of course, called for by the Department of Defense.) There was another side to the coin, however. Because of the increasing dependence of the government on science and technology, be it for weapons systems, space exploration or in other areas, control over the democratic process would slip from the peoples' elected representatives. Public policy would be controlled by a scientific-technological elite. Experts, respected for their scientific and technological know-how, would decide what should be done and how best to do it.

3   By 'technocracy' Roszak meant a system of social organization in which all aspects of political, economic, cultural and, indeed, private life had to be rationalized, planned, updated and rendered more efficient. It was a so-called 'rational response' to the bigness and complexity of modern industrial societies. To achieve its objectives the technocracy depended on specially trained experts. A technocracy was thus a society in which government based and justified its decisions on the views of technical experts, whose authority was derived from the claim that their knowledge was

scientific. And beyond the authority of science, as Roszak put it, there was no appeal.

4   The technocracy appeared to be outside the sphere of politics, but in fact it was in the hands of experts who, working behind the scenes, sought to control every aspect of public and private life in the name of science. We vote for political parties believing that, by choosing between them, we can influence the course of public policy. We are mistaken, says Roszak. For the traditional political process is no longer in control of society. The experts do not impose or maintain their totalitarian rule by force. Rather they persuade us that they are right by appealing to the authority of science to justify all they do, and they secure our compliance by providing all the creature comforts and security that modern science and technology can produce.

5   Expertise rested on its appeal to reliable, scientific knowledge, and reliable, scientific knowledge derived from objectivity. Therefore to know the world, the expert tells us, we must cultivate objective knowledge. Objectivity is a state of consciousness that demands detachment as opposed to personal involvement, that seeks access to reality free from any subjective distortion, that prizes facts above values (although Roszak does not actually mention this last element in this extract).

6   Since society had become totally ensnared in a technocratic system, and took it unquestioningly for granted, the only way to dislodge that system was to attack technocracy at its roots. The scientific world-view must be subverted. It was committed to an egocentric and cerebral world of consciousness. It had to be replaced by an approach, in Roszak's view, in which non-intellectual capacities, feelings, emotions reigned supreme. These capacities exalted visionary splendour and human communion. It was they, not the objectivity of science, that had to become the arbiters of the good, the true and the beautiful. For Roszak the conflict between the counter-culture and technocracy was comparable to that between Greco-Roman rationality and Christian mystery.

7   There are two fundamental points on which Roszak and Eisenhower agree (notwithstanding the gulf between them in almost every other respect!). First, that society was, or was in danger of, being governed by a scientific-technological elite, whose power lay outside the usual political process. This they saw as a threat to a democratic society. At a more fundamental level both the President and the radical critic affirmed the importance of the freedom of the individual in the face of a technocracy. Eisenhower valued science and the scientist. He was concerned by the changes in the structure of scientific work and by the threat to the intellectual freedom of the individual posed by the military-industrial complex. He was also concerned by the way in

which militarism was shaping the horizons of people's thought (see p.75). It led them to forget that the purpose of the weaponry being developed was to defend far more important values that the American people held dear, notably individual liberty and the respect for democratic principles. Roszak also wanted to liberate the mind from obsession with the technology of war, which he blamed on the pursuit of science and objective knowledge. The space that he wanted to recapture for individual freedom of expression was that of personal consciousness and feeling.

My juxtaposition of Eisenhower and Roszak is deliberate, and the similarities that I have drawn attention to are to be taken seriously. My reason for following this approach is to stress that the counter-cultural critique of science was not just something driven by 'extremists'. On the contrary, there was a broad level of consensus in American society and in the scientific community that some important and disturbing changes had taken place in the relationships between science and society in the two decades after World War II. It was also generally agreed that, notwithstanding some of its more extreme manifestations, the counter-movement in science had put its finger on some of those worrying trends. If science was not to lose its credibility altogether, it was felt, something had to be done to make it more responsive to the needs of people, to make it more socially and politically responsible.

EXERCISE

With these considerations in mind, read the text by Edward Shils on the anti-science movement (*Resource Book 4*, B3).

1 Shils listed a number of charges brought against science (and technology) by the anti-science movement, ranging from polluting the environment to using chemical, biological and nuclear weapons. He then argued that, in fact, what was being criticized was not science but scientists. Why did this distinction matter?

2 What, in Shils's view, were the charges that the 'anti-science' movement levelled against scientists?

3 What, in Shils's view, had the New Left added to this critique?

4 Identify the three kinds of response to the anti-science movement that Shils attributed to scientists.

DISCUSSION

1 Shils insisted that most members of the anti-science movement were not against science as such, but against scientists. This definition of the problem is of the first importance. It differentiates Shils from

Roszak. Roszak argued, as we have seen, for abolishing science. But Shils was adamant that for most of the anti-science movement this was not the issue; they were not against science, but rather against the practices of scientists in America in the late 1960s. What was required, therefore, was not the abolition of science, but the transformation of the practices of scientists.

2   Scientists were alleged to have become subservient to the demands of the government, the military and private industry. They had become totally irresponsible, allowing their work to be used by the military-industrial complex in whatever way it saw fit. Concerned only with their own research, they had neither thought about, nor felt responsible for, the context in which that work was done. The anti-science movement, as described by Shils, thus believed that scientists had conceded to the 'three diabolical powers' the power to decide whether the results of their work be used for good or for ill.

3   Shils indicated that the New Left, of whom Roszak would be a perfect example, wanted to reject science altogether. For the New Left, science was just another ideology, an instrument of domination. To insist on the objectivity of science was to be wrong intellectually and morally – it was to prefer bureaucratic, large-scale, impersonal organization to spontaneity and individual self-expression. It was to promote living in what Roszak called a 'totalitarian technocracy' instead of building a small, intimate, egalitarian community which lived close to nature and which was master of its own destiny. In Shils's view the New Left was not representative of the counter-movement in science. The majority, he alleged, were not against science, but against those scientists 'who use it ill' (to repeat the words of the spell cast by the WITCHES with which I began this unit).

4   Many scientists, Shils insisted, were indifferent to the criticisms of science and ignored them. Others, mostly younger scientists, were socially concerned. They were angry about the damage, actual or potential, done by the discoveries of science and the inventions of technology. They objected strongly to the involvement of science with the military and they were bitterly critical of the scientific establishment, notably in the universities, for colluding in what they saw as the corruption of science. Finally, there was a third group of scientists, who, although not radical in their views, were troubled by the criticisms made by the younger generation of the way in which science had become enrolled into the military-industrial complex. They respected the justice of the criticisms, and felt vaguely guilty about their collaboration in the process. At the same time they believed that science could bring enormous benefits to humanity, and were deeply attached to its values as an intellectual pursuit. So they rejected both the New Left's uncompromising opposition to science and the violent criticism by the young against the scientific

establishment and its institutions. They had lost confidence in science and in its future but they were not quite sure where to go next.

The war in Vietnam and protests at MIT in the late 1960s

By now you should have an idea of the different kinds of argument that inspired the counter-movement in science, from the radicalism of a Roszak to the more measured approach of a Shils. Let us then return to the campus of MIT and consider some of the specific forms that opposition to the military-industrial-academic complex took there. Behind these protests lay a deepening opposition to the involvement of the Johnson administration in the war in Vietnam.

The war in Vietnam was a major conflict in south-east Asia in the 1960s in which the USA became increasingly engaged. Put very simply, involvement in the war was presented to the American public by their government as support for a democratically elected and friendly government in South Vietnam menaced by guerrilla insurgents from the north of the country (called the Vietcong), who had the support of Communist China. Opponents of American engagement in the war objected that it was essentially a civil war, and that the USA had no business interfering in the domestic affairs of another sovereign nation. As the battle dragged on with an increasing loss of life on both sides, a more pragmatic argument also came to the fore: the USA was engaged in a war it could never win, which was costing it dear in terms of the lives of its youth, and its international credibility and prestige. Better therefore to settle for peace on face-saving terms than to continue in a costly and hopeless pursuit of decisive victory.

FIGURE 27.4 *The suffering of American troops in the Vietnam War. Photo: Associated Press*

The widespread availability of television (see section A2 in *Resource Book 4*) and the access of journalists to the war zones brought images of death and destruction in Vietnam daily into the homes of Americans and of people throughout the world. This gave the horrors of war an immediacy and impact they had never had before. By the late 1960s President Lyndon B. Johnson had committed over 500,000 troops to the conflict. In 1968, with no visible end in sight, the National Selective Services Headquarters announced that as of 30 June all undergraduate students completing their first degree, as well as all students then completing their first year of graduate studies, would become immediately eligible for the draft. Until this time graduate students had been more or less exempted from active military service in Vietnam, on the grounds that their education was essential to the long-term health of the nation. Now many previously exempt categories found that they were eligible for military service.

The earlier, vocal hostility to the conflict reached a crescendo. Some students fled to Canada. Others protested by leaving higher education and moving into industry or service roles like high-school teaching, where they were less likely to be drafted. Yet others mounted a sustained assault on the war, and on the collusion of the scientific establishment in the military-industrial-academic complex.

MIT took the lead in proposing a day of protest scheduled for 4 March 1969. As the word got round, action spread to 30 universities. The movement at MIT started with some graduate students in the physics department, from where it was taken up by students in biology and then began to attract substantial support from faculty members in theoretical physics and other disciplines. In January 1969, 47 academics, including the heads of the departments of physics, biology and chemistry, signed a statement expressing their opposition to the war in Vietnam. This formed the basis for the discussions held on the MIT campus in Boston on 4 March.

EXERCISE

Please read the extracts from the statement prepared for the debate on 4 March 1969 (*Resource Book 4*, B4).

1   Did the faculty and graduate students reject science altogether or did they only want to change its direction?

2   What scientific and technological weapons were they particularly opposed to?

DISCUSSION

1   Judging from the evidence available in these texts, the teaching staff who signed the statement and the graduate students who endorsed it

were not against science as such, but against its use for military purposes. They wanted to turn science away from building weapons of destruction to more constructive ends, pressing it into service to solve social and environmental problems. In terms of the three groups identified by Shils (see previous exercise), they were neither indifferent to the counter-culture nor did they sympathize with what he called the New Left. They were socially concerned scientists rather than radicals who wanted to abolish science altogether. (Of course, it is highly likely that the formal statement was far too conservative for the more radical students on campus. We cannot assume, therefore, that the arguments of the New Left were absent from the movement; they might have been there, but just not reported by this source.)

2   The variety of weapons singled out for criticism included anti-ballistic missiles (ABMs) and nuclear, chemical and biological weapons.

Both ABMs and nuclear weapons were central to the enormous build-up of arms that maintained the balance of terror between the two superpowers, the USA and the Soviet Union. The first major use of chemical weapons was in World War I, where toxic gases like the so-called 'mustard gas' were used to attack troops in trenches, but chemical weapons were used extensively in Vietnam to defoliate the countryside by killing vegetation. We shall deal with chemical weapons in Vietnam in the next section. Biological weapons, which kill by infecting populations with lethal viruses, were developed in many countries, including the USA and the UK, after World War II. As far as is known no biological weapons were used in Vietnam.

We may wonder whether any of these protests achieved anything. Did they help to sever the tie between the university and the military-industrial complex? Or was it just 'business as usual' once the excitement had died down? It is clear, at least at MIT and several other universities (e.g. Stanford, in California), that even if ties with the military were not abolished they were sharply reduced and reorganized. At MIT the administration set up a special panel to investigate the funding patterns of two of its laboratories: the Charles Draper Instrumentation Laboratory, which operated in several buildings near the MIT campus, and Lincoln Laboratories in Lexington, in the suburbs of Boston.

In 1968 the Charles Draper Instrumentation Laboratory had an annual budget of $50 million, of which $30 million came from the Department of Defense. The remaining $20 million came from the National Aeronautics and Space Administration (NASA), the agency responsible for the US civilian space programme. The Charles Draper Laboratory's main tasks included developing guidance systems for US missiles and spacecraft. As for the Lincoln Laboratory, in 1968 its budget was about $65 million, almost all of which came from the Department of Defense. It had been set up at the height of the Korean War at the request of the Pentagon to develop air defence technology. Its reputation rested on its being a leading applied electronics laboratory devoted primarily to communications projects, missile system development and missile defence. About 40% of the research done at Lincoln in the late 1960s was classified.

In June 1969 a review panel, which included faculty members, students and trustees of MIT, submitted its recommendations on the future role of these special laboratories. It recommended that the laboratories and MIT should make an energetic effort to shift the balance of their research towards socially useful non-defence projects. It also suggested that there should be closer educational interaction between the laboratories and the campus. Intensive efforts were to be made to reduce the amount of classified work done. These measures were put into practice. So yes, the protests apparently did have an effect, albeit limited, on the nature of the work done at MIT.

Chemical weapons in Vietnam

Nineteen sixty-two is often taken as the year in which an environmental movement got under way in the USA. In that year a quiet, unassuming author, Rachel Carson, published her book, *Silent Spring*. It poignantly described the devastating effects of a common herbicide, dichlorodiphenyltrichloroethane (DDT), which was used in tons all over the world to protect crops from pests. Concern grew that chemicals which were being used to kill bugs were also polluting the air, entering the food chain, seeping into the water table and causing irremediable damage to many forms of life.

The use of chemical weapons by the USA in Vietnam was seen as particularly obnoxious by those who were already concerned about the destruction of the environment in their own country. The weapons were used with two main objectives in mind. First, a defoliation programme was undertaken. This was a guerrilla war in which the enemy made extensive use of the dense jungle and mangrove swamps in the countryside to infiltrate American-held zones and to hide from attack. Chemical weapons were used to kill the leaves of trees and of plants, depriving the Vietcong of cover and exposing their trails. Secondly, the weapons were used to destroy crops. It was argued that the Vietcong were benefiting from the support of the peasants in this predominantly agricultural country, who fed them and protected them from attack. By destroying their food supply they could be weakened physically and their morale could be broken.

Table 1 gives some idea of the areas (in acres) that were treated with herbicides in Vietnam for these strategic purposes. The rapid escalation in the use of poisons sprayed from the air to destroy vegetation and food is clear.

TABLE 1 *Estimated area* treated with herbicides in Vietnam*

Year	Defoliation (acres)	Crop destruction (acres)
1962	17,119	717
1963	34,517	297
1964	53,873	10,136
1965	94,726	49,637
1966	775,894	112,678
1967	1,486,446	221,312
1968	1,297,244	87,064

*The actual area sprayed is not known accurately because some areas were resprayed.

(Source: US Department of Defense data. From *Science*, vol.168, 1 May 1970, p.544)

This issue was deemed so serious that the usually staid AAAS decided to make its own investigation. It asked a Harvard biologist to conduct a survey of the effect of herbicides on the land and people of Vietnam. He and his colleagues reviewed the pertinent literature, consulted with numerous experts and made a five-week tour of inspection of the country. Some of their findings were reported in the AAAS's journal, *Science*, in the issue of 8 January 1971. They showed that the military use of herbicides had caused considerably more damage than anyone had previously imagined.

■ One-fifth to one-half of South Vietnam's mangrove forests, some 1400 square kilometres in all, had been 'utterly destroyed' and even in 1971, years after spraying, there was no sign of life coming back.

■ Perhaps half the trees in the mangrove forests north and west of Saigon were dead, and a massive invasion of apparently worthless bamboo threatened to take over the area for decades to come.

■ The Army's crop-destruction programme, which sought to deny food to enemy soldiers, had been a near total 'failure', because nearly all the food destroyed would actually have been consumed by civilian populations.

■ There was no definite evidence of adverse health effects, but further study was needed to determine the reason for a high rate of stillbirths in one heavily sprayed province and to account for the increase in two particular kinds of birth defect reported in a large Saigon hospital, abnormalities coincident with large-scale spraying.

FIGURE 27.5 Defoliation in Vietnam, Science, 8 January 1971, pp. 43, 44. (Top left) Aerial photograph showing an unsprayed mangrove forest in South Vietnam. (Top right) Aerial photograph showing a mangrove forest that was subjected to herbicide spraying in 1965. One spraying kills essentially all trees. The larger trunks appear to have been removed by the local population for firewood. (Bottom) A mangrove forest that was sprayed with herbicides some time before 1968. © 1971 American Association for the Advancement of Science

These and other reports caused a flurry of correspondence in the letters column of *Science*. Here partisans of both sides in the conflict clashed with each other, sometimes violently. Some of this correspondence is reproduced in *Resource Book 4* (B5). The material is not arranged chronologically but rather by type of argument.

EXERCISE

Read the letters in order and in each case identify the arguments for or against the chemical warfare programme in Vietnam. I have added one statement from a different, but related, context (at point IV).

DISCUSSION

The first letter accused those who objected to the war of being illogical. War was brutal and always entailed cutting off the enemy's supply lines. Vietnam was no exception. What is more, the USA was doing all it could to make sure that it was the Vietcong, not the local civilian population, that was deprived of food. Animals were not being severely hurt and humans were not directly affected. Those who objected to this policy had to recognize that, by restricting the options of the military commanders, they were causing the deaths of American and allied soldiers. Apparently the protesters were more concerned about protecting the environment than protecting their countrymen!

The second letter shifted the terms of the debate. The author would not engage with the argument we have just heard: for him it was irrelevant to try to justify the war in Vietnam by arguing that all wars are dirty, and that the harm done to the enemy was necessary to save lives on one's own side. That argument, he objected, presumed that the ends justified the means, that any technology was permitted if it saved US soldiers' lives. It was not, in his view. The question of whether a particular, destructive technology should be used was not a purely technical question, but a moral and political question. The previous correspondent was drawing an artificial distinction between science and morality, between technology and politics.

Chomsky took this argument further. He put morality and politics at the heart of the debate: we were killing people. In this text he was not openly criticizing the USA for doing that. Instead, he was objecting that the way in which the arguments were presented and the language in which the texts were written were such as to blank out all considerations of the pain and suffering of the victims of the chemical weapons programme. In other words, very much like Roszak, he was objecting to a detached, cold and unfeeling way of writing about the events, which masked their horror and avoided posing painful political and moral questions.

Then comes a remark by a young graduate student who worked on the MIT campus. This short extract brings home forcefully how some scientists did not simply distinguish the technical from the moral, but found full satisfaction and justification for what they were doing in the creative pleasure of developing a new technology, regardless of its uses. (The idea that a researcher worked on a new weapon because it was technically 'sweet', as scientists sometimes put it, without thinking of the immense suffering that it could inflict on human beings, was also often invoked by scientists to explain their innovative work on the atomic bomb during World War II.)

The next letter is by two renowned biologists (both Nobel prizewinners), which of course gave their protest added weight in the scientific community. They argued that the war was morally reprehensible, adding that it was a catastrophe for the nation, although they did not say why. Their aim was to use the weight of their authority as respected members of the establishment to get their colleagues to look carefully at the research they were doing, and if it had military potential to consider working on other problems.

The rebuttal to this plea that follows once again argued that anything was permissible so long as it saved American lives: the end justified the means. But it added another twist: that in making a political plea Luria and Szent-Györgyi had stepped outside their sphere of competence. The author wanted to limit the authority of scientists to the domain of science, leaving political issues to the politicians. He was insisting on drawing a sharp distinction between science and technology, which dealt with facts, on the one hand, and morality and politics, which dealt with values, on the other.

The selection of texts you have just read gives you some idea of the deep split that divided scientists in the late 1960s. In fact, there was clearly no debate possible between the two sides we have just listened to: it was a 'dialogue of the deaf'.

For one party, the question of what to do in Vietnam was purely technical. Given that the war was under way, it had to be won with a minimum loss of American lives. Any weapon that achieved this objective was acceptable (scientifically and technically acceptable, that is). What is more, a new weapon's interest, from a scientific point of view, was enhanced if its design and development were intellectually challenging and 'technically sweet'. As patriotic scientists their duty was to put the best weapons they could at the disposal of the generals out in the field. The choice of whether or not to use those weapons was up to them and the politicians. Scientists were not competent to pronounce on such matters.

For the other party, this approach was simply irresponsible. To draw a sharp line between ends and means was to fall prey to a technocratic form of rationality. It was to evade social responsibility by claiming that knowledge was objective and value-free. Science and technology were part of society and embedded deeply in a military-industrial complex. Scientists were just as capable as anyone else of making moral and political choices. To pretend otherwise was to delude oneself, and, worse, to collude unthinkingly in a brutal, inhumane and pointless war.

FIGURE 27.6 This picture of a Vietnamese woman and a child burnt by napalm, a jelly-like chemical substance which clung to clothing and flesh, was distributed worldwide, and became an icon of the protest movement against the Vietnam War. Photo: Associated Press

I want you now to pause for a moment and to put aside your historian's hat. The war in Vietnam is past history, but the points of principle raised in the extracts given above are not. Indeed, the dilemmas that so divided the scientific community and American society 30 years ago are also our dilemmas today. In some countries many of them are just as much a part of scientific and public debate in the year 2000 as was the use of chemical and other weapons in Vietnam in 1970. We have at our disposal at the dawn of the twenty-first century scientific knowledge and technologies that enable us to genetically modify food, to 'artificially' produce and transform humans and animals, to generate nuclear power and nuclear waste, and to destroy the entire world many times over. What limits should be imposed on the development and use of these technologies? Who should impose such limits in a democratic society? What is the social and moral responsibility of the scientists who do the research and develop these technologies? These issues are still very much with us. Keep an eye open for them and, if you have time, put together a small folder of press and magazine cuttings that display the variety of the arguments used for and against a contemporary scientific and technological development that particularly interests you. In that way, I hope, the significance and relevance of this unit will be enhanced for you.

3 WOMEN IN SCIENCE

The counter-movement in science was not only about opposition to the links between science and war that had been cemented by the military-industrial-academic complex. It was also about building a new, more democratic society, which was not controlled and dominated by a 'scientific-technological elite'. As we saw earlier, even for Republican President Eisenhower this elite posed an intellectual and political threat to democracy. Some members of the counter-culture, what Shils called the New Left, were convinced that the only effective way to deal with this threat was to reject science and its methods altogether. For them science was synonymous with domination and control. Its objective, rational methods could never be a force for fulfilment, since they demanded detachment and the suppression of all subjective feelings. Yet it was only by being in touch with those feelings that human beings could become whole people who were genuinely concerned about others and the world in which they lived.

This radical opposition to science, however, was not shared by many of those who opposed it from within. On the contrary, they were not against science as such, but its use for what they regarded as perverse ends. What was needed was a science for liberation not domination, a science geared to building a more humane and tolerant world, rather than a science mobilized for destruction and in pursuit of national prestige and personal glory. These critics wanted to break the structures of power within the scientific community and change its relationship to the civil society. They wanted to put in place a new kind of science which would serve the needs of the 'people' and not those of a scientific-technological elite, who they believed were enmeshed in the prevailing structures of power. Their aim was not to abolish science but to transform it. Read again the spell cast by the WITCHES which I quoted at the beginning of this unit. The group's name and its actions were certainly provocative. But it was not science that they damned, only those who 'use it ill'.

The demand that women play a greater role in science was part of this new awareness. In this section we will study two aspects of what was called a 'feminist science'. The first was the demand for greater access to a life in science for women, a demand fuelled by the feeling that women were being systematically excluded from a prestigious and rewarding professional activity. The second was the argument that women entering science would transform the very character of the knowledge being produced. They would bring new ways of looking at the world, ways that were peculiar to them and not available to men. We shall explore each of these arguments in selected texts. Then we shall study a couple of specific examples in which, it can be argued, scientific knowledge advanced because women had insights and asked questions that did not initially occur to men.

Why were there so few women in science?

A survey published in 1965 gave figures for the percentage of women employed in various fields of science and in engineering in 1950 and 1960 (Rossi, 1965, p.1197). The most striking finding of the survey was that, on average, only about 10% of people working in science were women. This was the case notwithstanding the increase in the number of scientists employed during the decade of the 1950s. Women benefited from this increase, but far less than men. Thus, in 1960, as in 1950, only one in ten scientists was female.

What women were realizing in the 1960s, then, was that not only were there relatively few of them employed in science, but more of the new openings were being filled by men. Science was a prestigious, creative and rewarding career. Many women asked why they should not be able to participate as actively in science as did men. Their frustration was heightened by the knowledge that even if they were trained as scientists it was extremely difficult for them to remain active members of the scientific workforce. Table 2 illustrates the point.

TABLE 2 *Voluntary withdrawal from the labour force in selected professions, by age and sex, expressed in percentages**

Profession and sex	Age 25–44	Age 45–64	Age 65 or older
Natural scientists			
Women	51	13	61
Men	2	1	57
Engineers			
Women	31	13	42
Men	1	4	58
Secondary-school teachers			
Women	34	13	65
Men	2	2	54
Physicians–surgeons			
Women	19	10	31
Men	2	2	25

*The figures are as of 1960.

(Source: Rossi, 1965, p.1199)

EXERCISE

Table 2 gives figures comparing the voluntary withdrawal of men and women from the workforce in 1960. What do you deduce from this data?

DISCUSSION

The first point to note is the striking difference between the proportion of men and women who voluntarily left the labour force between the ages of 25 and 64. This is true for all the professions selected by the author of the study. Whereas far and away the majority of men remained employed if they could throughout these 40 years, as many of one out of two of the women withdrew.

The second striking point is that far more women withdrew from the labour force when they were aged between 25 and 44 than in the two decades afterwards. For example, 34% of female secondary-school teachers stopped working during this period, while only 13% of women aged 45–64 left the profession. Between the ages of 25 and 44 one would be expected to capitalize most on one's past education and to lay the foundations of a career. In the case of women, these are also the years when they are of child-bearing age.

Thirdly, we see that the withdrawal rates between the ages of 25 and 44 were highest in the natural sciences. According to this data, one out of two women (51%) who entered the field of science had left it voluntarily, or 'voluntarily', by the age of 44 years.

You will notice that I put the word voluntarily in inverted commas the second time I used it. This is to warn you that, according to some researchers, the decision to leave a professional life and abandon a career in these productive years was not a free choice at all. It was not voluntary, but a decision imposed by the social structure of the workplace and the expectations that women had of themselves. We are now going to look at some of those points and connect them with other material that you have already encountered in this block dealing with 'women's liberation'.

EXERCISE

Please read the extracts in *Resource Book 4* (B6), which are taken from the interpretation placed by Alice Rossi on the statistics reproduced in Table 2.

1   What changes in the social expectations of women does the first paragraph describe?

2   What do the next two paragraphs tell us about the expectations that men and women had of a woman's place in a couple?

3   The next paragraph links these expectations back to the way girls behaved at college (i.e. university) and to the way they were treated by their parents when they were adolescents. How did the author establish the connection?

4   The final paragraphs identified two steps that had to be taken to increase the number of women in science. Did the author see this as requiring a change in men's attitudes as well? Did she think that the 'triple roles of member of a profession, wife, and mother' were incompatible with each other and that women had to choose between them?

DISCUSSION

1   The author believed that there had been a major change in the expectations that the public authorities had of women in the USA. In the late 1940s and the 1950s women's domestic role was stressed, that is, their role as wives and mothers who were supposed to stay at home and care for their families. This 'national mood' had changed in the early 1960s. Women were then being encouraged to enter the workplace, notably in fields for which there was a 'critical shortage of manpower', including science.

2   These paragraphs show how the division of labour between men and women that was encouraged by the authorities in the 1950s became

internalized by both partners in a couple. It is possible that women felt they could not both be successful wives and mothers and have professional careers. Husbands, Rossi asserts, may have reinforced this by resisting any wishes expressed by their wives to leave home and enter the workplace.

3   The next paragraph suggests that the definitions of the proper places in society for men and women filtered down from parents to children. Rossi believed it was the conflicts that men and women perceived between domestic and professional roles that affected not only the way young girls behaved at school but also the way in which their parents treated them as adolescents. Parents saw their sons as potential professional men, and guided them accordingly, while they viewed their daughters as potential wives and mothers, and prepared them for a domestic role. By successfully transmitting these values and perceptions to their offspring, parents built a new generation in their own image.

4   The next paragraph is an appeal to action. It was intended precisely to disrupt the transmission to women of role models that identified being a woman with renouncing a career. Rossi suggested that the first thing to be done was to encourage a measure of role-reversal, to encourage men to take more responsibility at home and to encourage women to enter professional life. Her second suggestion was that the conflicts women felt between having a career and being a wife and mother should be treated as a social problem to be dealt with by social engineering. She was specifically against telling girls to be 'realistic', to lower their expectations and to reconcile themselves to having either a family or a career, but not both. Women, like men, should be able to feel no conflict between being a good parent and building a professional career, and the necessary social measures had to be taken to ensure that their attitudes could change.

You may wonder what broader social developments lay behind the shifts in policy described in the first paragraph of the extract. There is no simple or straightforward answer to this, but two changing conditions stand out. First, World War II ended in 1945. Men were returning from the front, being demobilized and re-entering the workplace. The government saw its priority as full male employment, and laid great stress on women's domestic role in order to encourage them to stay at home and not to seek jobs or to build careers.

The launch of *Sputnik* by the Soviet Union in October 1957 forced a reassessment of these policies. The fact that the Soviets had been the first to put an artificial satellite into orbit was a serious blow to American pride. It also showed that the Soviet Union was a formidable scientific and technological power to be reckoned with. An extremely powerful rocket was needed to launch *Sputnik* into space. That same rocket could be used for an intercontinental ballistic missile carrying nuclear weapons which, launched from Moscow, could destroy New York. The US authorities came to believe that, to meet the Soviet threat, they had to invest massively in their scientific and technological base. That is why in the early 1960s, as Rossi tells us, a new emphasis was put on the need for women to enter careers in teaching, science and engineering to overcome the 'critical shortage of manpower'.

Of course, I do not necessarily expect you to agree with the views expressed by Rossi in this extract (although many of you undoubtedly will)! In fact, the question of whether you agree with Rossi is irrelevant for our purposes here. Remember we are reading these texts as historians. Rossi's statements are to be treated for our purposes as a historical document, to be situated in its time and place, and to be analysed. The first thing that you need to do is to establish just what your source is claiming. Then you need to treat the statements made as a 'sign of the times', a snapshot, which in this case I have judged as typical of the sentiments expressed by some women in the mid-1960s. You should then go on to relate the document and its author to the general social movement that you are analysing. What is not needed from you, as a historian, is to decide whether what is written is 'true' or 'false' in terms of today's standards and knowledge (although, of course, you can confront it with other arguments and evidence from the same period). Above all, it is not important for you, as a historian, to decide whether you agree with the author or not (although you might do that when you put aside your historian's hat, and discuss social policy with your friends).

I have chosen Rossi's text as an introduction to the question of women in science as it was written in the mid-1960s and because I find it sober, well-balanced and backed with useful statistical data. It is also a text that appeared in the in-house journal of the AAAS, *Science*. It was thus intended to be read by the mainstream scientific community. I would now like you to analyse texts produced by feminists active in the 'Science for the People' movement in the USA around 1970. These were written in a less detached, more militant style.

EXERCISE

Please read *Resource Book 4*, B7.

1   In the view of these authors, in what three ways were young girls being discouraged from entering science?

2   Why were women who then chose a scientific career finding it difficult to remain in science?

3   Can you identify six ways in which, the authors asserted, women in science were treated differently from men?

4   What did the authors mean when they wrote that the female scientist was continually defined 'in relation to her sex'?

DISCUSSION

1   The authors alleged that young girls were:

■   educated into subordinate roles and stereotypes;

■   encouraged to be 'intuitive' whereas men were trained to be 'logical';

■   counselled in high school to enter a family role or a caring, service profession, such as teaching or nursing.

2   The charge was made that access to advanced training was being restricted by setting quotas on the number of women who were allowed to enter graduate school, and that even if this hurdle was overcome women had to choose between family and career, something men never had to do.

3   Women were discriminated against:

■   by being systematically placed in subordinate positions;

■   by rarely being given authority (for example, having their own laboratories or holding supervisory positions);

■   by rarely being given first authorship on papers. (Writing scientific papers for publication is the most important way of building one's professional credibility and visibility in science. It is the single most important way of climbing the ladder of success. The order in which authors' names appears on multi-authored papers is often taken as a sign of who made the most important contribution to the results reported.) The authors alleged that women's names were systematically put after those of men even if they did most of the work and so deserved prominence;

■   by being paid less than men doing the same job;

■   by being denied tenure, that is, a long-term stable contract of employment at a university;

■   by being barred from certain jobs, notably in industry.

4   The point being made here is that women in science were characterized in relation to their sex rather than in relation to their intelligence or competence as scientific workers, as was the case for men. Whereas the fact that he was a man was never taken into consideration for a male scientist, the fact that a female scientist was a woman was constantly remarked on and even entered into judgements of her professional ability.

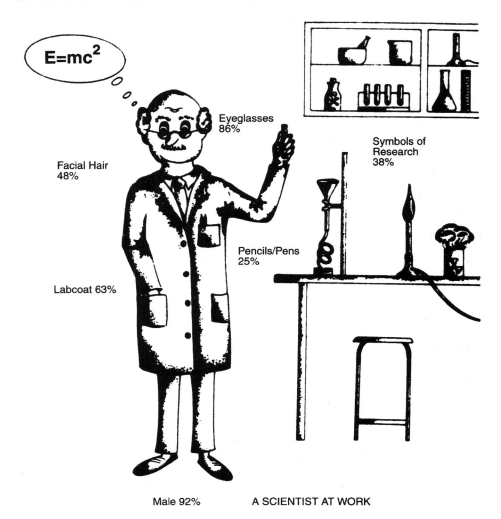

FIGURE 27.7 *Results of a 'draw-a-scientist' test. Most schoolchildren draw a man. Reproduced in Londa Schiebinger,* Has Feminism Changed Science?, *Harvard University Press, 1999, p.74, from Jane Butler Kahle,* Images of Scientists: Gender Issues in Science Classrooms, *Curtin University of Technology, Perth, Australia, 1989*

EXERCISE

Look again at Table 2 (p.99) in the light of the extract from the Women's Group which you have just read. How would the Women's Group explain the voluntary withdrawal of women from the scientific workplace?

DISCUSSION

The extract from the Women's Group suggests that the high rate of voluntary withdrawal by women from a scientific career may have been because of the limited opportunities that women had to advance their careers by being barred from senior positions, not being given tenure and so on. The statistics in Table 2 can thus be interpreted as meaning that, faced with these frustrating hurdles and the 'need' to choose between family and career, women of child-bearing age were dropping out of science and resigning themselves to marriage and motherhood.

EXERCISE

Now read the second text from a woman active in Science for the People (*Resource Book 4*, B8).

1   How did the author define the relationship between men and women in a scientific laboratory?

2   Where, in her view, did women's alienation in the laboratory spring from?

DISCUSSION

1   The author saw the relationship between the sexes as 'suspiciously similar' to that in a classical nuclear family. She regretted that, in the laboratory as in marriage, woman was subordinate in terms of status and authority to the powerful male. A woman was expected to perform nurturing functions. Her security and well-being depended entirely on the male, and she was supposed to accept less prestigious and uninteresting tasks, leaving her male superior to do more important things.

2   Women scientists felt alienated because of the contradiction between what they had been led to believe work in science would be like and what they actually experienced in the laboratory. Science was presented as a system in which rewards were distributed primarily on the basis of merit. Yet women found that they were constantly put in a subordinate position. Having been conditioned to think that if something did not work out as foreseen it was her fault, the woman presumed that she was, in fact, inferior to those who succeeded where she had failed. That prevented her relating the gap between expectations and reality to a system of male domination that was already in place in the laboratory, and she was therefore unable to oppose it.

We have now almost reached the end of this section dealing with the access of women into science. I hope you have gained a good understanding of the arguments and motivations that moved these members of the counter-culture. To round off our study, let us relate these arguments regarding science to the more general movement for 'women's liberation' which was launched in the Sixties.

EXERCISE

Please read again the texts by Betty Friedan (*Resource Book 4*, A10) and Kate Millet (*Resource Book 4*, A21).

1 What did Friedan mean by the 'feminine mystique'?

2 What traces are there of Friedan's argument in the texts you have read earlier in this unit?

3 What did Millet mean by 'patriarchy'?

4 How do her arguments extend those in the texts you have read earlier in this unit?

DISCUSSION

1 The 'feminine mystique' was an image that women had of what they ought to be, a role that they felt they had to conform to, which identified femininity with domestication.

2 Friedan's objection that women 'live through their husbands and children' is similar to Rossi's portrayal of the place of women in marriage (*Resource Book 4*, B6, second paragraph). Friedan, like all of the women quoted in this section, was demanding that women (just like men) should not feel guilty about combining a career with having a family.

3 Patriarchy is described as a way of organizing social life such that males rule females, a system represented as being in the natural order of things, as a 'birthright priority'.

4 Millett's arguments would suggest that the unequal distribution of status and power in the scientific workplace was not just an extension into the laboratory of the domestic role expected of women. It was far more general and deeply entrenched than that. It was also an expression of the patriarchal structure of society, indeed of all 'historical civilizations', that is, of all civilizations that have existed to date.

Seeing the world differently: the thalidomide tragedy

You may have noticed that, along with her complaint that society was patriarchal, Millett suggested that the anti-war movement expressed a 'revolt of youth against the masculine tradition of war and virility'. Many feminists did indeed argue that the use of science for military purposes was connected to men's need to dominate others and affirm their virility.

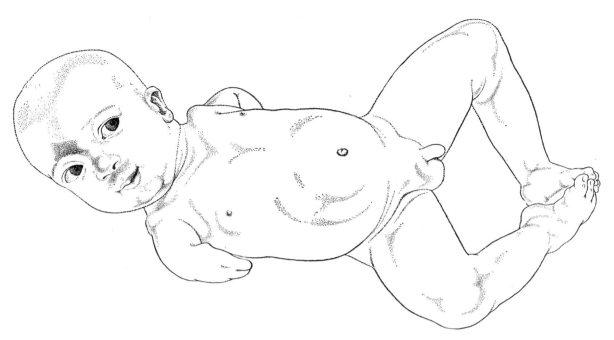

FIGURE 27.8 *Drawing of thalidomide baby. From H. Taussig, 'The Thalidomide Syndrome', Scientific American, August 1962, p.31. A victim of thalidomide syndrome typically has short, deformed and useless arms and hands. The actual case shown in this drawing displays the haemangioma, or strawberry mark, on the forehead, nose and upper lip, which is the most characteristic (although harmless) feature of the syndrome. Other abnormalities that may occur include deformed legs and feet and a wide variety of deformations of the ears, digestive tract, heart and large blood vessels*

A women's science, it was indicated, would be of a different kind, more caring and concerned about people and the environment.

In this section of the unit we are going to focus on a tragic event, the birth of about 7000 seriously deformed babies in the early 1960s, as a way into this kind of discussion. I will first give you the basic factual material you need to understand the arguments. Then you will read extracts from a text written by a historian of medicine, which gives an account of how a tragedy of this kind could have happened.

Beginning in 1959, and with increasing incidence in 1960 and 1961, doctors in Germany noticed that a large number of seriously deformed babies were being born. Photographs and X-rays of the infants showed that the long bones of their arms had almost completely failed to grow. Their arms were so short that their hands extended almost directly from their shoulders. Their legs were less affected, but did show similar signs of distortion of growth. The deformity of their limbs was characteristic of a malformation known as phocomelia. This is derived from the Greek words *phoke* meaning seal and *melos* meaning limb. Phocomelia was so rare that most doctors never saw cases of it. Then, suddenly, hundreds of afflicted infants were being born, not only in Germany, but also in Australia, Canada and the UK.

No evident explanation for the disease could be found. It was known that women who caught German measles at a critical period of their pregnancies could give birth to deformed babies. Was phocomelia similarly a viral disease? Or was it caused by radioactive fallout? By exposure to X-rays during pregnancy? By medicines taken with or without prescription?

The mothers of the afflicted children and their doctors were questioned in detail about the treatment they had had, the medicines they had taken and the food they had eaten during pregnancy. One of the investigators, Widukind Lenz, noted that in about 20% of the cases the mother reported taking a drug called Contergan. His suspicions aroused, he specifically asked all the patients in his sample if they had used the drug. Fifty per cent said yes. Many mothers explained that they had not mentioned it previously because they believed it to be harmless.

Within three weeks, by the end of November 1961, Contergan had been withdrawn from the market in Germany. The West German Ministry of Health issued a firm but cautious statement that Contergan was suspected of being responsible for phocomelia. Radio and television spread the news widely throughout the population.

Lenz's studies had established that, in many cases, malformed babies were born if their mothers had taken Contergan between the 28th and 42nd day after conception. During this period the human embryo, no more than an inch long, was forming its arms and legs. The malformations arose because the drug arrested and deranged these growth processes at a crucial phase in the development of the unborn child.

The active ingredient in Contergan was a substance called thalidomide. This had first been synthesized in the early 1950s and was intended for use as a sedative. It was tested on laboratory animals and showed no harmful effects. Thalidomide was given the trade name Contergan, and by 1960 it had become a favourite sleeping tablet in West Germany. It was inexpensive, sold over the counter without a prescription and widely used in homes, hospitals and mental institutions. Thalidomide was combined with other medicines for use against minor ailments like coughs and colds, and also migraine and neuralgia.

Pharmaceutical companies elsewhere were soon making or marketing thalidomide under licence. Distillers (Biochemicals) Ltd sold it as Distaval in Great Britain, Australia and New Zealand. To emphasize its safety their publicity showed a small child taking a bottle from a medicine shelf. In September 1960 the Merrell Company applied to the American Food and Drug Administration for clearance to market thalidomide-containing compounds in the USA. The Merrell Company's application was initially rejected on the grounds that the drug company had not supplied all the information required. At this stage no one had yet connected thalidomide with the few cases of phocomelia then being registered in Germany.

Thus, the application was not refused because the drug was seen to be dangerous, but for administrative reasons. When Merrell resubmitted its application, the first indications of the drug's dangers were being reported in the German press. Frances Oldham Kelsey, a physician and pharmacologist who worked at the Food and Drug Administration, took note of these reports and, fearing that the drug might have damaging side-effects, asked for more information from the pharmaceutical company. Before her questions had been answered, the increased number of cases of phocomelia had been recognized in Germany and the drug was removed from the market.

Kelsey was alerted to the possible risks of the drug by its proposed label, which suggested that it could be used against nausea in pregnancy. From her work with quinine in the malaria campaign in World War II she had come to realize that, from a pharmacological point of view, the foetus or newborn baby may be an entirely different organism from the adult. She was thus particularly sensitive to the fact that medicines that were harmless for adults could be lethal for unborn children. Kelsey accordingly delayed the acceptance procedure in the USA, thus averting an even greater catastrophe. Given the speed with which pharmaceutical companies can saturate a market with a new drug, and people's tendency to take medicines for even minor aches and pains, there is no doubt that, but for Kelsey's alertness, many deformed babies would have been born in the USA before anyone realized the dangers of thalidomide.

Two factors combined to make it very difficult to trace phocomelia to thalidomide. First, since the drug showed no harmful effects in tests on animals, and was freely available without prescription, it was regarded as an absolutely safe and efficient way to help people suffering from a number of relatively minor ailments. Secondly, it was assumed that embryos would react to drugs in the same way as adults. To overcome these factors, it required the determined efforts of researchers like Lenz, coupled with the then-revolutionary perception of Kelsey, who insisted that embryos and adults reacted differently to drugs. Today we take it for granted that unborn children are far more vulnerable than their mothers to a variety of substances, including alcohol and nicotine, particularly in the early weeks of pregnancy. This was not the case in the 1960s.

Mind-sets and the thalidomide tragedy

Now that we have some idea of the story of thalidomide, and at least one kind of explanation for the tragedy, we are ready to take the analysis a little further. A historian of science has recently explained 'blindness' to the harmful effects of thalidomide on unborn children by a number of deeply rooted preconceptions in the minds of the medical profession. She points out that not even alcohol was seriously considered to be a danger to the unborn child until very recently, and she goes on to connect this to a particular image that doctors had of the womb.

EXERCISE

Please read the extract reproduced in *Resource Book 4*, B9. It is taken from the medical history section of the extremely prestigious British medical journal *The Lancet*.

1   Why was it believed in the mid-twentieth century that alcohol did not harm the human embryo?

2   What other argument reinforced the view that the placenta was the perfect barrier against damaging influences of the environment?

3   How does the author define a mind-set?

4   What mind-set did she think led to the thalidomide disaster?

5   How, in her view, was that mind-set dislodged?

DISCUSSION

1   By the mid-twentieth century earlier evidence that alcohol had serious effects on the foetus tended to be ignored. This was because it was assumed that the placenta, the membrane in which the unborn child is enclosed in its mother's womb, gave perfect protection to the foetus. The placenta was thought to be impermeable to toxic substances except in such doses as would kill the mother. As a result women were not advised against drinking alcohol during pregnancy. Similarly, many drugs were barely tested on pregnant animals, if at all.

2   According to the author, the Victorian idealization of the womb as a privileged part of the woman's body also led to the view that the unborn child was safe from external influences.

3   A mind-set is a shared way of thinking that limits perception and understanding. It acts as a kind of filter, leading us to ignore evidence that does not fit our theories and beliefs.

4   The mind-set, or style of thought, that brought about the thalidomide disaster consisted of the idealization of the womb and placenta along with the belief that the placenta was impermeable to harmful substances.

5   The mind-set crumbled due to the accumulation of so much startling and contradictory evidence in the public domain that it simply could not be ignored any longer. By the 'public domain' the author meant the domain that lies outside the realm of laboratory experimentation. In other words, the prevailing mind-set of the medical profession was destroyed by growing public awareness of the rising incidence of malformed babies in hospitals throughout the world.

Mind-sets in primatology: the feminist's science

It appears that neither men nor women played a dominant role in breaking down the presuppositions about the safety of the foetus in its mother's womb. These presuppositions had led doctors and drug companies to neglect research on the potentially harmful effects of chemical substances on the unborn child. Yet it is noteworthy that one of the first people to recognize the risk in the USA was an experienced female physician, Frances Kelsey, who demanded evidence that the drug was safe in pregnancy. It seems quite plausible to argue that, being a woman, this was the kind of question that she, rather than a man, would be inclined to ask.

One area of science in which a prevailing mind-set was completely revised, thanks to women asking new and different questions, was the science of primatology. Indeed, women's presence in, and influence on the field has been considerable. In the 1960s no women at all graduated from university with a doctorate in primatology. By the 1990s the situation had changed completely. The demand made by the women's movement for greater access to advanced education during the 1960s, coupled with the fascination of studying non-human primates and the enormous popular impact of studies of these animals in their natural habitats, led to increasing enrolment in graduate programmes. Women gained over 50% of the PhDs in primatology in the 1970s, some 60% in the 1980s, while by the end of the century some 80% of the people obtaining doctorates in primatology were women.

Although zoologists include humans among the primates, primatology as a science has generally concentrated on laboratory and field studies of various kinds of ape, baboon and monkey. It is a rich and complex scientific discipline and it is dangerous to generalize about it. What follows is a brief and necessarily very selective account of some of the ways in which women have reset the agenda of research.

Apes are fascinating partly because they are disarmingly similar to ourselves; the 'monkey cage' is always the most popular stop at the zoo, and the place where adults and children alike spend many pleasurable hours finding similarities between the antics of the occupants and their own behaviour. But it goes further than that. There is a tendency to go on to identify the familiar traits that we see in the behaviour of non-human primates with what is 'natural' for all members of the primate family, including ourselves. By studying apes, baboons and monkeys primatologists have thought to have access to the basic drives shaping the interactions between all primates, uncluttered by the subsequent layers of culture that human societies have imposed on them. Many women entering the field have insisted that the analysis of those drives has been shaped by men's uncritical preconceptions about the appropriate social roles of males and females.

Studies of social stability and group cohesion were one area in which female primatologists were particularly concerned to unearth and disrupt mind-sets. These studies sought to identify the underlying 'glue' that held society together. Put very simply, they argued that male dominance along with female sexual receptivity were the foundations of primate societies. Males fought among one another for leadership and control, the 'prize' being access to sexually receptive and docile females. Females were essentially passive resources whose status was determined by their ability to bond the dominant males to the group. As the feminist and social theorist Donna Haraway puts it in summarizing one version of this theory, 'Females were bound to the group by the dominance of males; males were bound by the sexuality of females. Both were bound to each other by a logic of control. The product was the reproduction of primate society' (1992, p.85).

For women and feminists working in primatology, this model of social behaviour was impregnated by conventional, masculinist stereotypes of men and women and of the relationships between the sexes. These stereotypes constituted a mind-set that biased their research on primate behaviour. For feminists this was not merely a question of bad science (and they were at pains to expose the methodological weaknesses of these studies). It was also a question of ideology and politics. For by suggesting that this model captured the 'natural' characteristics of primates, it legitimated, in the name of science, the view that male dominance and female docility were unchangeable characteristics of primate behaviour, and that they were essential for social cohesion.

The most important shift in perception achieved by feminists was a reassessment of the social role of females. By foregrounding females rather than males, and by concentrating attention on their social world, a better balance between the behaviour and adaptations of the two

FIGURE 27.9 Reconstructions of the early humans presumed to have made the Laetoli footprints – fact or fantasy? Reproduced in Londa Schiebinger, Has Feminism Changed Science?, Harvard, 1999, p.128. Photo: Courtesy Department of Library Services, American Museum of Natural History, New York, negative number 4936

sexes was achieved. Careful research showed that the sex differences emphasized in the traditional model did not stand up empirically. To put the point polemically, it was found that anything that males could do, females could do too. Like males, female monkeys were found to be competitive and to take dominance seriously. Like males, female monkeys were found to be adventurous and to wander, and not simply to be conservative and 'housebound'. Like males, female monkeys were found to be sexually assertive. These views may seem evident to us today. When they were first affirmed in the early 1970s by the anthropologist Jane Lancaster they were considered radical.

This step was soon followed by another. The stress on showing that 'females can do too' retrieved the female primate from the obscurity to which the masculinist mind-set had condemned her. That battle won, attention turned to understanding better the specificities of the female's position in primate societies. Without devaluing the role of either the male or the female, scholars sought to grasp the functioning of the group 'from the female monkey's point of view'.

Thus, Linda Marie Fedigan, a physical anthropologist who made field studies of free-ranging monkeys in Texas, noted that research on dominance had neglected to investigate systematically the actual processes whereby female primates chose their partners. By concentrating on how those choices were made by her subjects, Fedigan exposed the limitations of the earlier mind-set, which had constructed female primates as 'passive resources like peanuts or water', and which saw them as simply choosing the most successful male in the dominance stakes as partners for reproduction (Haraway, 1992, p.323). This was an oversimplification. Reproductive strategies were crucial to the survival of the species, but involved far more than just choosing the dominant male. Other considerations were also important, including age, demography and the environment. Fedigan concluded that females did compete with one another, but that their reproductive strategies involved assessments of costs and benefits that were simply not captured by the traditional, masculinist model.

The view of the female primate as child bearer and child carer has also been radically revised by feminist primatologists. Jeanne Altmann, for example, in her studies of baboon mothers and infants, was struck by the ability of female primates to do several things at once. Her observations of baboons in the Amboseli National Park in Kenya led her to abandon the idea that child care was something separate and boxed off from the other activities of the mother. Altmann found that baboon mothers spent their time managing the competing demands made on them by various activities. Being a mother involved 'juggling' with such things as nursing, eating, carrying, disciplining and protecting from danger. It also required establishing a flexible 'budget' or hierarchy of importance between these different demands.

These few examples have, I hope, given you some idea of how the field of primatology has been transformed by challenges to the existing mind-set made by a new generation of women who began entering the field in the 1970s.

EXERCISE

To complete this section please read the extract from Londa Schiebinger's book, *Has Feminism Changed Science?*, in which she deals with primatology (*Resource Book 4*, B10). In what ways have feminist scientists changed the mind-set in respect of primatology?

DISCUSSION

Schiebinger stresses that the mind-set that shaped the masculinist research programme treated females as socially important in primate society mainly because they were dedicated to their offspring and were sexually available, above all to the more powerful males. They were generally docile and non-competitive. The most important change brought about by the feminists has been the re-evaluation of the role of the female. By treating her as socially influential in her own right, the female primate was no longer seen as passive and dependent, but as assertive, competitive and intelligent.

In this section I have dealt with two very different aspects of the critique of science waged by feminists beginning in the Sixties. First, there was the question of discrimination, the argument that women were being systematically discouraged from pursuing a scientific career and that, if they managed to overcome the obstacles to entry, they were treated as inferiors within it. Secondly, and more fundamentally, we saw how preconceptions about women (and men) were embedded in the very content of science itself. The key concept here was the idea of the mind-set, defined by Dally as 'a shared view of reality that controls, organises, and limits perception and understanding' (*Resource Book 4*, B9). The thalidomide tragedy was linked to doctors' preconceptions about the nature of the womb; parts of primatology were shown to be dominated by stereotypes of male and female roles and attitudes, which legitimated prevailing structures of power and of exclusion.

These examples take us back to Roszak's critique of science. They raise important questions about the circumstances under which science can produce objective knowledge. They alert us to the complexity of scientific practice at the research frontier, and to the struggle, not only with 'nature', but also with oneself, that the pursuit of objectivity entails. The feminist critique of science, initiated in the 1960s, is in a constant state of refinement and self-analysis. It has illuminated aspects of science and of its practices, which have left an indelible mark on our understanding of the relationships between power and truth.

4 CONCLUSION

In the first two units of this block a number of general questions were raised about the relationship between mainstream culture and counter-culture. There Arthur Marwick told us that, in his view, the '"counter-culture" formed no consistent, coherent, opposition or alternative force' to mainstream culture (Block 6, p.19). 'Counter-culture', notwithstanding the rhetoric of some of its proponents, was not diametrically opposed to mainstream culture. Rather, in his opinion, it shared many of the general features of the culture it was criticizing, most evidently a certain level of material well-being made possible by science, technology and economic growth in the democratic societies of the West.

Our analysis of counter-movements in science tends to bear out this interpretation. Yes, we have encountered arguments to the effect that science and its methods should be rejected entirely, and replaced with a very different, mystical, subjective approach to reality. This approach inspired the writings of Roszak and took shape in the emergence of hippie culture and communal styles of living. Here, one might argue, mainstream culture was being rejected, and radically alternative forms of individual freedom and social organization were being explored. But this was not the only, or the most important line of attack. Rather, as we have emphasized in this unit, the core of the counter-movement *in* science did not want to abolish science but to transform it. The aim of those who made up this group was to demilitarize the scientific enterprise, to reorient funding patterns and research priorities away from military objectives and towards socially beneficial goals.

The aims of members of the women and science movement, as spelt out in this unit, were entirely coherent with this. Indeed, what many women objected to was being excluded from a prestigious activity that they found personally stimulating and professionally rewarding. Some of them also believed that many of the research priorities of science reflected male interests and men's position in society. Women, so the argument ran, would inject a new sensibility to nature and society into the scientific enterprise, and place different questions and priorities on the research agenda.

The counter-movement in science was spearheaded by the first post-war generation of young men and women, many of whom had experienced levels of affluence, personal comfort and health undreamt of by their parents. They confronted a scientific establishment that had seen the horrors of war and totalitarianism at first hand, and whose members had devoted much of their effort since 1945 to building the military strength that, they felt, was essential to preserve democracy and maintain world peace. That peace was based on the fear of mutually assured destruction of one superpower by another, but it created an island of stability in the USA and Western Europe in which economies could grow and the quality of life could improve for many. With that achieved, the new generation, and the senior scientists and academics who supported them, felt that the time had come to call a halt to the militarization of science and, indeed, of society. They did not reject science altogether. They sought rather to exploit the new possibilities opened up by the vast investments in science and technology since 1945. Taken out of the hands of the scientific establishment, and redirected away from destruction and domination, science and technology were to be used to build a more just, more democratic society, a society in which people could live together in harmony with one another and with the natural environment.

REFERENCES

PUBLIC PAPERS OF THE PRESIDENTS OF THE UNITED STATES, *DWIGHT D. EISENHOWER, 1960–61* (1961) Containing the Public Messages, Speeches, and Statements of the President, January 1, 1960 to January 29, 1961, Washington, DC, US Government Printing Office.

HARAWAY, D. (1992) *Primate Visions: Gender, Race and Nature in the World of Modern Science*, London, Verso.

LESLIE, S.W. (1993) *The Cold War and American Science: The Military-Industrial-Academic Complex at MIT and Stanford*, New York, Columbia University Press.

ROSSI, A.S. (1965) 'Women in science. Why so few?', *Science*, vol.148, 28 May, pp.1196–202.

SUGGESTIONS FOR FURTHER READING

You may find it helpful and interesting to look at one or more of the following:

ARDITTI, R., BRENNAN, P. AND CAVRAK, S. (eds) (1980) *Science and Liberation*, Boston, South End Press.

GREENBERG, D. (1967) *The Politics of Pure Science*, Chicago, University of Chicago Press.

HISTORICAL STUDIES IN THE PHYSICAL AND BIOLOGICAL SCIENCES, Volume 18:1 (1987) Papers from a symposium on cooperative research in government and industry held at the University of California, Berkeley, July/August 1985.

KEVLES, D.J. (1971) *The Physicists: The History of a Scientific Community in Modern America*, Cambridge, Mass., Harvard University Press.

LESLIE, S.W. (1990) 'Profit and loss: the military and MIT in the postwar era', *Historical Studies in the Physical Sciences*, vol.21, no.1, pp.59–85.

SCHIEBINGER, L. (1999) *Has Feminism Changed Science?*, Cambridge, Mass., Harvard University Press.

TAUSSIG, H.B. (1962) 'The Thalidomide Syndrome', *Scientific American*, vol.207, no.2, August, pp.29–35.

Acknowledgement

Grateful acknowledgement is made to the following sources for permission to reproduce material in this unit:

Table 1: Orians, G.H. and Pfeiffer, E.W. (1970) 'Ecological effects of the war in Vietnam', *Science,* vol.168. 1 May 1970. American Association for the Advancement of Science; *Table 2*: Rossi, A.S. (1965) 'Women in science. Why so few?', *Science,* vol.148. 28 May 1965. American Association for the Advancement of Science.

Every effort has been made to trace all the copyright owners, but if any has been inadvertently overlooked, the publishers will be pleased to make the necessary arrangements at the first opportunity.

UNIT 28
RELIGION AND COUNTER-CULTURES IN THE 1960s

Written for the course team by Susan Mumm

Contents

STUDY COMPONENTS				
Weeks of study	Texts	TV	AC	Set books
1	*Resource Book 4*	TV28	–	–

Aims and objectives

The aims of this unit are to discuss the following questions:

1   Was there a change in the religious climate of Western society in the 1960s?

2   Was there a relationship between the development of the counter-culture and the upsurge of interest in alternative religions?

3   Why did New Religious Movements (NRMs) gain prominence in the 1960s?

4   Were mainstream churches influenced by the NRMs, and, if so, how did they respond to the challenge posed to the established religious culture by NRMs?

By the end of this unit, you should be able to:

1   assess whether there are elements of 1960s alternative religions that show counter-cultural influence;

2   explain the difference between the concept of 'cult' and 'NRM' and show why scholars of religion avoid the first term;

3   reflect on the enduring impact of counter-cultural religion on the social landscape;

4   employ some of the techniques and methods of analyses utilized in academic religious studies.

1   INTRODUCTION

In August 1967, an unusually large scrum of interviewers, camera operators, and photographers gathered at Los Angeles International Airport, waiting to glimpse the most important person in the world at that moment. He was more famous even than the Beatles and the Rolling Stones: he did not have to be a fan of theirs, for they were his devotees. Finally, he descended the narrow metal steps and appeared to the world's gaze: a short man with a long beard and dishevelled hair, dressed in a white robe and carrying flowers. When the media questioned him he

FIGURE 28.1   *Maharishi Mahesh Yogi on his arrival at Heathrow Airport, 29 September 1967, in transit between Los Angeles and Copenhagen. He appears as he did to the mass media in LA, wearing a smile and carrying flowers. (Photograph: Hulton Getty)*

laughed, giggled, and offered humanity a technique which would bring personal fulfilment, spiritual transcendence and world peace.

This is how the Maharishi Mahesh Yogi appeared to the TV-viewing and newspaper-reading world when the Beatles announced their membership of his Spiritual Regeneration Movement (SRM). When the announcement was made, the ensuing media mayhem focused on the attraction of Eastern religions for the young, and especially for the counter-cultural young. This particular group (the SRM) had been established the year before the Beatles formed, and was disbanded a few months after they split up; the Stones of course keep rolling. The author of Units 14–15 has discussed whether Transcendental Meditation (TM, as the SRM became known) is a religion, but certainly in 1967 both its supporters and its detractors described the movement in religious terms, and the media depicted it as an important new religious movement.

Other paths to enlightenment were also popular in the decade: New Religious Movements (NRMs) which ran counter to mainstream religions. But, despite the fact that they often recruited from the counter-culture, not all of the NRMs could be clearly associated with the counter-culture. Some seemed to stand outside both the counter-culture and the mainstream as a kind of counter 'counter-culture' culture in opposition to both. Earlier units in this block have examined the idea of the counter-culture as a social and historical phenomenon, questioning its very existence and emphasizing its plurality. Here I will examine aspects of these counter-movements in religion, understanding the term counter-culture as something similar to, but wider than, the youth culture of the 1960s. It will be clear as you read on that for the most part, this unit will define religion *functionally* (refer back to Block 4, p.35, if you need a reminder of what this means). In this unit the focus will be on the mutual impact of religion and the counter-culture, paying particular attention to NRMs. The approach employed will be that of the case study, building on some of the concepts introduced in Units 14–15.

2 THE COUNTER-CULTURE AND THE SEARCH FOR MEANING

Earlier units in the block have discussed the larger issue of what the counter-culture or, more probably, counter-cultures were. Here we will take for granted the existence of some sort of counter-culture, and begin with a popular commentary on its nature, first published in 1969 by Theodore Roszak, a Californian academic. In *The Making of a Counter Culture: Reflections on the Technocratic Society and Its Youthful Opposition*, he wrote that:

> the interests of our college-age and adolescent young in the psychology of alienation, oriental mysticism, psychedelic drugs, and communitarian experiments comprise a cultural constellation that radically diverges from values and assumptions that have been in the mainstream of our society at least since the Scientific Revolution of the seventeenth century.

> *(Roszak, 1970 edn, p.xii)*

This passage should seem familiar; it is part of a longer passage you encountered in *Resource Book 4*, A22. While Roszak's reliability as a historical source is a question that we will return to, his exposition of the interests of the young is useful for our purposes, because it summarizes so succinctly some of the major characteristics of NRMs that developed in the 1960s. This unit will discuss three of the four elements of the cultural constellation identified by Roszak: oriental mysticism, psychedelic drugs, and communitarian experiments. It is arguable that the fourth eleme. (the psychology of alienation) should also be examined in any handling of religious belief, but I will not be doing so, except incidentally and occasionally.

EXERCISE

But first, we need to identify the elements of the counter-culture that were relevant to the flowering of religious diversity in the 1960s. The list in Units 25–26 (pp.16–17) concentrates on events and trends, while this one needs to focus on attitudes and beliefs. Jot down what you see as the key elements of counter-cultural attitudes.

DISCUSSION

What follows is my list, necessarily imperfect and incomplete. As you encounter the readings in the unit, ask yourself to what extent the groups being described fit with, or deviate from, the characteristics noted here.

■ a search for new structures

■ a rejection of the status quo

■ anti-materialism

■ a search for self-identity and self-fulfilment

■ a spiritual quest

■ a desire for a supportive community

■ disillusionment, alienation

■ a quest for meaning

■ a desire to change the world

■ the mainstream left them feeling unfulfilled and exploited

■ a desire for self-enhancement

You may have noticed that some of the elements listed above are phrased negatively, while most are described in positive terms. I have done this deliberately, as a way of reminding you that depictions of the counter-culture travel from negative to positive and back again. In its early phase, the counter-culture was depicted mostly as rebellious: a reaction against mainstream values, Western materialism, parental values, and the political system, to name a few. By 1967 the focus had shifted somewhat. Popular attention was turning to what the counter-culture was perceived to be advocating: equality, non-violence, experimentation and spontaneity, tolerance of alternative lifestyles, environmentalism, right livelihood, enlightenment and transcendence. I would argue that the really distinctive feature of the counter-culture was the high value it put on individual personal experience, which led directly to its diversity: since inner experience was diverse, there could be no one path to truth. This acceptance of other ways encouraged the blossoming of NRMs. NRMs, as with most of the counter-culture, were seen as stressing love, acceptance, and personal transformation.

EXERCISE

Please read the extract from Roszak (*Resource Book 4*, C1). While reading, ask yourself:

1   What, in Roszak's opinion, is the attitude of the counter-culture to science?

2   What can you deduce about Roszak's sympathies?

3   What is 'radical' about the counter-culture's interest in religion?

Before you start on the first question, I would like to suggest some cautions as to the use of Roszak as a source; you've already encountered one historian's assessment of his work in Units 25 and 26. Of course, we can't simply accept Roszak's assertions at face value, any more than we would unquestioningly accept those of any writer. Like any other source, this one is limited by its presuppositions, and lacks the critical distance that only time can give. But precisely for that reason it is also valuable: it tells us what a generally acute observer of the social scene at the time thought was going on. Sometimes, and especially in the social history of religion, it is every bit as important to study what people *thought* was occurring as to piece together what was *actually* going on. While Roszak might in fact tell us less than we would have liked about what was actually happening, he is certainly a useful articulator of societal assumptions about the counter-culture, in his self-appointed role as liberal cultural commentator.

DISCUSSION

1   Roszak claims that the counter-culture and its spokespersons, such as the Beat poet Allen Ginsberg, are rejecting the scientific 'technocratic' orientation of the modern West in favour of something that is decidedly opposed to scientific objectivity: an inner world of religious seeking and mystic experience. Science, in the eyes of the counter-culture, has become the tool of political and social evil. Urban life in the modern West, and especially the horrors of the Vietnam War, provide the proof that governments imbued by the technocratic, scientific spirit are unable to govern morally. In addition to the technocracy's moral failure, it is profoundly hostile to religion, and denies the life of the spirit.

2   I think that Roszak's sympathies are, for the most part, with the counter-culture. Although he attacks its crudity and ignorance, he reserves his anger for the secular intellectualism that he believes culminated in the barbarities of the Vietnam War. In his final paragraph, he suggests that the counter-culture is rediscovering something of value that the technocracy cannot comprehend. Rituals of the spirit are more enriching to humanity than the rituals of science and politics.

3   What is 'radical' about religion in the counter-culture is the reclaiming of mystery which, since the Enlightenment, had been rejected in favour of 'a militantly sceptical secular tradition'. Perhaps what Roszak means by this can best be illustrated by an anecdote about the French astronomer Laplace (1749–1827). When he explained his theories to the Emperor Napoleon, he was asked, 'But what about God?' Laplace answered, 'I have no need of God in my hypothesis.' It is this attitude that Roszak predicts the counter-culture will overthrow.

3 COUNTER-CULTURAL RELIGION: SOME DEFINITIONS

EXERCISE

Before we go any further, we need to deal with one very problematic term: *cult*. You've already encountered it in the discussion of Scientology in Units 14–15 (Block 4, p.29). What images come to mind when you read the word? Jot down some examples.

DISCUSSION

What associations did you make? Shaven-headed men in saffron robes, chanting and singing on a street corner? Followers of an American clergyman drinking cyanide in a remote corner of South America? Impressionable teenagers being exploited financially or sexually by an unscrupulous, charismatic leader? Young people selling flowers in airports? Branch Davidians in Texas burning to death in a barricaded compound?

If the images the word 'cult' evoked from you were very different from those suggested above, I would be pleased but also surprised. Such extreme, and mostly negative, images constitute the public perception of a 'cult': a religious organization that is foreign, bizarre, exploitative, and potentially damaging to adherents. Since the 1960s almost all NRMs have had to struggle against the popular images that this label generates. But students of religion define 'cult' very differently. This definition is usefully simple:

> A cult is a religious group that presents a distinctly alternative pattern for doing religion and adhering to a faith perspective other than that dominant in the culture. What is a cult is relative to a culture. Thus one understands the attempts in some cultures to curb the influence of such cults as the Methodists, the Presbyterians, the Episcopalians, and the Roman Catholics because they deviate so widely from established Hindu, Buddhist, and Islamic religion.
>
> *(Melton and Moore, 1982, pp.17–18)*

When a culture begins to feel threatened by encroaching new or minority religions it may respond by labelling these groups as cults. 'Cult' becomes nothing more than a pejorative term, a way of condemning a group without having to justify its rejection. Most of those who study new religions avoid the term 'cult', finding that the negative connotations that the word has acquired make it unhelpful as part of an academic vocabulary. They suggest that less emotionally loaded terms are preferable, such as *NRM, minority religion, alternative religion*, or *new religion*. Of course, these terms are also far from perfect: many 'new' religions are based on ancient faith traditions, and some of them are unhappy with being classified as 'religions' at all. Remember the discussion in Units 14–15 of both TM and Scientology: the TM movement does not class itself as a religion while Scientology, of course, has the opposite problem, fighting continually against attempts to refuse it the status of a religion.

What the negative publicity around NRMs has meant is that most of the things we think we 'know' about such groups are actually wrong, or at best partial. I would suggest that a more fruitful approach to the question 'what is an NRM?' would be to look at how they are classified by scholars of religion. The best-known model comes from the work of the late Roy Wallis, an important sociologist of contemporary religion. Wallis's approach varies from the popular one in that it doesn't divide NRMs into 'good' religions and 'bad' cults. The judgement made is not a moral one, unlike that of most anti-cult activists, who tend to define as a cult any group that they don't agree with. Instead, Wallis classifies groups by their intellectual response to a central problem for religion.

EXERCISE

Examine Wallis's typology, reproduced in Figure 28.2. (A typology is simply a system of classification of ideas by their 'type', or nature.) What key feature of these groups does Wallis use as the basis of his divisions? Don't be concerned if you are unfamiliar with some of the groups he gives as examples.

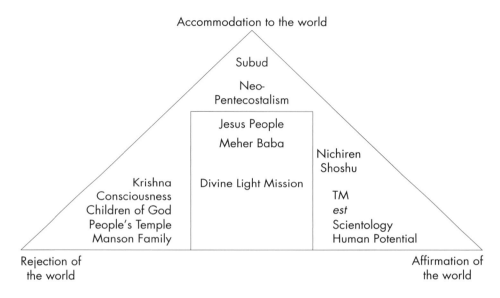

FIGURE 28.2 *Orientations of the new religions to the world. From Wallis, 1984, p.6.*

DISCUSSION

His division of NRMs into three groups is based on their attitude toward society, which in religious language is often called 'the world' ('world' meaning not the physical entity of the planet, but the wider culture's societal values). It is not based on their theology or their impact, negative or positive, upon society. Thus, you will find groups derived from Christianity in all three categories, as well as non-Christian ones.

It will be useful at this point to examine what Wallis actually means by his three groups.

World-rejecting religions see the world as evil and corrupt, and believe that it is doomed to speedy destruction. Normally, the only survivors of this expected apocalypse will be the members of the group. An extreme but well-known example of this type was The Family, which developed under the influence of Charles Manson and came to prominence after some members carried out the 'Helter-Skelter' murders in California in the late 1960s. Manson taught his followers that he was a combination of both God and Satan, and was destined to be the new Messiah. He prophesied that a revolution by the black underclass in the USA would be followed by chaos, ended by Manson's personal rule over a new society. In this society, women would exist only to serve men's needs and to produce children, and whites would rule blacks. Some might argue that in this dystopic vision Manson was defending the status quo of 1960s America. A bizarre touch was added by his teaching that the Beatles were four angels proclaiming the end of the world, and that their songs were prophecies which carried secret messages for The Family. While we must condemn his teachings as racist and sexist as well as murderous and theologically ludicrous, this is not the point. The Family fits well into the typology as an example of a world-rejecting NRM.

World-affirming religions hold the view that humanity is not sinful or hopelessly corrupt (as with world-rejecting groups) but is unawakened. These groups teach that the human spirit contains enormous untapped power which people can be taught to use through involvement in the spiritual practices of the group. World-affirming movements include what are sometimes called 'quasi-religions' or 'therapeutic religions'. They have fewer of the characteristics usually associated with religion. Such groups often have 'no "church", no collective ritual of worship, [and] may lack any developed theology or ethics' (Wallis, 1984, pp.20–21). You should look back at the discussion of TM in Units 14–15 here to see if it carries the characteristics of a world affirming religion (Block 4, pp.21–4).

World-accommodating religions occupy the middle ground in their attitude toward the world. While the world is not wholly good, as it is marred by sin, it isn't totally evil either. Believers can still live in it while remaining faithful to their religion. Did you wonder why some of the central group in the diagram were boxed off? Wallis has placed a box around those NRMs that are examples of more mixed responses to the world, where the tension between the acceptance and rejection of the world is clearly evident; in other words, they are less accepting of the world than the groups above them. I won't give you examples of world-affirming or world-accommodating groups now, as we will study an example of each in case studies later in this unit.

Interestingly, Wallis also claims that both world-rejecting and world-affirming groups rise to some extent from the failure and disintegration of the counter-culture of the 1960s. This is an important issue for the unit, and one I would like you to keep in mind as you learn more about NRMs.

EXERCISE

Read the extract 'The cults are coming!' (*Resource Book 4*, C2), from an American anti-cult book by Lowell Streiker first published in the 1970s. Then read 'Numbers of movements' by Eileen Barker in *Resource Book 4,*

C3. (This expands upon the extract you have already read in Study Weeks 14–15.)

1   Compare the tone and approach of each text.

2   Ask yourself what message each is conveying about the appeal of the NRMs.

3   Both authors make a different point about the potential of NRMs to form a real threat to society. Do you think either point is valid?

DISCUSSION

1   First of all, these are very different kinds of documents. While Barker is writing under the auspices of the Home Office, Streiker is introducing the second edition of a popular anti-NRM book. We can assume that the intent of the writers is equally at odds.

The language used is strikingly different, as are the forms of argument. Streiker deals in assertion, with a vague undertone of menace; many of his metaphors are military and suggest concerted action on the part of new religions. Barker's tone is drier and less emotional. It should not surprise us that their sources are also different: Streiker looks for evidence in the products of popular culture, such as films; Barker's document is largely empirical.

2   Barker's statistics form a useful starting place for reconsidering some widely held beliefs about NRMs. While Streiker seems to suggest that all NRMs (and a lot of other groups as well) can be lumped together and that they have an appeal that few young people can resist, Barker's calculations indicate that very few people ever join an NRM. However, much larger numbers may have shown some interest or have been attracted to some elements of some NRMs, such as the practice of hatha yoga, meditation, or communal living.

3   In a sense, both authors make a valid point: Streiker is right in seeing an increased interest in alternative religion in society and increasing influence for NRM forms, and Barker is equally correct in reminding us that very few people ever make a complete commitment to an NRM, and that none of the groups have any potential for 'taking over' a culture.

I chose these two documents because they typify the two major tendencies of writing about NRMs. Streiker is typical of the popular approach to the issue of alternative religions – the sort of coverage of 'cults' that one is likely to encounter in the media – while Barker represents the academic specialists in the sociology of religion. The polarization of these two approaches creates constant tension, and I would be surprised if you found a book or article on the subject of NRMs which did not fall more or less squarely into one camp or the other.

4 COUNTER-CULTURAL RELIGION: DOORS TO ENLIGHTENMENT?

It could be argued that what really launched the counter-culture as it is commonly understood was its interest in the expansion of consciousness through chemical and psychological means. One important precursor of this counter-cultural obsession was the novelist Aldous Huxley, who wrote *The Doors of Perception* in 1954. The book chronicled his experimentation with drugs (primarily mescaline) and advocated the use of drugs as a way of experiencing truths hidden from ordinary people. Incidentally, the pop group The Doors was formed when several rock musicians met in a TM class. They took their name from Huxley's book, thus nicely linking alternative religion, drug use, and popular music in the counter-cultural milieu.

EXERCISE

Please read the extract from *The Doors of Perception* (*Resource Book 4*, C4).

1   Why does Huxley advocate drug use?

2   Who would benefit from this experience?

DISCUSSION

1   He sees drugs as unlocking a door into non-verbal consciousness, which he assumes is deeper, more profound, and perhaps truer, than verbal awareness. The idea was that one could use drugs to free the non-rational self, and experience abnormal or transnormal states of consciousness, which Huxley understands as spiritual states. He almost suggests that the well-rounded intellectual should not be without this experience.

2   To my mind, Huxley appears rather élitist: although he does say at one point that everyone should experience drug-enhanced consciousness, much of the passage makes it clear that he assumes that 'inner-naughts' would be people of education and considerable leisure. But as the end of the passage laments, few of the professional classes he is writing for demonstrated any interest in opening the 'Door in the Wall'. What Huxley fails to point out is that as mescaline – in limited supply and expensive – must be purchased in order to participate in this exercise, spiritual experience is becoming a commercial transaction available only to the wealthy.

Now please read this brief extract from a later book by Huxley, *Heaven and Hell.*

> For an aspiring mystic to revert, in the present state of knowledge, to prolonged fasting and violent self-flagellation would be as senseless as it would be for an aspiring cook to ... burn down the house in order to roast a pig. Knowing ... what are the chemical conditions of transcendental experience, the aspiring mystic should turn for technical help to the specialists – in pharmacology, in biochemistry, in physiology and neurology, in psychology and psychiatry and parapsychology.
>
> *(Huxley, 1956, p.128)*

In *Heaven and Hell* Huxley argues that the practices of mystics and saints in earlier periods, including flagellation, fasting, prolonged meditation, all strove to bring about the altered states of consciousness through inefficient chemical means of bodily deprivation. While they often achieved the desired mystical state, they damaged their bodies in the process. Drugs would perform the same alteration of consciousness, but more quickly, thoroughly, and painlessly. Added to drugs, however, would be techniques learned from the hard sciences and the behavioural sciences.

What Huxley advocated as an experience primarily for an intellectual, moneyed élite, Timothy Leary popularized and democratized. Leary, an academic psychologist, became the self-proclaimed high (in every sense of the word) priest of the drug culture. He advocated the use of LSD (lysergic acid diethylamide, often abbreviated to 'acid') rather than the rarer mescaline, as LSD was a drug which any competent chemistry student could concoct at a relatively low cost. He also preferred LSD because it was more powerful. Originally, Leary valued LSD as a therapeutic tool, claiming that a single acid trip was the equivalent of two years in therapy. Soon, however, he began to argue that drugs were a sacrament in a new inner religion, writing, 'The LSD trip is a religious pilgrimage.' As we will see later with the Maharishi, one attraction for counter-cultural youth was fast results. Just as meditation could lead to instant bliss, LSD was advocated as a way of achieving immediate spiritual knowledge. Speedy, easy, and apparently safe, acid offered enlightenment without the suffering and self-denial that traditional religions usually demanded as the price of mystical experience. Like Huxley, Leary assumed that if LSD was a direct path to enlightenment, the older spiritual paths would become obsolete.

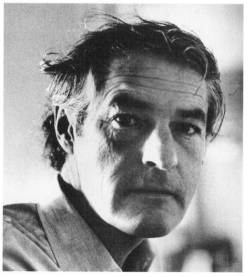

FIGURE 28.3 *Self-proclaimed high priest of the drug culture and underground cult figure, Timothy Leary, September 1971. (Photograph: Hulton Getty)*

EXERCISE

Please read the first page of Leary's autobiography *High Priest* (*Resource Book 4*, C5).

1 What impression does the passage leave?

2 Jot down what message you think the structure of the page is intended to suggest.

3 What do you make of the language?

DISCUSSION:

1 For many of you, the first impression may have been one of intense distaste, or confusion as to the author's message. I have to admit that I profoundly dislike Leary's writing; I find it sloppy, self-indulgent, and unconvincing. But at the same time I acknowledge that he was generally seen as a spokesperson for the counter-culture, so it is worth reading him for that reason alone. We will have trouble understanding any group unless we read and take seriously what they found significant and meaningful. I think we can get something of value from this passage if we persist.

2 The obvious oddity is the page layout. Leary's text is centred, with quotations from Genesis and a novel distributed down the sides of the page. If you are familiar with traditional Biblical or Talmudic commentaries, you will immediately recognize this structure. Theological texts of many traditions use this form in order to emphasize the authority of the central text, by cross-referencing it to other sacred or authoritative texts. I think it is intended to suggest that Leary's text is a new gospel, a message of salvation for the chemical age. The old revelation, and both the Bible and literature rank as this, are being superseded by Leary's message. Think how well the title of the book, which is an autobiography, after all, links in with this.

If you read the central text and the sidebars in conjunction, you will notice that they are thematically linked. God the creator still exists, but now the act of creation is that of the Big Bang and is described as a psychedelic as well as an organic experience. God's message is within the body, not without, as was traditionally taught in religions that emphasize revelation. It is encoded in the genes, which carry millions of years of evolutionary sensation. And LSD can unlock the past which is carried within every individual. This revelation will allow individuals to escape from the technocracy: 'the fake-prop studio of the Empire game'.

3   I hope you caught the Biblical quotations (often slightly altered) that Leary embeds in his own text. I counted eight of these, witting or unwitting testimony to Leary's own Catholic upbringing, but there may be more. The point is that by incorporating and altering a text that was traditionally considered to be inspired, Leary is playing with the suggestion that his own text is psychedelically 'inspired' as well. Notice that despite the often-assumed relationship between the counter-culture, psychedelia, and Eastern religions, the dominant tradition underlying this passage is Christianity.

Finally, you almost certainly observed the use of Leary's infamous catch-phrase, which it could be argued became the mantra of much of the counter-culture: 'Turn on, tune in, drop out'. Don't be too concerned by his definitions of these terms: Leary redefined the slogan virtually every time he used it. You've already come into contact with it in the *Playboy* interview in Study Week 26. Try to get the general drift of the meaning of the words in this context.

EXERCISE

Now look at another extract from Leary (*Resource Book 4*, C6). This one comes from a chapter entitled 'Start your own religion', in *The Politics of Ecstasy* (a book which has been called the 'Bible' of the alternative movement).

1   Compare its message and language to the extract you've just read.

2   Is Leary proposing anything revolutionary in religious terms?

DISCUSSION

1   This is a much more readily intelligible document than the extract from *High Priest*. The chapter from which this section is taken is essentially an instruction manual for forming a rural commune (which Leary calls a 'clan') based on a hallucinogenically-assisted spiritual quest. We will come back to the religious commune as a feature of the counter-culture later in the unit, when discussing the Jesus People. For now, I merely want to point out that several thousand counter-cultural communes were formed in our period in North America alone: it is estimated that more than half of these were religiously motivated (Bates and Miller, 1995, p.371).

You will notice that some of the metaphors are the same as in the other document: the evolutionary path and cellular memory are still important, as is the idea of mass culture as something that is both shallow and false ('the studio-prop game'; 'the TV-studio game').

Notice how Leary defines religion: in both documents it is described as consciousness expansion, and as something that derives from the body, rather than from the mind or spirit.

2 Not really. Oddly enough, as you read through the passage, you may be reminded of other guides to the spiritual life: the early sixth-century Benedictine Rule (an early Christian monastic rule), for instance, also contains warnings about the love of money, the need to abandon private ownership, the monitoring of sexual behaviour, the need for a role model, whether that be patron saint or Leary's 'mythic figure', the rejection of urban life, and the importance of communal ritual. If you strip away the interest in drugs, you find something which very crudely articulates ideas similar to those employed for many centuries in more traditional religious communal organizations, such as monasteries, convents, and ashrams.

Early users of hallucinogens paid great attention to what they called 'set and setting'. In other words, the intention or mindset (abbreviated to set) of the person had to be right; individuals looking for thrills or an easy high were discouraged from participation. In the pioneering days of experimentation with hallucinogenic drugs, most users seem to have been in search of spiritual revelation: monks and theological students were eager subjects in the first clinical tests. It is important to remember that such experimentation was originally entirely legitimate: the extra-laboratory use of LSD wasn't criminalized until the mid-1960s. Setting meant that the physical environment had to be rich (beautiful countryside or a lavishly decorated temple were two favourite locations), evocative, and tranquil. Religious users of psychedelic drugs claimed that 'bad trips' were only experienced by those who ignored the importance of set and setting, or who took drugs with improper motives. Of course, another important factor was dosage and purity, both of which suffered greatly as newly criminalized hallucinogenic drugs became market commodities on the streets.

Some of Leary's claims for the religious potential of acid need balancing against the opinions of his contemporaries. Here's the view of the novelist and journalist Tom Wolfe, looking back on the period in *Mauve Gloves and Madmen, Clutter and Vine*.

> Very few people went into the hippie life with religious intentions, but many came out of it absolutely *righteous*. The sheer power of the drug LSD is not to be underestimated. It was quite easy for an LSD experience to take the form of a religious vision, particularly if one was among people already so inclined.
>
> (Wolfe, 1976, p.133)

Wolfe seems to be suggesting that people found what they were looking for in drugs: for those with a religious background or religious interests, this could well be a spiritual experience. But I think he also implies that there was nothing intrinsic to LSD that would have made religious 'trips' the normative hallucinogenic experience: those who found God did so because they were looking for God.

What now? The case studies

So far, as well as trying to make a case for a less value-laden terminology, we've had a brief look at what the counter-culture rejected – the 'technocracy', what Unit 27 calls the military-industrial complex. We've also been introduced to one aspect of counter-cultural practice that was embraced by many – drug culture. But where did disillusion and drug-enhanced consciousness leave 1960s youth culture, religiously speaking? I shall try to answer that question through the use of two case studies and by focusing on two contrasting ways of faith. The groups I have chosen to study are two extreme examples of religions which recruited most of their early following from the counter-culture.

One major religious tendency was the Eastern-influenced meditation groups, of which the Spiritual Regeneration Movement, or SRM, was by far the largest and best known in the West (they claimed a million initiates in their first two decades). In the first case study we will concentrate on SRM activity in Britain, taking advantage of its ties to pop culture in the UK. SRM was selected for the case study for several reasons: because of its size; because of the amount of media attention it attracted (due to the common assumption that Hindu and quasi-Hindu groups were synonymous with counter-cultural religion); because it is a good example of a 'world-affirming' religion; and because it did not remain static, but has continued to change and evolve in ways that many of you are probably aware of, such as the establishment of the politically active Natural Law Party.

The second case study was chosen because of the high level of contrast it presents to the first. World-rejecting rather than world-affirming, the American Jesus People, or JP, communes came out of the Protestant fundamentalist tradition, demanded total commitment through a communal lifestyle and the abandonment of secular ambitions, and engaged in a highly publicized movement which caught the attention of the mainstream denominations, who wrongly saw in it hope for the revitalization of their own traditions.

You might be concerned about the seeming ephemerality of the SRM and the JP. But it can be argued that the attitudes toward religion and society exemplified in these case studies have continued to exert an important influence. The biggest religious surges of the 1970s were the growth of evangelical-Pentecostal-charismatics, and the popularity of quasi-religious therapeutic movements, both of which owe their major intellectual debts to the groups we will study in the remainder of this unit. Former JP members have been a major influence on the formation of the radical right in the USA in the late Seventies and early Eighties; radical right influences (seldom completely stripped of their religious underpinnings) have moved on to display new vitality in many Western countries, including the UK. The neo-Eastern groups have been an important formative influence on what is now usually known as 'New Age' spirituality, and the individualistic pursuit of private spiritual interests, which most commentators see as the dominant religious mode today.

I would like to end this section of the unit with a remark made by John Lennon, in August 1967: 'We aren't sorry that we took LSD but we realize that if we'd met the Maharishi before we had taken LSD, we would not have needed to take it.' Lennon puts very succinctly the case for the use of drugs in the religious quest, taking for granted the possibility and legitimacy of such use. This brings us to the next phase of counter-cultural religious development: the growing popularity of Eastern meditation groups from the mid-Sixties as casual drug experimentation began to turn sour for many.

5 COUNTER-CULTURAL RELIGION: TWO CASE STUDIES

The Spiritual Regeneration Movement and pop culture

We began this unit with a description of the arrival of the Beatles' spiritual guide at LA airport in the summer of 1967. The quote from John Lennon above reminds us of the direct relationship between the counter-culture, the drug culture, and the fashionable Eastern and Hindu-derived religions. It also suggests that by this time Lennon had concluded that drugs are an inferior way of achieving one's spiritual goals. In the same interview, Lennon made another illuminating remark, which once again highlights the assumed relationship between spiritual revelation and drugs; again note the use of Leary's catch-word in the following: 'If we [the Beatles] went round the world preaching about Transcendental Meditation, we could turn on millions of people.' The use of the language of drugs ('turn on') in a statement about the missionary potential of TM makes the earlier drug/religion linkage very clear. The NRMs of the 1960s and early 1970s can be seen as closely linked to the counter-culture, and it is also possible to argue that some later NRMs are, in part, successor movements to the counter-culture.

After the announcement by the Beatles and the Maharishi's greeting by rapturous thousands in the USA, the SRM enjoyed for a time perhaps the highest visibility of any non-Christian religion in the West. The Maharishi became the spiritual advisor of many key figures in popular culture, including not only members of the Beatles and the Rolling Stones, but also the Grateful Dead and Jefferson Airplane. Donovan, the Beach Boys, and Mia Farrow joined the Beatles at the guru's ashram (meditation centre) in India in 1968, where their initiation into the more mystical aspects of meditation was zealously covered by the international press. While these high-profile adherents soon lost their faith in the Maharishi, their public devotion to his teachings had enabled him to spread his ideas to a very large, youth audience who were the consumers of popular culture.

FIGURE 28.4   *George Harrison with ISKCON devotees at Apple Studios, 1971. (Photortgraph: Camera Press, London)*

EXERCISE

Look at the example of testimony from a former SRM member (*Resource Book 4*, C7).

1   Why and how did this woman become involved in Transcendental Meditation?

2   What did she value about the meditation techniques?

DISCUSSION

1   This woman clearly sees her involvement in TM as part of a religious quest, in which she experimented with a number of techniques which might help her discover the 'answers to life'. Notice that traditional religious organizations do not form any part of this quest, but that a book by Leary and a community of like-minded friends do. This is typical of counter-cultural religious experience. One of the things those who entered the counter-culture dropped out of was

organized religion – at least in its conventional forms. A minority of those in the counter-culture, however, dropped into alternative religions, and it is those we are concerned with in this unit. Depth, duration and intensity of involvement both in counter-culture and with NRMs varied, of course.

She describes her recruitment as a gradual process and as part of a therapeutic milieu. TM is attractive to her because of its association with Eastern mysticism, the involvement of her friends, and its ready availability. Notice that there is no suggestion that she is ever personally invited to join the movement, but her previous experiences plus her reading combine to make her receptive to the posters' invitation. She is actively looking for answers, not passively responding to pressure from believers. This individualistic and active approach is typical of the counter-cultural religious experience.

2   The real appeal of TM was its effectiveness. It appeared to work. There were positive emotional changes from the very beginning of her involvement, and supernatural experiences seem to have reinforced her sense of the reality of the experience. She found meditation provided her with fast and pervasive changes of consciousness: reread the striking last sentence of her testimony. Incidentally, counter-cultural metaphor was often connected with scientific developments of the late twentieth century: even Leary's 'tune in ...' carries its symbolic meaning in light of the development of radio and television. While the counter-culture may have liked to see itself as anti-technocracy, it was necessarily saturated in the consumer technology, and its metaphors, of the time.

The problem of source bias

One real difficulty when studying NRMs is the bias or prejudice in the sources we have available to us. While earlier units have pointed out that all historical sources are biased in one way or another, the emotions surrounding issues such as religious conversion and de-conversion seem to result in especially problematic documents. The student of such groups finds eyewitness accounts of life in NRMs in two main sources: there is a small amount of recruitment material and an enormous body of anti-cult literature. The recruitment material has an obvious interest in portraying the group and its members as positively as possible. Anti-NRM literature is usually generated by former members of groups. As material written by ex-members and published in anti-cult books, it tends to depict NRMs as destructive or exploitative. Given its provenance, it should not surprise us that it tends to be as wholly negative as the other is positive. The very process of leaving the group involves a reaction against its values, denial of its authenticity, and retrospective bias. Reflect upon the way people may describe something they have abandoned: the temptation to portray a false step as wrong or without value is very strong. A good example is to think how recently divorced persons react when asked to describe their former spouses.

The first person account you've just read comes from an anti-'cult' polemic; a book so extreme that it concludes that NRMs succeed because of demonic involvement. I chose to use Joan Harrison's account because its author (Harrison herself, not the author of the book who quotes it) makes a real attempt to be fair-minded in her description of her recruitment, and it contains relatively little retrospective bias, but I think that if you read it carefully, you will realize that it does have a subtly negative tone. She is, after all, an *ex*-TM teacher.

What is the solution to the problem of source bias? There probably isn't a perfect one: all that we can do is be acutely aware of the probable biases of the individuals or groups generating the material, and be sensitive to how those biases, which are based on beliefs, have been used to shape the evidence.

EXERCISE

Look back now to the checklist on page 123 showing key elements of counter-cultural attitudes. To what extent do you see these elements reflected in Joan Harrison's account?

DISCUSSION

I think you will see that this former devotee reflects central aspects of counter-cultural attitudes in her story, especially the search for self-identity and self-fulfilment, the idea of a spiritual quest, the search for meaning, and a desire for self-enhancement. You may find different elements of counter-cultural attitudes in her account, but I hope you agree that several are evident.

One of the appealing features of the majority of Eastern-derived meditation groups, including the SRM, was how easily they fitted into a counter-cultural lifestyle. TM is an excellent example of what I am going to call a *low-commitment NRM*. One became initiated after the payment of a fee (one week's income), and participation in a ceremony taken from the Hindu puja (see Units 14–15), where the mantra (sacred chant, invested with mysterious qualities) was assigned. After this, the only requirement was to meditate for 20 minutes once or twice a day.

The SRM did not demand asceticism or self-denial or even the rejection of Western materialism; thus it fitted easily into relatively consumerist counter-culture lifestyles. The Maharishi said:

> My technique does not involve withdrawal from normal material life. It enhances the material values of life by the inner spiritual light. ... We do not even think of giving up anything ... We do whatever our needs demand, but we are regular in Meditation, and when we become filled with the Bliss, the Being, – the need is no longer there.

The SRM preached a brand of syncretism very attractive to the counter-culture with its emphasis on tolerance, diversity, individualism, and its suspicion of claims of absolute truth.

> The same age-old message of Buddha, the same age-old message of Christ, the same age-old message of Krishna. Get within, experience the Kingdom of Heaven, experience Nirvana, experience Eternal Freedom, come out with that freedom, live a life of freedom in the world, the same age-old message.

(both quotes from the Maharishi in Mason, 1994, pp.45–6, 52, 92)

Notice especially the last sentence of that quotation from the Maharishi. Does it remind you of anything you read in the last section? The idea of God being within the individual, of unity with the cosmos through a transcendent experience, parallels Leary's claims for LSD. Both suggest that the individual with a raised consciousness is an atom of God, or even God itself. But TM had the advantage over the uncontrolled experience of LSD in that it offered not one altered state of consciousness, but five, clearly structured and ordered, and open to advanced practitioners: the best known is probably the claim of levitation, or 'astral flying'.

The SRM also rejected the Christian emphasis on redemption through atonement or suffering, especially that of Jesus on the cross. The Maharishi claimed that other religions create what he called 'theories of suffering' in order to try to explain it and to make suffering positive. This is false, according to the SRM. Suffering, in its teaching, results from the world-wide neglect of meditation. Essentially, life is bliss, and relearning the forgotten technique of meditation will enable one to reclaim bliss. Meditation and righteousness will fill the world with harmonious vibrations and bring about world peace.

The SRM, renamed the Society for Creative Intelligence in 1970, later began to de-emphasize religion in favour of scientific research into the claimed psychological and physiological benefits of meditation. At the same time, the language of mysticism was replaced by that of science. However, we can recognize the roots of the movement in its most recent incarnation, that of the Natural Law Party, which fields candidates in the local and national elections. One of its central tenets is that establishing meditation centres in world trouble-spots will bring about universal peace.

While the SRM was clearly a religious movement in the 1960s, today TM is most often classified as a *quasi-religion* (see the discussion of world-affirming religions, p.128). These are groups that ride the fence between the sacred and the secular. Instead of holding services, quasi-religions have meetings or classes. Their primary goal is therapeutic; to make the lives of their members more enjoyable, through an emphasis on wholeness rather than on duty. They base their ideologies on scientific claims. Another term used for such groups is *manipulationist sects*: here the idea is that the techniques taught to members allow them to make positive changes in their lives, and that the techniques properly carried out cannot fail; thus the term 'manipulationist'. Much of the modern therapy movement could be said to have borrowed heavily from the quasi-religions/manipulationist sects in this respect. The following quotation is a good description of their attitude to science.

> The appeal to science found in many of the quasi-religious ideologies suggests that, although modernisation may have led to alienation and loss of meaning, the new quest for meaning is heavily influenced by the modernisation and secularisation of contemporary society against which it revolts.
>
> *(Griel and Ruby, 1993, pp.231–2)*

In other words, for some people the possibilities of personal transformation which used to be the province of traditional religious faiths are now being offered more attractively and more credibly by quasi-religious appropriations of science. In some ways, the whole issue of whether TM is a religion or not is irrelevant, given that its roots are in Hinduism. Many Hindus say that Hinduism is not a religion, but a *dharma* – a way of life. This was discussed in the Bowker extract (*Resource Book 3*, A3) which you read in Study Weeks 14–15.

Jesus People communes and the rejection of the counter-culture

The second cluster of NRMs I want to examine is that which became known collectively as the Jesus People (JP). This umbrella covers a large number of different groups: they were often called Jesus Freaks or Street Christians. The movement emerged in California in the mid-Sixties and seems to have started when a number of youthful evangelical Christians opened missions directed at street people and counter-cultural dropouts. Like the meditation NRMs, the JP groups varied widely, in theology, in tactics, and in degrees of success. However, they all emphasized converting youth. Their basic techniques were 'witnessing' – describing their own experience of a changed life – and street preaching. Instead of operating out of churches, as mainstream Christian denominations had done for a long time, they went out into the youth subculture and preached on beaches, at rock concerts, in coffee-houses, and on the streets themselves.

It would be an impossible task to list, let alone describe, all the groups that became identified with the JP. Most started in the wake of (or in reaction to) the 'summer of love'. Some were short-lived, some became incorporated into existing religious organizations, and a few developed a character of their own which deviated quite sharply from their origins. What binds them together is their fundamentalism.

What is fundamentalism? One sociologist of religion gives us a polysyllabic but useful definition:

> We can think of fundamentalism as a value-oriented, anti-modern, dedifferentiating form of collective action – a sociocultural movement aimed at reorganising all spheres of life in terms of a particular set of absolute values.
>
> *(Lechner, 1993, p.79)*

Don't be dismayed by Lechner's vocabulary. What he is saying is that fundamentalism seeks to bring people back to what its advocates see as a set of universally true values that are rooted in the past. These values are true for everyone at all times, and are usually perceived as being antagonistic to the values of the mainstream culture.

EXERCISE

At this point I would ask you to recall again the list of counter-cultural values earlier in the unit (p.123). Make a similar list describing the key elements of fundamentalist religion and then compare it to Lechner's list below.

- emphasizes action, not merely beliefs

- embodies a vision of a rightly ordered society

- contains a profound critique of modern society, especially pluralism

- its solution is to revitalise the 'true faith'

- involves a literal interpretation of sacred texts

- goal is to restore a sacred or golden past

(Lechner, 1993, pp.79–80)

EXERCISE

Is there any similarity between the values of fundamentalism and of the counter-culture?

DISCUSSION

I think that most of you would probably respond 'no' to that question. You might even point out that the central value of diversity found in the counter-culture is actively rejected in the fundamentalist suspicion of pluralism, and its emphasis on one true path. You may have gone on to ask a key question: given that counter-cultural values seem so different from those of the fundamentalists, how do fundamentalist groups recruit from the counter-culture? I don't want to answer this question right now, but we will come back to it at the end of the section, when some possible solutions to this apparent contradiction should have emerged.

One characteristic of the JP is that because they recruited on the streets rather than on university campuses, they attracted adherents from a somewhat different social milieu than most other NRMs. Members of JP communes tended to be more working class in background, less likely to have university degrees, and more likely to have been heavy drug users than converts to other NRMs. Sociologists studied a large JP commune in 1972, located in rural North America. Of the hundred or so permanent members, 97 per cent reported having used illegal drugs prior to conversion: most of these used illicit substances daily or more frequently than once a day. The group touted conversion to their beliefs as a sure means of releasing oneself from drugs: Jesus was a cure for addiction, offering a 'permanent high' that drugs could not match. The academics studying this particular group suggested that this counter-cultural commune was still maladaptive, but that those involved had simply switched addictions (Simmonds, 1977, pp.123–5). Much recent research would seem to reinforce this: accounts of the Anglican Nine O'clock Service in Sheffield in the 1990s, for example, stress its rave-like atmosphere and the 'high' that members got from the 'fix' of participation in its services. Of course, this connection between drugs and religion has a long and honourable tradition, dating from prehistoric times. Marx's famous statement on religion serving as the opiate of the people is also worth considering in this context, although it is often overlooked that in addition to the stultification produced by opiates, Marx argues that they serve to make tolerable what would otherwise be too painful to endure. Thus religion in capitalist society can be seen as ameliorative in its relief of very real pain, rather than simply befuddling.

A prominent JP group which targeted 'the dropouts, the drifters, the burnouts, and the headcases' was the Christian Foundation. Started by Susan and Tony Alamo in southern California, it focused on evangelizing among hippies and junkies. Established on a ranch near LA, adherents practised communal living on a very large scale, with several hundred living there in the early 1970s. They did manual work in local industries, and as is common in most religious communities, all earnings went to the group. This group is still active, having moved to Arkansas in 1973 after brushes with militant anti-cult groups and deprogrammings (to be discussed in Section 6), although there are still branches in several cities. Their theology is conservative evangelical Christian, with a strong emphasis on judgement and damnation; at times there is a suggestion that only members of the Foundation will escape the day of judgement. This is certainly a world-rejecting group, as defined by Wallis.

Probably the best-known of JP groups was the Children of God. Started by David Berg and his teenaged children in the mid-Sixties, again in California, it began as a very strict, conservative fundamentalist group, differing from the Foundation only in its emphasis on love rather than on judgement. However, it too can be seen as rejecting with considerable violence the mainstream values of American society.

EXERCISE

Please read this extract from an open letter from Berg to the parents of his followers, entitled 'Who are the rebels?' (*Resource Book 4*, C8).

1   Who are the rebels here, according to Berg?

2   What is the letter saying about the relative values of the counter-culture and of mainstream society?

DISCUSSION

1   Some of the more extreme groups, such as the Children of God, taught their members that it was not them, but their parents, who were in rebellion. By rebelling against God's laws, their parents had created an anti-God society. Church members in general were reviled as 'systemites'. Notice that the youth are exempted from responsibility by virtue of their ignorance of the truth. Berg promised to lead his followers from the ignorance foisted on them by their rebellious parents to a true understanding of God's plan for the world.

2   As for the relative values of the counter-culture and mainstream society, I trust you noticed the spiritual polarity that this text sets up: their parents, the churches, and the establishment on one side, and the youthful followers of Berg on the other. I hope you also noted the overtones of Leary's denunciations of modern society in the beginning of the sixth paragraph here. In actual fact, Berg's group soon began to deviate so markedly from the basic tenets of Christian theology that by the early 1970s, it had moved beyond the JP movement altogether, just as the SRM had abandoned its spiritual purposes in favour of scientific research by the same date.

Very different from the Children of God was the Christian World Liberation Front (CWLF), based originally at the Berkeley campus of the University of California. It was the most intellectually oriented of the JP groups, and did much of its recruiting on university campuses. The group published a popular underground newspaper, *Right On!,* and had a flair for attracting press coverage, staging mass baptisms in the ocean, swimming pools, and public fountains. Street-theatre was also an important aspect of the group's recruitment efforts. The CWLF's members fronted several of the many JP rock bands, such as The All Saved Freak Band, and the group established many communes (usually called Houses), some of which still exist.

This brings me to an important point. The JP groups we are examining in this case study are all organized communally. Communal groups, unlike the SRM, are *high-commitment NRMs.* They expect believers to abandon their homes, families, jobs, and former values, in order to conform to a highly codified set of behavioural and doctrinal norms in a group setting. Communal organizations, regardless of faith group, are usually considered to be the most demanding form of religious expression.

If you have made a video-recording of TV28, *Two Religions: Two Communities*, this would be a good point at which to watch it. (I do realize that the programme may not have been broadcast yet or you may have seen it already – so don't worry if it does not fit into your study programme at this point.) If you do watch the programme now, look for clues as to how religious communities structure themselves in order to ensure stability and continuance. Despite the very different theologies of the two groups examined in the programme, I think you will find that the strategies for work, life and devotion employed by the two groups display significant similarities.

Any communal organization has to come to grips with two central issues if it is to survive and grow. These are the issues of financial sustainability and the control of sexuality. Communal organizations, religiously motivated or not, usually come to grief on one or other of these issues. Financial stability is the easier issue. Most of the groups we are looking at (and the communities in TV28) initially funded themselves by a combination of donations from the public and by members' contributions. Members were expected to donate all their money and goods to the group upon joining, and to take only what they needed from the communal stocks. Private possessions were usually discouraged. In some JP groups, this was taken to the extreme of no one owning their own clothes: every morning, members would select clothing from a box of garments common to their sex. Normally, the solicitation of donations from the public and from the mainstream churches soon ceased, as communal groups disliked the public scrutiny usually associated with this form of fund-raising. Self-sufficiency became an important goal, and the mostly working-class members learned skills or took on jobs that were not very dissimilar from those of their counterparts in 'the world'. All the groups I've mentioned are now completely self-supporting. You will immediately see that the need to be self-supporting limits the size of the groups. As they tend to locate themselves in rural areas, saturation of the local employment market comes quickly. This is why most of these communes have a number of centres scattered around North America, and to a lesser extent, Europe.

Gender and sex roles in religious communes are even more potentially problematic than money. This is the issue which most often determines the survival or failure of the group. Typically, NRMs respond by defining gender roles very strictly. Communal groups redefine sex roles by emphasizing one aspect, and rejecting or minimizing others.

Most JP communes were established in rural areas. Some of the most world-rejecting quickly acquired survivalist overtones, but most gained a measure of financial stability by providing services such as restaurants, manual labour, and small craft skills to the local agricultural economy. The *millennial* aspect is important in understanding the motivation to form, or join, a rural commune. Millennialists believe that God is returning to earth soon to end society as we know it and to establish a theocracy, where God and true believers will reign. Because JP millennialists believed that Jesus would return in their lifetime, they were reluctant to see value in long-term enterprises like university or professional training. Many JP groups were tainted by anti-intellectualism, and saw any enterprise that didn't lead to the salvation of souls as a waste of time. 'I quit college after three and a half years and I'm glad, because the only thing that's going to stand is God's Word', was a typical remark (Ortega, 1972, p.93).

JP groups were particularly hostile toward theological education. Most of those involved in the JP movement (with the exception of the Christian World Liberation Front) tended to insist upon a very literal interpretation of the Bible; they believed in a literal Hell and a real Satan who attempted to control individuals. While sharing the racially tolerant views of their peer group, almost all (excepting again the CWLF) were adamantly opposed to feminism and gay rights as unbiblical. Their method of biblical exegesis seldom extended beyond *proof-texting*. Proof-texting is taking a single text from the Bible as the 'proof' which can be used to approve or condemn the topic under discussion. Most groups were anti-drug, and claims that conversion could instantaneously break the cycle of addiction were common. This wasn't unique to the JP, of course: most fundamentalist groups of any faith made this claim.

EXERCISE

In the passage that follows, one member of a JP commune (the Rapping Post) described the life.

I've lived in communal situations for the last two years now. I really like communal living. I've found that most Christian houses are kind of like boot camp in the Navy. I was made from a super civilian to a super military man within three months. I think that a lot of these new Christians need this heavy training of discipline of the flesh; in fact just understanding just what God wants and requires of you in these first three months in heavy communal living is really good for them.

(Ortega, 1972, pp.90–1)

1   What does this communitarian suggest are the advantages of group living?

2   Does the mixture of language and metaphor surprise you at all?

DISCUSSION

1   The speaker here emphasizes the attraction of the discipline and control of communal living, a remark I found interesting because it highlights one possible reason for the popularity of the JP with some members of the counter-culture. On the face of it, this seems contradictory: surely the counter-culture was all about rejecting these values? But for those who see the NRMs of the period as a rejection of the counter-culture by those who had been damaged by it, this kind of statement supplies some evidence.

2   The speaker uses an almost unimaginable metaphor in the context of the counter-culture: learning to live in a religious commune is like basic training in the military. The advantages of discipline and obedience are stressed, but still in a mildly drug-linked language: communal living itself is 'heavy'.

EXERCISE

Please read the extracts from 'Jesus now: hogwash and holy water', by an American poet, James Nolan (*Resource Book 4*, C9).

1   How does Nolan's background affect his response to the JP?

2   What are his criticisms of the movement?

3   Does he see it as having any value?

DISCUSSION:

1   Nolan is open in his admission that his own fundamentalist background is a major factor in his largely negative perception of the Jesus movement: 'I O.D.'d on peanut butter when I was 10 and fundamentalism when I was 12 and haven't been able to stand the taste of either since.' The author, despite his turning away from

religious fundamentalism toward the political left, suggests that the experience was formative.

2   He sees the JP as politically naive, and potentially politically reactionary, intellectually escapist, financially compromised, and as leading nowhere.

3   Despite his hostility to the movement, he does concede that it offers a haven to those who haven't been able to cope with the drug culture. In this he agrees with the sociologist Roy Wallis, who we saw earlier as describing NRMs as a refuge for those who have been damaged by the failure and disintegration of the counter-culture. Nolan's description of the communal JP house (which is painfully 'unhip') would seem to bear this out.

EXERCISE

Of course, joining an NRM could also be seen as a rejection of values other than those of one's parents. Consider the message of the following song, sung by the Children of God in their early days, in the light of the aspects of the world rejected by this group.

> Down, down, the sun's going down,
> The axe is laid to the tree.
> Proud America she spins around,
> She shall be brought to her knees.
> Look at the way they raised us,
> Look at the way they raised us.
> They think their money has amazed us.
> America's sinking fast in the sand.
>
> The system is fucked and it's getting me down.
> Oh, Lord, I can't stand it.
> The system is fucked and it's getting me down.
> Oh, Lord, I can't stand it.
>
> (quoted in Patrick and Dulack, 1976, p.30)

Now look at another NRM hymn, this one composed by the Shakers, another fundamentalist, celibate communal group, in the early nineteenth century.

> Of all the relations that ever I see
> My old fleshly kindred are furthest from me
> So bad and so ugly, so hateful they feel
> To see them and hate them increases my zeal.

O how ugly they look!

How ugly they look!

How nasty they feel!

(quoted in Kanter, 1972, p.90)

DISCUSSION

Firstly, I find the juxtaposition of the two hymns useful, as it helps to make the point that extreme reactions against the biological family are not new in alternative religions. In nineteenth-century Britain and America, both Anglican and Roman Catholic nuns came under repeated attack (literally and in public discourse) for 'abandoning' their families. Indeed, there is considerable evidence that for some recruits the anti-family attitudes of such groups hold considerable appeal. In more recent times, the new family of the NRM has replaced the old nuclear family, and is seen by many members as an improvement on it.

Secondly, notice that the Children of God hymn attacks not only the family, but American society as well. The material wealth of the West, the song suggests, cannot save it from apocalyptic destruction. The logic of salvation in such a case must necessarily be separatist, where true believers can work together for spiritual, not earthly, rewards.

EXERCISE

Read the letter sent by a new recruit to a JP group to her parents (*Resource Book 4*, C10).

1   What strikes you about the language in which the letter is written?

2   Look for evidence of sex-role attitudes, family background, and the general cultural milieu of the writer.

3   What do you think attracted her to the group?

4   How was she recruited?

DISCUSSION

I think most parents would be slightly alarmed to receive this in the post!

1   Let's start with the language: much of the letter echoes Biblical phrasing, with a heavy element of cliché. The Biblical resonances are the most striking aspect of the letter's phraseology. The negative terminology she applies to her body and to her old life is also interesting: a university degree becomes 'carnal knowledge', she herself becomes 'this soul', her body is 'this flesh of your daughter', Christmas becomes 'the worldly holidays'. This kind of language is more often seen in Eastern-influenced groups like ISKCON (the Hari

Krishnas) than it is in modern Christian groups, although a medieval monk might have felt at home with most of it. It reminds me of the terminology used by Margery Kempe, the medieval Christian mystic (c.1373) and author of the first autobiography written in English, who refers to herself throughout as 'this creature'. The power of the 'group-think' is impressive; this young woman has a whole new vocabulary and set of categories since joining this NRM.

Notice that the group she has joined doesn't even have a name ('we go by no name') and it is clearly migrant, living communally but not settled in a single location. She has no concern over what happens to her possessions and seems to reject any lifestyle that offers more than a bare subsistence as worldly. The number of times that the 'world' is mentioned, and always negatively, would also incline us to identify this group as world-rejecting.

2   Sex roles seem to be clearly defined and very traditional. Women sew the clothes worn by the group by hand, and must dress modestly in body-concealing clothing. Men dress in what they see as Biblical clothing: robes, sandals, and wear beards. Although it is not spelled out in the letter, this group, as with most JP communes, demanded complete celibacy outside of marriage, and segregated the sexes rigorously in their daily lives. She also makes it clear that she has absorbed the group's fundamentalist teaching about the religious role of women: preaching is something that is not permitted to them; they provide the backup support that allows the men to go out and preach.

Her previous jobs were in the service sector, as a dental assistant and as a hairdresser. Her family was religious, but she now believes that while the Bible was pounded into her (an interesting and suggestive phrase), they didn't really know God. In terms of general cultural background, I get the impression that she was confused and drifting at the time of her first encounter with the group. She clearly was living away from her family, and doesn't seem to have had strong ties in the city she left: there is no mention of saying goodbye to friends or leaving a job, for example.

3   She was attracted by the exotic appearance of the two brothers, who look like pictures of the disciples, and who seemed to her to be living a life similar to that of the first followers of Christ. She suggests that she saw in their religious practice an authenticity and an immediacy that the mainstream denomination of her family did not offer.

4   Recruitment is more direct than a simple poster on the walls (unlike the meditation groups we looked at earlier): presumably these unusually dressed men preached or witnessed to her, and invited her to join their group. At the time of writing this letter, she is sure that her decision to abandon everything to join an NRM was the right one,

and is enjoying life in the group, even the adventure of scavenging food (this nameless group was known to the general public as 'The Garbage Eaters'). Her uncertainties have been put to rest by the simple message of the group and she appears to have complete confidence in the rightness of their mission.

You may have agreed that most people would react with alarm to receiving a letter like this. But it wasn't only the families of individual devotees who found themselves having to respond to the challenge of the NRMs. The responses of the mainstream churches to the movements are also important, and the next reading begins our examination of this issue, which will be carried into the next section of the unit.

EXERCISE

Read the *Time* cover story 'The Jesus revolution' (*Resource Book 4*, C11) and study the selection of photographs from the article reproduced in Figures 28.5–8.

1   What is the overall tone of the article?

2   What impression do the photographs convey?

3   Who are the revolutionaries described here, and is the label appropriate?

4   How are the mainstream churches responding to the movement?

FIGURE 28.5   *Wearing sackcloth, daubed with ashes, members of the Children of God conduct a vigil on Los Angeles' skid row. (Photograph: D. Gorton ©Time Inc.)*

FIGURE 28.6   An exuberant congregation at Bethel Tabernacle in Redondo Beach, California. (Photograph: D. Gorton ©Time Inc.)

FIGURE 28.7   A young person suffering from paralysis is carried to a mass baptism in the Pacific at Corona del Mar. (Photograph Julian Wasser ©Time Inc.)

FIGURE 28.8   *A California teenager gives the 'Jesus sign' during a beach baptism. (Photograph: Julian Wasser ©Time Inc.)*

DISCUSSION

1   The tone is generally upbeat, in decided contrast to the Nolan article. The author sees the Jesus movement as returning American youth to the 'fold' of American values, albeit with less emphasis on material success. Historical links are made to earlier American revivals, and the author believes that the movement is giving youth a sense of meaning that they had been unable to find in their parents' lifestyles. The overall impact on American culture is assumed to be positive, as religious fundamentalism is thought to be better than apathy or drug use. The movement will affect the mainstream churches.

2   Most of the photographs depict young people of vaguely hip appearance. They are in groups, not alone. The photos depict a much stronger youth message than does the text, which discusses not only the JP, but conventional fundamentalists such as Billy Graham and the pre-eminently square 1950s singing star, Pat Boone. The

crowded frames suggest that the movement is popular and growing, giving the impression of a significant cultural phenomenon.

3   The writer of this article casts a wide net when describing the Jesus movement. Some of the representatives of the JP mentioned, such as the country singer Johnny Cash, seem not to belong to a discussion of religion among a youthful counter-culture. If this is revolutionary, it can be best seen as counter-revolutionary, as the author claims that the movement is returning American youth to the basics of their tradition. The author sees three threads forming the movement, and it is debatable whether counter-cultural elements can be detected in all three.

4   As for the responses of the mainstream churches to the movement, this again is depicted as largely positive, although the number of churches that simply ignored the JP was large. When looking at a movement which seems (however briefly) to have potential for significant social change, it is essential to ask who is funding and promoting it. Funding for communal living often came from the liberal Christian denominations. Ironically, the liberal denominations benefited the least from the JP in the long run. The fundamentalist evangelicals, who tended to reject the JP as long as they retained their counter-cultural appearance and language, usually became the churches of choice for former JPs as they rejoined the mainstream.

As the article suggests, many on the conservative wing of social opinion had high expectations of the JP in the early Seventies; it was thought that the movement had attained such momentum that it could be an agent of social change in America. Even mainstream evangelicals like Billy Graham imagined this; what happened is that most JP groups were eventually absorbed into the evangelical mainstream. Turnover in the Jesus Houses was high, as people paired off and married, or moved into more traditionally organized households. Communal life doesn't ordinarily work well in a context of monogamous marriage. Groups ordinarily are either celibate or advocate some form of group marriage. Because members of JP communes, due to their fundamentalism, could accept only complete celibacy or totally monogamous marriage, the Jesus Houses slowly disintegrated and their more committed members drifted into the suburban evangelical mainstream where their social conservatism came to encompass political conservatism as well. Of course, exceptions still exist; there are JP communes in the USA and Britain with anything up to several hundred members, whose counter-cultural roots are still very evident in middle age.

6 COUNTER-CULTURAL RELIGION AND THE MAINSTREAM CHURCHES

Of course, the mainstream churches did not spend the 1960s concentrating only on the issue of disaffected, counter-cultural youth, although retaining the young is a major preoccupation of any faith group, for obvious demographic reasons. But if I were asked briefly to summarize the main areas of development in the churches during this time period, I would choose (1) the impact of Vatican II on Roman Catholicism, (2) the discussions about ecumenism between a number of Protestant denominations, and (3) the emergence of the charismatic movement (usually manifested as glossolalia: speaking in 'tongues') both in Catholicism and in the liberal Protestant churches. You might remember these three trends as reform, reunion, and renewal.

There is no question that when we compare the size of the mainstream churches in the 1960s to the NRMs, the churches remain strikingly predominant in number and membership throughout the period. But despite that, the churches expressed increasing concern about counter-cultural religion as the decade progressed. I think there were two main reasons for this: the first was that even though the NRMs were minute in size, they were growing rapidly, and the mainstream denominations were not. Second, the churches realized that they were no longer calling the cultural shots, as had been the case in the 1950s – they seemed to be conservators of a tradition that was increasingly irrelevant to the young. The long-term consequences to any religion that cannot attract the next generation should be evident.

It is interesting that the liberal mainstream churches tended to accept counter-cultural religion much more easily than the fundamentalist churches. From what you understand of fundamentalism, can you suggest why this was? I would tend to argue that unlike fundamentalist denominations, the mainstream churches had a much higher tolerance of pluralism; while they found NRM religious expression often odd, crude, or even repellent, they saw in the counter-culture's very interest in religion a possibility of hope for the future of belief.

One major area of mainstream response to NRMs remains to be examined in this unit: this is the issue of *deprogramming*. Deprogramming (the term is a metaphor derived from computer programming) involved the forcible removal of an individual from the premises of an NRM, against his or her will, and their involuntary confinement in a secret location until their religious affiliation was renounced. In a few extreme cases, allegations of rape or violence were made against hired deprogrammers; several have served prison terms for kidnap and related offences. But despite the distasteful nature and doubtful legality of deprogramming, in the backlash against NRMs it was claimed that this was the only way that individuals could be persuaded to leave the group they had joined. Deprogrammers were almost invariably hired by parents, frustrated by their inability to convince judges or psychiatrists that their children had been 'brainwashed' and no longer had the ability to make rational religious decisions. *Brainwashing* was a term originating in the Korean War, when it was believed that American GIs captured by the Communists had their entire value systems transformed through the techniques of mind control. Such captives tended quickly to revert to their former opinions and attitudes upon release from captivity; although this was usually forgotten by those who employed the term. Brainwashing assumed that the individual's free will had been completely paralysed. The metaphors embedded in both deprogramming and brainwashing assume a mechanistic view of the mind and will.

It was around 1970 that a backlash against counter-cultural NRMs began to emerge. The group first targeted was a JP movement we've briefly examined, the Children of God. Anti-cult groups sprang up like mushrooms in the early Seventies, but like FREECOG (Free Our Children from the Children of God), most were driven by the concerns of parents whose children had joined minority religions. You might be surprised that the first groups targeted were actually coming out of the Christian tradition, rather than the more exotic Eastern-derived NRMs, but this makes sense, I think, in the context of Wallis's typology. The Children of God were very world-rejecting; this could make them more threatening to parents than membership in a relatively world-accepting or world-affirming meditation group, which did not demand that their child take on a wholly new, and very demanding, way of life. Personal hurt, lifestyle rejection and membership in a demanding religion combined to make these religious choices unacceptable to parents.

Remembering Eileen Barker's statistics on NRM memberships in Britain, I think it is hard to believe that the 'cults' were ever going to pose a real threat to Western secular society. But certainly the NRMs got swept up into what sociologists and historians sometimes call a *moral panic*. A moral panic is a fear widely spread in a society that the society's moral values are being effectively destroyed by an influential (and often secretive) minority or by inescapable historical forces. In this last section of the unit I would like you to keep this definition in mind, and see if you can identify how 1960s interest in NRMs degenerates into cult scares in the early 1970s.

The main success of anti-cult groups has been to make NRMs appear crazy, exploitative, or frightening to the general public. This generates public prejudice against NRMs, and the ensuing moral panic legitimates coercive action such as deprogramming. What is often forgotten is that people choose NRMs to serve their needs. The group helps its members, at least for a time, to have their wants met in a supportive and internally meaningful environment. NRMs had a lot to offer those members of the counter-culture who joined them. Recruits enjoyed a sense of belonging, often in a communal structure: instant friendships were a compelling inducement for many devotees; members didn't need skills, everyone was needed because the community relied on the work of all members. Membership in an NRM allowed individuals to release themselves from the otherwise overwhelming pressures of their society to achieve material success or to display sexual attractiveness (Bromley and Shupe, 1981, p.84).

It was seen as sinister that NRMs aggressively recruited among teenagers and young adults. However, it made sense for alternative religions to recruit youth because of two factors: their idealism and their freedom from marital and occupational constraints. The desire of NRMs to appear more successful than they really were meant that the alarm generated in parents by their inflated membership figures made it difficult for many 'anti-cult' activists to realize how small most NRMs were. In addition, the high turnover experienced by NRMs must be kept in mind: the typical stay of full-time members was brief, with most members leaving the group within two years. Deprogramming was attractive to parents because it did not stigmatize them or their child: activity in an NRM could be attributed to brainwashing, rather than suggesting that there was something wrong with either the family or the devotee. As Shupe and Bromley contend,

> The brainwashing ideology provided an honorable basis for accounting for the individual's past bizarre behaviour, one which did not imply inherent personal weakness or family problems, and when properly implemented, posed no danger of future recurrence. Brainwashing/deprogramming as a package explanation placed blame for the individual's problems or mistakes squarely on the 'cult'.
>
> *(Shupe and Bromley, 1980, p.127)*

Later deprogramming was taken to even more extreme lengths, as deprogrammers began to kidnap and 'liberate' young persons for many more reasons than unorthodox religious affiliations. Deprogrammers forcibly removed monks from Catholic monasteries, and also made attempts to 'deprogramme' such things as sexual preference and undesirable choice of marriage partners. In short, anything disapproved of by parents could come to be seen as the result of 'brainwashing' in the moral panic of the early 1970s.

EXERCISE

Please read the extract from *Let Our Children Go!* (*Resource Book 4*, C12). The author, Ted Patrick, was the earliest, and for a long time the best known, of the professional deprogrammers. Shortly after the book from which this extract is taken was published, he left his government job to deprogramme full time.

1   What is Patrick's reason for becoming a deprogrammer, and how does he justify his activities?

2   How does deprogramming (from the example given in the text) work?

DISCUSSION

1   Patrick describes himself as falling into deprogramming accidentally, as a personal response to the unhappiness of parents who contacted him. He clearly allies himself with those, like Streiker, who see NRMs as endemic and a threat to America's vision of itself as a society. Because he perceives this threat to be so real and so pervasive, he assumes that extreme means are justified in response. He claims that the conversion techniques of NRMs are 'psychological kidnapping': a phrase which seems to suggest that adult conversions to new religions are always spurious, always the result of mental manipulation by the group. Some of his claims seem implausible: for example, people cannot sustain labour for twenty hours a day for long without physical collapse; added to undernourishment this would mean that NRMs would be full of invalids whom the group would have to support; no communal organization would find a nine-year-old a valuable asset, except as part of a family group; and so on.

2   He describes the content of deprogramming as talk, with physical restraint and involuntary confinement. While US law allowed parents to remove minor children from NRMs, this rarely was at issue: the 'children' of the anti-cult literature are ordinarily legal adults. The goal of deprogramming was a return to the parents' values and faith.

In order to achieve this goal, members of NRMs were locked in rooms with windows nailed shut, furniture and objects which could serve as weapons were removed, and the devotee's ordinary clothes were taken away in order to reduce the chance of escape.

The actual content of deprogramming was criticized by sociologists of religion as unjustifiable coercion (compare this to Patrick's description):

> While the primary strategy was argument, wearing the deprogrammee down through restricted movement, closely guarded and rationed sleeping periods, ideological and counterideological harangues, outright brow beating, threatened and even occasional physical violence ... and the psychologically draining uncertainty resulting from a possibly extended 'captivity' played an important part in the deprogramming 'therapy'.
>
> *(Shupe and Bromley, 1980, p.76)*

I think the different agendas implicit in both descriptions of the process are obvious.

It may have occurred to you as you read the descriptions of deprogramming, that it varies very little from the Christian custom of exorcism. If so, well done! As with the rite of exorcism, the devotee is presumed to be totally under the control of a separate entity (the NRM) and can only be restored to his or her 'right mind' through a set of rituals that replace the old preoccupations and habits of thought with new ones.

EXERCISE

Read the 'Statement on deprogramming' by the National Council of Churches (NCC) in *Resource Book 4*, C13. The statement was published as an official policy document of the NCC, an umbrella organization that speaks for most mainstream American denominations (fundamentalist groups are the major exception).

1   What is the NCC's position on deprogramming?

2   What does it see as the central issue?

3   Are we studying conversion or brainwashing when learning about NRMs?

DISCUSSION

1   Here the assumption is that joining an NRM is usually the result of a valid, even if often temporary, conversion experience. Deprogramming is thus never appropriate.

2   This conversion experience, given the American emphasis on religious liberty, must be respected. Thus, kidnapping devotees out of NRMs is as criminal and reprehensible an act as kidnapping to extort money. The document concludes by saying that anyone over the age of eighteen ought to be able to make their own religious choices without fear that force will be used to make them renounce their faith, whatever it may be.

3   It is probably obvious by this point in the unit that my position is similar to that of the NCC. Since individuals join NRMs of their own free will, and the statistics on retention indicate that they leave in large numbers, it is hard to justify the belief that members of NRMs are kidnapped or detained against their wishes. They join alternative religions to meet their own spiritual and psychological needs, and leave (if leave they do) when those needs have changed, or are no longer being met by the group.

7 NRMS AND THE COUNTER-CULTURE: SOME SUGGESTIONS

The social meaning and long-term significance of counter-cultural NRMs is still a matter of considerable debate. Earlier in the unit, I introduced you to Wallis's argument that many of them emerged as a response to the failure of the counter-culture (p.128). I want to conclude by offering some other explanations for the emergence of so many NRMs in the 1960s and early 1970s; I will leave it to you to decide which, if any, most adequately serve as an explanation. But if you remember the discussion of historical causation in Section 6 of Units 25 and 26, you may well conclude that a multi-causal approach is the most helpful. It at least avoids the pitfall of simplistic 'cause and effect' explanations of very complex behaviours, such as NRM membership.

Some historians of religion have seen NRMs as adaptive and integrative, rehabilitating drug users and reassimilating dropped out, transient youth. NRMs use the language of dissent against the dominant culture while training individuals to retake their place in it. This is called the *integrative thesis.*

Robbins, who subscribes to this theory, describes NRMs as:

> a kind of haven or asylum from *both* the system *and* the counterculture in which individuals could temporarily sustain the deviant *style* of the counterculture while changing their practical values and behaviour in the direction of conventional expectations.
>
> *(Robbins, 1988, p.29)*

Another group of explanations for the popularity of NRMs in the 1960s clusters around the family and its malaises. Membership in an alternative religion can be seen as either symptom or cause of *family disorganization/family deprivation.* This thesis is particularly unprovable because of the 'blame the other guy' nature of the argument: parents place the blame for bad family dynamics on the decision of a child to 'abandon' the family for an NRM, while the sociologist might suspect that the choice of NRM provides evidence of needs unmet in the family circle. More recently, some academics who study NRMs have modified the family deprivation theory to emphasize the devotees' need for stable sex roles, seeing NRMs as a religious response to family breakdown, fuelled by a 'fierce intolerance for the ambiguity surrounding gender roles' in the modern West (Palmer, 1994). But are these explanations adequate for the momentous changes often demanded by membership in a NRM?

The *social drift theory* suggests that disillusioned activists moved from the counter-culture to alternative religions as the political and social systems of society proved their resilience against radical attacks. Instead of converting society, activists began to seek the role of convert, and the plethora of NRMs made shopping for a congenial god increasingly possible. Linked to the social drift theory is the belief that drugs, rather than politics, led counter-cultural members to religion. It has been suggested that some moved from drugs to mysticism not because drugs were failing but because their effects were too overwhelming and chaotic. Religious discipline allowed former devotees of the drug culture to both make sense of, and to reject as no longer necessary, their former experimentation with chemicals. However, is this convincing outside of southern California, where the model emerged? Someone joining an NRM from Saskatoon or Basingstoke presumably had considerably less exposure to radical university politics and hallucinogens.

The *social pathology model* sees NRM involvement as an attempt to cope with overly demanding social conditions (such as highly competitive job markets and expectations of academic success) and personal problems. NRMs offer an accepting environment while seeming to solve the problem of cultural malaise. This is similar to the hypothesis, popular among sociologists of religion, of *crisis periods*; that youth join NRMs at difficult turning points in their lives (often in the first year of university, for example, or just after graduation). They are attracted to the NRMs' 'answers' to their problems, and tend to leave the groups once their personal conflict has been resolved. The proponents of this theory point out as evidence that most of those who join an NRM leave again within two years. These models seem to fit particularly well with the upsurge of interest in NRMs during the 1960s: with the counter-culture offering a series of alternatives to the traditional life pattern, the tensions over life choices may have been exacerbated for those caught up in it.

8 CONCLUSION

I hope this unit has given you a better sense of the issues surrounding the rise of new religions in the 1960s. I have argued that the religious climate in the 1960s does change, with an increased tolerance for pluralism and personal exploration, fed by the media's fascination with Eastern and unconventional patterns of doing religion. The failure of the counter-culture (or at least the psychedelic wing of it) to provide a sustainable and ordered structure of being and practice was also an inducement for many to re-orient themselves towards religion. But because counter-cultural youth made such unorthodox religious choices, their very religiosity was sometimes seized upon as potentially threatening, culminating with a moral panic over the issue of 'cults' and deprogramming by the end of our period.

While the mainstream churches remained numerically dominant throughout the Sixties, they evinced increasing concern with counter-cultural religion, which seemed to be demonstrating signs of life and vitality absent from their own traditions. But for most participants in counter-cultural religion, the disorder inherent in the counter-culture itself meant that they eventually rejoined the mainstream, joining its churches as well as its corporations. But this does not mean that counter-cultural religion was absorbed by the mainstream without affecting it; it played an important part in the formation of the current cultural environment. As well as influencing New Ageism and fundamentalism, it can be seen as a precursor of the growing preoccupation in the present with totally non-affiliated religion, the pursuing of private spiritual interests.

REFERENCES

BARKER, EILEEN (1989) *New Religious Movements: A Practical Introduction,* London, HMSO.

BATES, ALBERT and MILLER, TIMOTHY (1995) 'The evolution of hippie communal spirituality: The Farm and other hippies who didn't give up', in TIMOTHY MILLER (ed.) *America's Alternative Religions,* Albany, State University of New York.

BECKFORD, JAMES (1985) *Cult Controversies,* London, Sage.

BROMLEY, DAVID G. and SHUPE, ANSON D. (1981) *Strange Gods: The Great American Cult Scare,* Boston, Beacon.

GRIEL, ARTHUR J. and RUBY, DAVID R. (1993, 2nd edn) 'On the margins of the sacred', in THOMAS ROBBINS and DICK ANTHONY (eds) *In Gods We Trust: New Patterns of Religious Pluralism in America,* New Brunswick, Rutgers, pp.219–32.

HUXLEY, ALDOUS (1956) *Heaven and Hell,* London, Chatto & Windus.

'The Jesus Revolution', *Time Magazine,* 21 June 1971.

KANTER, ROSABETH MOSS (1972) *Commitment and Community: Communes and Utopias in Sociological Perspective,* Cambridge, Mass., Harvard University Press.

LECHNER, FRANK J. (1993, 2nd edn) 'Fundamentalism revisited', in THOMAS ROBBINS and DICK ANTHONY (eds) *In Gods We Trust: New Patterns of Religious Pluralism in America,* New Brunswick, Rutgers, pp.77–98.

MASON, PAUL (1994) *The Maharishi,* Shaftesbury, Dorset, Element.

MELTON, J. GORDON and MOORE, ROBERT L. (1982) *The Cult Experience: Responding to the New Religious Pluralism,* New York, Pilgrim Press.

ORTEGA, RUBEN (1972) *The Jesus People Speak Out,* London, Hodder and Stoughton.

PALMER, SUSAN JEAN (1994) *Moon Sisters, Krishna Mothers, Rajneesh Lovers, Women's Roles in New Religions,* Syracuse University Press.

PATRICK, TED and DULACK, TOM (1976) *Let Our Children Go!*, New York, E.P. Dutton.

ROBBINS, THOMAS (1988) *Cults, Converts and Charisma: The Sociology of New Religious Movements*, London, Sage.

ROSZAK, THEODORE (1970 edn) *The Making of a Counter Culture: Reflections on the Technocratic Society and Its Youthful Opposition*, London, Faber and Faber, first published 1969.

SHUPE, ANSON D. and BROMLEY, DAVID G. (1980) *The New Vigilantes: Deprogrammers, Anti-cultists, and the New Religions*, Beverly Hills, Sage.

SIMMONDS, ROBERT B. (1977) 'Conversion or addiction: consequences of joining a Jesus movement group', in JAMES T. RICHARDSON (ed.) *Conversion Careers: In and Out of the New Religious Movements*, London, Sage.

WALLIS, ROY, (1984) *The Elementary Forms of the New Religious Life*, London, Routledge & Kegan Paul.

WALLIS, ROY and BRUCE, STEVE (1986) *Sociological Theory, Religion, and Collective Action*, Belfast, Queens University Press.

WILSON, BRYAN (1970) *Religious Sects*, Toronto, McGraw Hill.

WOLFE, TOM (1976) *Mauve Gloves and Madmen, Clutter and Vine, and other stories, sketches and essays*, New York, Farrar, Straus and Giroux.

SUGGESTIONS FOR FURTHER READING

You may find it helpful and interesting to look at one or more of the following:

KANTER, ROSABETH MOSS (1972) *Commitment and Community: Communes and Utopias in Sociological Perspective*, Cambridge, Mass., Harvard University Press.

MELTON, J. GORDON and MORE, ROBERT L. (1982) *The Cult Experience: Responding to the New Religious Pluralism*, New York, Pilgrim.

PALMER, SUSAN JEAN (1994) *Moon Sisters, Krishna Mothers, Rajneesh Lovers, Women's Roles in New Religions*, Syracuse University Press.

TIPTON, STEVEN M. (1982) *Getting Saved from the Sixties: Moral Meaning in Conversion and Cultural Change*, Berkeley, University of California Press.

Acknowledgement

Grateful acknowledgement is made to the following for permission to reproduce material in this unit:

Figure 28.2: Wallis R. (1984) 'Orientations of the new religions to the world', *The Elementary Forms of the New Religious Life*, Routledge & Kegan Paul.

UNIT 29 CHANGE AND CONTINUITY: MUSIC IN THE 1960s

Written for the course team by Trevor Herbert and Fiona Richards

Contents

STUDY COMPONENTS				
Weeks of study	Texts	TV	AC	Set books
1	*Resource Book 4*	TV29	AC12	–

Aims and objectives

The aims of this unit are to:

1   provide you with some idea of what was happening in musical terms during the 1960s by looking at three different types of music that were being made and listened to in Britain and the United States at the time: popular music, modern classical music and early music;

2   look at how these musical developments relate to social and cultural changes in the 1960s;

3   consider some challenging musical issues of the 1960s;

4   expand on the analytical techniques you encountered in Study Weeks 3 and 22.

Sections 1 and 5 are an introduction and conclusion to the unit. Objectives for Sections 2–4 are as follows.

■   By the end of Section 2 you will have considered four pieces of popular music in terms of an established culture and a counter-culture and should be able to demonstrate how the sounds of the pieces relate to the context of the Sixties.

■   By the end of Section 3 you will have studied a movement from a work by one composer, Sir Peter Maxwell Davies. You should have gained an understanding of the piece in purely musical terms and should also be able to relate it to its period.

■   By the end of Section 4 you should be able to:

1   say what the terms 'early music' and 'Early Music Revival' mean, and what the main issues associated with them are;

2   spot some of the basic differences in various performances of the same piece of music and be able to explain, in a straightforward way, what those differences are (this is something that you may already have begun to do in your work at summer school);

3   relate the impact of the Early Music Revival to the main theme of this block: the relationship of a culture (in this case the *status quo* of the classical music establishment) to a counter-culture (in this case the proponents of the Early Music Revival).

Study note

You will find that the three categories of music in this unit are very different from each other, but we hope that you will enjoy finding out about them as well as listening to them. It is important that you try to spot similarities and relationships that lie behind the music, and, indeed, that you try to see the activities in this unit in the context of the block as a whole.

In your work in Unit 25 you were offered a chronology of important events in the Sixties (*Resource Book 4,* A1). You can refer back to this chronology for an overview of the many different types of musical activity that were taking place during this period. There is also a glossary at the end of this unit where you will find musical terms that were not covered in Units 3 and 22. Glossary terms are highlighted in bold type in the body of the unit.

As with the other music units in A103, you will always need to have a cassette player to hand. TV29 accompanies this week's work, and develops some of the issues raised in Section 4 of the unit.

1 CULTURE AND COUNTER-CULTURE/ CHANGE AND CONTINUITY

Throughout this block we are examining the 1960s in terms of the relationship between a cultural *status quo* and more radical forces which we might call counter-cultures. In Unit 29 we move from counter-movements in religion and science to counter-movements in music. It is possible and indeed helpful to think of music in these terms, but it is important to acknowledge that not everything changed in the 1960s. Popular singers like Frank Sinatra, Bing Crosby and Mat Munro, whose songs and styles had found favour a generation earlier, coexisted with the pop-group format of groups such as The Beatles and The Rolling Stones. At the same time there was a renewal of interest in musical styles that were more self-consciously traditional. 'Trad jazz' groups such as Acker Bilk and his Paramount Jazz Band, Monty Sunshine's Band, and the Temperance Seven were consciously drawing on past practices and styles even though they overlaid them with a new gloss. Similarly, the revival of interest in folk music was based on reflection on old and established stylistic devices. Modern, folk-inspired singer/songwriters such as Bob Dylan and Joan Baez may have enunciated contemporary and radical messages, but the musical forms that carried them owed more to a continuum of the folk-song tradition than to anything novel.

So we must not forget that continuity was also a feature of the musical activity of the 1960s. Just as several types of popular music continued to be enjoyed while acutely different new music was being introduced, so similar contrasts – continuities and changes – occurred in the world of 'classical' music. Many of the world's cities were centres of radical, modernist, **avant-garde** music. Simultaneously, a renewal of interest in the music and musical practices of the **medieval** and **renaissance** periods led to what became known as the Early Music Revival. This movement, which must have seemed innocuous and even quaint to many in the 1960s, generated a powerful legacy which led to a fundamental reappraisal and reorganization of the music industry, of musical education and of attitudes to the performance of all **art music** of the past. Yet at the same time, the great classical music institutions – the opera houses, the symphony orchestra, the music **conservatories** and so on – did not simply continue to exist but actually expanded in number. For example, the period saw the development of provincial opera companies such as the Welsh National Opera and the Scottish National Opera.

In Unit 25 you were introduced to the notion that there was not one, but several, counter-cultures in the 1960s. 'All of the different movements, forms of protest and expression which made up "counter-culture" were opposed to something, or several things, in "mainstream" culture; but they also had roots in, or connections with, established culture' (p.26). In Unit 29 you will look at three different types of musical activity in the light of this statement.

It is possible that the existence of two creative forces – the continuity of well-established styles and practices on the one hand, and the emergence of the new and radical on the other – provided a creative tension that placed one in sharp relief against the other, so as to make the characteristics of each that much clearer. Thus, pop groups seem more evidently new when compared to **ballad** singers, avant-garde classical music more outrageous in comparison to traditional symphonic music, and the singing of fifteenth-century songs by early music enthusiasts more archaic and tangential in comparison to the glossy environment of opera prima donnas.

Summary points

1   Musical activity in the 1960s was rich and varied. Traditional styles coexisted alongside the new sounds.

2   There was no single counter-culture, but several movements which posed challenges to historical continuity.

2 POPULAR MUSIC

Many studies of rock music in the 1960s discuss it in terms of the music representing some sort of revolt against a dominant, existing culture. By 1963/64 the rock music breakthrough was well established, and elements of rebellion were present in the lyrics and manner of delivery of a number of groups. Given that rock music was a predominantly youth culture, there was strong revolutionary potential here, and challenges to authority undoubtedly did happen. But *musical* rebellion and even aggression do not necessarily constitute *real* rebellion against society.

Culture and counter-cultures

CASSETTE 12, SIDE 1, ITEMS 1–3

This section consists of one extended listening exercise. Here, once again, is the quotation taken from Unit 25: 'All of the different movements, forms of protest and expression which made up "counter-culture" were opposed to something, or several things, in "mainstream" culture; but they also had roots in, or connections with, established culture' (p.26). And here are some of the items which appeared on Arthur Marwick's list of aspects of established culture that the 1960s counter-cultures were reacting against (pp.24–5):

- rigid social hierarchy

- stuffy and repressed attitudes to sex

- respect for authority – the family, the government, Western religions, the nation state

- prevalence of racism

- universal, if often uncomprehending, obeisance to canonized art.

There are three pieces of music to listen to in this section:

Item 1: Simon and Garfunkel 'The Dangling Conversation' 1966

Item 2: The Beatles 'Within You, Without You' 1967 (extract)

Item 3: Jimi Hendrix 'Star Spangled Banner' 1969.

What I'd like you to do is listen to each of these pieces in turn and write down your thoughts on each piece in the light of both the above quotation and the list of features of the established culture. In what sense can they be seen as musical reflections of a counter-culture, and to what extent do they have their roots in established culture? Take your time with this exercise – you might have to spread it over a couple of study sessions. The words of the Simon and Garfunkel and The Beatles songs are shown overleaf:

The Dangling Conversation

It's a still life water colour
Of a now late afternoon,
As the sun shines through the curtain lace,
And shadows wash the room.

And we sit and drink our coffee,
Couched in our indifference
Like shells upon the shore,
You can hear the ocean roar
In the dangling conversation,
And the superficial sighs,
The borders of our lives.

And you read your Emily Dickinson,
And I my Robert Frost,
And we note our place with book markers
That measure what we've lost.

Like the poem poorly written,
We are persons out of rhythm,
Couplets out of rhyme,
In syncopated time.
And the dangling conversation,
And the superficial sighs
Are the borders of our lives.

Yes, we speak of things that matter
With words that must be said,
Can analysis be worthwhile?
Is the theatre really dead?

And how the room is softly fading,
And I only kiss your shadow,
I cannot feel your hand,
You're a stranger now unto me
Lost in the dangling conversation
And the superficial sighs
In the borders of our lives.

Within You, Without You

[...]

We were talking about the love that's gone so cold,
And the people who gain the world and lose their soul,
They don't know, they can't see.
Are you one of them?

When you've seen beyond yourself, then you may find peace of mind
is waiting there
And the time will come when you see we're all one, and life
flows on within you and without you.

DISCUSSION

1   Simon and Garfunkel

This is not an overt expression of counter-cultural sentiments, but is rather pensive and nostalgic. In musical terms, it is lyrical, gentle, almost stark in its melodic simplicity. The accompanying instruments are guitars, percussion, strings and harp. The song has its roots in an established culture, and its evocative sounds are in stark contrast to the second

FIGURE 29.1   *Swordmandel.*
(Photograph: Mike Levers/The Open University)

FIGURE 29.2   *Tabla.*
(Photograph: Mike Levers/The Open University)

extract you heard. However, in terms of the song's lyrics there are clear innovations. The move away from simple, repetitive lyrics to a piece of carefully constructed poetry has been one of the most striking characteristics of Paul Simon's work. As he has continued to write and perform, his resourcefulness and imagination in this area has become even more marked.

2   The Beatles

By 1967 The Beatles were hardly viewed as a group who were posing challenges to society. However, this song, from the album *Sergeant Pepper's Lonely Hearts Club Band* has distinctively new qualities – the sort of qualities which might suggest an immediate appeal to alternative cultures. It uses Indian musicians and foregrounds the complex rhythmic sounds of the East. The instruments involved in this extract are the **swordmandel** (a **zither**-like plucked instrument), **tabla** (drums), **dilruba** (a stringed fiddle-like instrument), and **tamboura** (a type of **sitar** – a lute-like instrument) (see Figures 29.1–4). Added to this are the sounds of classical string instruments – a real blending of cultures. This is obviously a long way from the typical Western pop song – there isn't a four-square beat, there's no clear underlying harmonic structure and

FIGURE 29.3   *Dilruba.*
(*Photograph: Mike Levers/The Open University*)

FIGURE 29.4   *Tamboura.*
(*Photograph: Mike Levers/The Open University*)

FIGURE 29.5   *Jimi Hendrix performing at the Isle of Wight music festival, September 1969. (Photograph: Hulton Getty)*

when the voice enters there is an almost chanting vocal line. Incidentally, the only Beatle actually appearing in this song is George Harrison.

Before you move on to part 3 of this discussion please turn to *Resource Book 4*, D1, and read the article by George Martin, producer for The Beatles, in which he describes the making of this song.

3 Jimi Hendrix

If music can be a reflection of cultural change, then progressive rock, and in particular the music of Jimi Hendrix, might be seen to be the dominant expressive form of the counter-culture's values, a musical embodiment of the challenges to society. Born two years before Ray Davies, whose music you will encounter shortly, Hendrix's icon status was achieved both because of his extraordinary and innovatory talents, and because of his untimely death in 1970 as the result of a drugs overdose.

Hendrix was renowned for his sheer physical presence – for erotic actions on stage, suggestive lyrics, hyper-amplified music and theatrical antics including guitar smashing and burning. He shot to fame at the 1967 Monterey Pop Festival after dousing his guitar in lighter fuel. In August 1969 Hendrix performed at the Woodstock Music and Arts Fair, New York's massive celebration of the counter-culture. The highlight of his band's appearance was his version of 'Star Spangled Banner'.

Right from the start of this extract you know that it has subversive elements. It's not the usual pleasant, or rousing, or celebratory, version of the National Anthem, though at first you can hear the tune quite clearly, even with the feedback and over-amplification. However, it soon starts to deteriorate, the tune ripped apart, shattered into nasty fragments, aggressively spiky shards of hideously distorted sounds. The torn bits of music represent the tearing up of old values, a symbolic act of liberation on the part of a black man at a time of civil unrest. However, there is no real threat to the state. The aggression is purely *musical* aggression – the music is troubled and violent on the one hand, assertive and triumphant on the other.

What these three extracts share is that they all have highly original, challenging musical characteristics. In that sense they all offered a challenge to existing ideas about music – what it should be – and its role within society. The new sounds they offered were part of a real transformation in listening habits which was taking place in the 1960s. However, in no sense did any of these pieces of music offer any real opposition to the existing structure of society. In fact, the music of all these performers has now become part of an established culture; listened to by exactly the type of bourgeois society against which they may originally have been reacting.

Music of its time – The Kinks

The Kinks are a difficult group to place – notorious in the 1960s for aggressive, violent behaviour on stage and sexual exploits offstage, while singing of village greens, cups of tea, tin soldier men and the legendary summer afternoon of 1966. Banned from visiting the United States between 1966 and 1969, they missed Woodstock, maintaining that the so-called 'freedom' of the Sixties was a myth, that the so-called 'counter-culture' never really infiltrated society and that the establishment continued to rule. Partly as a result of this ban the group stood outside the acid-rock generation, instead making songs about suburban and village Britain and playing to smaller audiences than The Beatles or The Stones. According to jazz singer and music critic George Melly:

> they stood aside watching, with sardonic amusement, the pop world chasing its own tail, and they turned out some of the most quirky, intelligent and totally personal records in the history of British pop.

> *(quoted in Moore, 1993, p.90)*

And yet their music has a sound which is characteristic and evocative of the Sixties – it can be said to belong to a distinct period in music history.

The line-up of the group consisted of lead singer and guitarist Ray Davies, the composer of most of the songs, brother Dave Davies on guitar, drummer Mick Avory and Pete Quaife as bass guitarist. This

FIGURE 29.6   *The Kinks from left to right: Mick Avory, Ray Davies, Dave Davies and Pete Quaife. (Photograph: Hulton Getty)*

combination, with its four distinct layers of sound, was the standard **rhythm and blues** line-up of the 1960s.

In 1994 Ray Davies published his autobiography, *X-Ray*, in which he records his memories of his career in the Sixties. We're going to look at the music of one of his best-known songs, 'Waterloo Sunset', in the light of his writings on music and society, taken from this autobiography, in order to see how his music both reflects and stands outside its time.

CASSETTE 12, SIDE 1, ITEM 4

The words of 'Waterloo Sunset' are shown below – listen to the song, Item 4 on the cassette, with the words before you read any further.

Waterloo Sunset

Dirty old river must you keep rolling,
Flowing into the night.
People so busy, make me feel dizzy
Taxi lights shine so bright

But I don't need no friends
As long as I gaze on Waterloo Sunset
I am in paradise. *Sha la la*
Ev'ry day I look at the world from my window, *Sha la la*
Chilly, chilly is the evening time
Waterloo Sunset's fine.

Terry meets Julie Waterloo Station,
Every Friday night.
But I am so lazy don't want to wander
I stay at home at night.

But I don't feel afraid
As long as I gaze on Waterloo Sunset
I am in paradise. *Sha la la*
Ev'ry day I look at the world from my window, *Sha la la*
Chilly, chilly is the evening time
Waterloo Sunset's fine.

Millions of people swarming like flies round
Waterloo Underground.
But Terry and Julie cross over the river
Where they feel safe and sound

And they don't need no friends
As long as they gaze on Waterloo Sunset,
They are in paradise.
Waterloo Sunset's fine.

The lyrics

Ray Davies ('I', 'he', 'his' and 'him' are all used by Davies to mean himself):

> I decided to throw away all the books and printed material and let the music tell me about him...
> He made people think that he was singing for them, and his experience was also theirs...
> I could tell lies in my little songs because in many ways my style had been my own invention and my subconscious was allowed to work through me and yet somehow bypass the listener: I could keep the secrets of my motivation completely to myself. The strange thing was that my songs were being heard all over the world by millions of people and yet nobody really knew what these songs were really about.
>
> *(Davies, 1994, pp.4, 125, 196)*

EXERCISE

Read through the words of the song in the light of Davies's statements (above). He says that he makes you feel that he is singing for you and that his experience is also yours, but on the other hand he says that nobody really knows what his songs are about. Think about these comments and then write down what you think the song is about. What is Davies's position and what secrets are hidden in the song? Here you are drawing on the skills that you learned in Study Week 2 – a song text is, after all, a piece of poetry.

DISCUSSION

Damon Albarn, lead singer of the 1990s group Blur, has described Davies's songs as being 'geographical'. A strong sense of place is one of the striking elements of this song, vividly set in Waterloo, with images of the dirty River Thames, people milling about, taxi lights, the underground station and the sunset, inspirational to many before Davies. The words do on the one hand seem to address the listener – we are given glimpses of very personal feelings, and yet Davies is an observer as well as a participant, looking down on the scene, distanced. There's a poignancy about the words, a sense of melancholy as well as a sense of security. He speaks of Terry and Julie as though they are well known to him, but *we* don't know who they are. So although the song is for the listener, it also has resonances of a private world. We'll return to this subject at the end of this section.

The tune

Ray Davies (again talking about himself):

> I played some of his old records and liked them, even though his obviously untrained voice sounded as if he had suffered from sinus trouble, to such a degree that it conjured up the image of a man standing in front of a microphone holding his nose. I played a selection of his early hits ... then some ballads, which had obviously been recorded later, when his singing voice had matured. It retained that familiar melancholy style, but sounded deeper.
>
> *(Davies, 1994, p.3)*

CASSETTE 12, SIDE 1, ITEM 5

Listen to the first verse of 'Waterloo Sunset', Item 5 on the cassette. How does the tune contribute to the meaning of the words of the song? Listen not only to the *shape* of the tune, but also to the *timbre* of Ray Davies's voice, again bearing his own words in mind. The words of verse 1 are shown below:

> Dirty old river must you keep rolling,
> Flowing into the night.
> People so busy, make me feel dizzy
> Taxi lights shine so bright
> But I don't need no friends
> As long as I gaze on Waterloo Sunset
> I am in paradise.

DISCUSSION

The words and the tune seem so closely entwined that it's difficult to separate the two. There are two parts to the melody – (a) and (b), as marked against the words in Figure 29.7 (opposite). The (a) pattern repeats, and dominates the song.

The nostalgia of the words in the verse is matched by gently dropping, gently syncopated phrases, lazy in their evocation of the reluctance of the observer to participate in the commuter bustle. And Davies's slightly nasal voice, with the mellow, low notes at the ends of phrases, contributes to this effect. Later on in the song an echo effect enhances this even further. The other noticeable vocal contributions are the **falsetto** harmonies above the tune, lissomly floating 'oohs' and 'las', so characteristic of many Sixties songs.

> Dirty old river must you keep rolling,
>
> Flowing into the night. } a
>
> People so busy, make me feel dizzy
>
> Taxi lights shine so bright } a
>
> But I don't need no friends b
>
> As long as I gaze on Waterloo Sunset
>
> I am in paradise. } a

FIGURE 29.7

The bass line

Ray Davies:

> And I understand that Bach heave-hoed his missus with such regularity that an abundance of little Bachs were unleashed upon an unsuspecting planet that was already 'fugued out' by Johann's over-active left hand. Ah, but what bass notes...
>
> *(Davies, 1994, p.70)*

Davies swoons over the power and complexity of J.S. Bach's bass notes, an example of which you heard in Study Week 22, on AC10. With Bach it may be a cello or a keyboard instrument supplying the bass line. Here it's the bass guitar, the significance of which to the rock band cannot be underestimated – it provides the deepest notes of the texture and underpins the whole, as you heard in 'When I'm 64', in TV3.

CASSETTE 12, SIDE 1, ITEM 5

Rewind the cassette to find Item 5 again. In what ways do you feel the bass line contributes to and permeates the song? Use the words in Figure 29.8 as your guide – write on them as you hear the bass guitar. It may help to use graphics to show the direction of the bass line.

Dirty old river must you keep rolling,

Flowing into the night.

People so busy, make me feel dizzy

Taxi lights shine so bright

But I don't need no friends

As long as I gaze on Waterloo Sunset

I am in paradise.

FIGURE 29.8

DISCUSSION

My marked-up words are shown in Figure 29.9.

falling bass line before words start

Dirty old river must you keep rolling,

Flowing into the night.

People so busy, make me feel dizzy

Taxi lights shine so bright

bass not so prominent here, though there are more descending lines

But I don't need no friends

bass here – falling again

As long as I gaze on Waterloo Sunset

I am in paradise.

heavy bass notes where underlined

FIGURE 29.9

The bass line in this song is both a propelling and binding element – the opening eight notes form a very distinctive falling pattern, 'setting the scene', as it were. This falling motif recurs at other points as marked (with 'But I don't need no friends' and then to emphasize the words 'gaze on Waterloo Sunset I am in paradise'). You also hear it at the end of the chorus, leading the way back to the next verse.

The guitar lines

Ray Davies:

> My playing had developed into a slow, soulful and slightly contrived style handed down to me by the blues-playing jazzers, whereas Dave had what can only be described as a jack-in-the-box technique, full of crazy staccato phrases which perfectly mirrored his more aggressive speech pattern.
>
> *(Davies, 1994, p.82)*

Ray Davies's description does go some way towards differentiating between the different playing styles of him and his brother, though in a lyrical song such as this you would hardly expect to hear a 'jack-in-the-box' element – exactly what he means is much more apparent from archive footage of the group on stage. While the emphasis of this song is on the words and the melody, the 'slow, soulful ... style', inner guitar parts add to the overall effect, either picking out melody lines or strumming chords. The role of the guitar isn't simply to flesh out the harmony, but to interact with the voice.

CASSETTE 12, SIDE 1, ITEM 5

Rewind the cassette to find Item 5 once more. This time indicate against the words in Figure 29.10 the places where you hear the electric guitar playing the main tune of the song (shown as **'a'** in Figure 29.7) and the places where it plays a slightly different **counter-melody**.

	Melody or counter-melody
Dirty old river must you keep rolling,	
Flowing into the night.	
People so busy, make me feel dizzy	
Taxi lights shine so bright	
But I don't need no friends	
As long as I gaze on Waterloo Sunset	
I am in paradise.	

FIGURE 29.10

DISCUSSION

This is how my answer looks:

	Melody or counter-melody
	melody a
Dirty old river must you keep rolling,	
Flowing into the night.	*counter-melody starts at 'night' and continues throughout lines 3 and 4*
People so busy, make me feel dizzy	
Taxi lights shine so bright	
But I don't need no friends	
As long as I gaze on Waterloo Sunset	*counter-melody from 'Waterloo Sunset' to end of verse*
I am in paradise.	

FIGURE 29.11

The sound and meaning of the whole

Ray Davies:

> At this time it was like there were three people inside me: the loving suburban husband and father who happened to be a pop star; the confident celebrity who took pleasure in spreading his own form of good-will to his fans up and down the country, while at the same time preparing for major litigation; and, finally, the lost soul who was desperately insecure and looking for friendship which would not turn into some kind of betrayal and end up hurting me.
>
> *(Davies, 1994, p.335)*

What is it that makes 'Waterloo Sunset' both an expression of and the antithesis of 1967, the year when it was written? This was the year in which The Beatles released the *Sgt Pepper* album, the year of the Monterey Pop Festival, of protest songs and of a prevalent drug culture among young people. The concept of a counter-culture perhaps found its most obvious expression in the extrovert, aggressive sound of Jimi Hendrix's guitar playing, while The Beatles' songs became progressively more abstruse – 'I am the Walrus' was a far cry from 'She Loves You'. Instead, Ray Davies, the 'lost soul' and 'suburban husband', produced a gently rolling song of melancholy and compassion. But present-day nostalgia for the Sixties means that the nostalgia inherent in Davies's songs in many ways becomes representative of the 1960s. The band line-up of The Kinks is typical of its age, but the music is imbued with its own characteristic features. You will continue your work on what makes a song, or a poem, or a picture, representative of its age in Unit 30, when you look at some of the techniques used by Andy Warhol.

EXERCISE

Finish your work on 'Waterloo Sunset' by reading Ray Davies's own explanation of the song in *Resource Book 4*, D2. When you have done this read his short story of the same name, D3 in *Resource Book 4*. In 1997 Davies produced a book of short stories named after the song 'Waterloo Sunset'. He said that:

> it was going to be lots of short stories dashing around on different topics but then I found this character who was similar to me, in fact he was me. Then I thought I don't want to get into all that again, I did that in *X-Ray*, so I just changed it to a failed rock star, Les Mulligan ...
>
> (The Birmingham Post, *18 October 1997, p.29)*

The stories grew out of the sentiments behind Davies's songs, and some share the same titles. They are linked by two main characters: Les Mulligan (songwriter making a comeback) and businessman Richard Tennent who is trying to make this happen. Other characters also recur from time to time, one of whom is Fox, an artist and criminal. In the story 'Waterloo Sunset' (the penultimate story in the book) Fox meets Richard, who tells him about Mulligan (referred to as the 'total wreck'). At the same time nostalgic images from the song permeate the story. ■

3 MODERN CLASSICAL MUSIC

While sweeping changes to the popular music scene were crucial musical features of this period, movements in other areas were also exciting and innovative. Like the popular music scene, 'classical' music saw composers moving in very different directions. Think back to Steve Reich's *Clapping Music* in TV3 – New York in the Sixties saw Reich (b.1936) experimenting with **phasing**, a compositional procedure in which he played around with the idea of rhythmic or melodic patterns gradually moving out of sync with one another. At the same time traditionalists such as Dmitri Shostakovitch (1906–75) in the former USSR continued to work with long-established genres such as the symphony (which you encountered in Unit 22). Luciano Berio (b.1925) in Italy was experimenting with phonetics in his compositions while Toru Takemitsu (1930–96), whose *Rain Tree* you heard in TV3, was incorporating traditional Japanese instruments such as the **biwa** and the **shakuhachi** into the Western orchestra.

Travel to India and Africa was tremendously influential for a number of composers, and there were also connections between classical and rock musicians. Figures such as John Tavener (b.1944) and Karlheinz Stockhausen (b.1928) crossed paths with The Beatles, for example. In this country Benjamin Britten (1913–76) produced his commemorative *War Requiem* in 1962 for the newly built Coventry Cathedral while Harrison Birtwistle (b.1934) delved deep into the past for inspiration, drawing on ancient legends and music of earlier periods.

Peter Maxwell Davies – *Eight Songs for a Mad King* (1969) No. 7 – 'Country Dance'

The work that I have chosen for study in this section is by a British composer, Sir Peter Maxwell Davies (b.1934) (henceforth referred to as Max, the name by which he is generally known), an *enfant terrible* of the Sixties, whose music often shocked and aggravated, and who, as I write in 1998, is still one of the foremost British composers. In the 1960s Max was involved with the formation of an instrumental ensemble called the Pierrot Players, whose initial aim was to perform new works by Max and one of his contemporaries, Harrison Birtwistle, and also to give 'authentic' performances of *Pierrot Lunaire*, a work composed by Arnold Schoenberg in 1912. (The concept of authentic performance will be explored in Section 4 of this unit.)

FIGURE 29.12 *Sir Peter Maxwell Davies. (Photograph: Clive Barda/P.A.L.)*

CASSETTE 12, SIDE 1, ITEM 6

Before we examine the musical detail of this piece and consider what Max is doing with his material, I'd like you to listen to the whole piece without direction and without preconceptions. As you listen to it, jot down what you hear, as you hear it, just using a few words or a single sentence. For example, you might describe the piece as starting with:

~ gentle piano, swung rhythms

You will hear the piece as Item 6. The words are shown below:

> Comfort ye, comfort ye, my people
> with singing and with dancing,
> with milk and with apples.
> The landlord at the Three Tuns
> makes the best purl in Windsor.
> Sin! Sin! Sin!
> black vice, intolerable vileness
> in lanes, by ricks, at Courts.
> It is night on the world.
> Even I, your King, have contemplated evil.
> I shall rule with a rod of iron.
> Comfort ye.

DISCUSSION

This is my answer in response to a pretty startling piece:

~ gentle piano, swung rhythms

~ interrupted by mad singing, almost grunting, wailing

~ instruments come in

~ jazzy music – dance (**foxtrot**), with weird duck-like voice over the top

~ dance gradually breaks down, gets slower and slower

~ 'operatic' with piano

~ piano gets wilder; clashing sounds

~ low voice, some quiet percussion sounds, then voice all over the place

~ quiet ending – **harpsichord**, cello, high voice

CASSETTE 12, SIDE 1, ITEM 6

Now rewind the cassette and listen to the whole piece again, concentrating on hearing the different types of music in my list. This time I've set out the words in Figure 29.13 with my list alongside at the appropriate moments.

Eight Songs for a Mad King – No. 7 'Country Dance'	
Words of piece	**My comments**
	~ *gentle piano, swung rhythms*
Comfort ye, comfort ye, my people	~ *interrupted by mad singing, almost grunting, wailing*
	~ *instruments come in*
with singing and with dancing, with milk and with apples. The landlord at the Three Tuns makes the best purl in Windsor.	~ *jazzy music – dance (foxtrot), with weird duck-like voice over the top*
Sin! Sin! Sin!	~ *dance gradually breaks down, gets slower and slower*
	~ *'operatic' with piano*
black vice, intolerable vileness in lanes, by ricks, at Courts.	~ *piano gets wilder; clashing sounds*
It is night on the world. Even I, your King, have contemplated evil.	~ *low voice, some quiet percussion sounds, then voice all over the place*
I shall rule with a rod of iron. Comfort ye	~ *quiet ending – harpsichord, cello, high voice*

FIGURE 29.13

If you found the piece disorientating in places don't be put off. That was the original intention. It's one of Max's *Eight Songs for a Mad King*, written in 1969 at exactly the same time as Hendrix's 'Star Spangled Banner' – and you may have noticed some similarities. This was a time when much of Max's music was violent and theatrical, designed to shock – an aural challenge to the audience. We're now going to look at some of the striking musical characteristics of this piece in more detail.

Theatre

Eight Songs for a Mad King is based on the actions and speeches of the often-assumed insane king, George III (1760–1820). The writer of the words, Randolph Stow, was inspired by a miniature mechanical organ which was once the property of George III. The organ played eight tunes, which George III would try to teach caged birds to sing. Stow was fortunate enough to see this organ in action in 1966.

FIGURE 29.14   Eight Songs for a Mad King *in performance, with Michael Rippon as George III. (Photograph: Chris Davis)*

It left a peculiar and disturbing impression. One imagined the King, in his purple flannel dressing-gown and ermine night-cap, struggling to teach birds to make the music which he could so rarely torture out of his flute and harpsichord. Or trying to sing with them, in that ravaged voice, made almost inhuman by day-long soliloquies...

(Stow, quoted in the score of Eight Songs for a Mad King, *1971, London, Boosey & Hawkes Music Publishers Ltd.)*

The work functions on several levels. The king's bullfinches are represented here by flute, clarinet, violin and cello. These players stand in cages on the stage and also operate mechanical birdsong devices. The king, with suitably 'mad' voice, has dialogues with his 'bullfinches' while a percussion player stands for the king's 'keeper'. The king's words incorporate some lines actually spoken by George III. The other protagonist in the drama is a keyboard player, playing both piano and harpsichord.

Exploitation

One of the features of this piece is the exploitation of the voice and instruments. In the work Max chose to stretch the players' techniques to the limit. Think back to Piece 5A in Unit 3 (Block 1, pp.126–7). This was a short caprice by Paganini which demanded virtuosic capabilities on the part of the violinist. You've also heard that Jimi Hendrix was truly innovatory in his own playing style. In this piece Max is equally demanding, particularly in terms of the vocal techniques he requires of the singer. This was one of the hallmarks of his music of the 1960s – howling voices, shrieking noises and the use of sounds which were not traditionally 'musical'. For an audience the sounds he created were either fascinating or horrifying, received rapturously by some and jeered at by others.

CASSETTE 12, SIDE 1, ITEM 7

Listen to the ending of the piece, Item 7 on the cassette. Write down what you consider to be the main way in which Max is exploiting the human voice at this point.

DISCUSSION

The vocalist is asked to produce an extraordinary range, from high notes which you don't imagine the male voice could possibly reach to notes which plumb the very depths. The words 'contemplated evil' span a vast range.

CASSETTE 12, SIDE 1, ITEM 8

Now listen to Item 8, the first part of the song. This time concentrate on the questions in Figure 29.15, which refer to the ways in which the voice is treated.

Words	Questions
Comfort ye, comfort ye, my people	At the beginning of the song the singer is given the instructions 'female vocalist'. What other effects does Max demand of the singer?
with singing and with dancing, with milk and with apples.	Does the singer sing definite notes? Describe the sort of sound you hear.

FIGURE 29.15

DISCUSSION

My answers are as follows:

- After the first 'Comfort ye' the singer almost seems to lose control. In the score, the second 'com-*fort*' actually includes the instructions 'like a horse', and 'my people' growls along at the bottom of the voice's range.

- The singer doesn't have definite notes. It's more of a shouting sound, but with some sense of pitch movement. You may have commented on a somewhat hollow or echoing sound here – in the score the singer is told to 'use cupped hands as megaphone and bawl'.

The singer is asked to use a variety of techniques, not all of which are necessarily 'singing' techniques, but which contribute to the portrayal of madness. One of the other ways in which Max does this is through notation.

Notation

Although there isn't the space to consider musical notation in any great detail in this course, the whole concept of notated music is a very interesting one and in Unit 3, Piece 2, you looked at a single melodic line which was originally notated with dots and dashes (Block 1, pp.103–9). In this work Max uses traditional Western notation, but also includes some instructions for improvised sections (just as Takemitsu did in *Rain Tree*). This is sometimes very straightforward. For example, he gives the pianist some chords, with the words 'improvise arpeggios over whole keyboard' (**arpeggios** are spread chords, so the pianist has fixed notes, but a free choice of the part of the piano in which to play the notes and a free choice of tempo). Or he tells the percussionist to 'intermittently stroke wood, metal and glass jingles'. At the climax of the work, as George III takes and then breaks the violinist's instrument, the notation is more symbolic. Figure 29.16 shows you this.

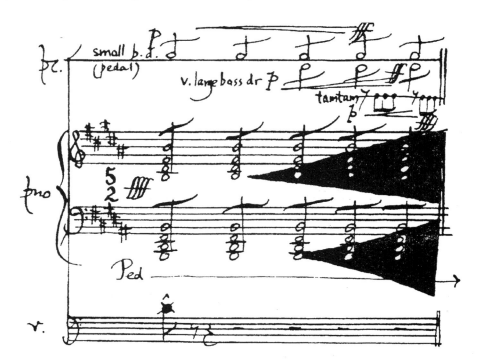

FIGURE 29.16 *A section of the notation of* Eight Songs for a Mad King. (© *Copyright 1971 by Boosey & Hawkes Music Publishers Ltd. Reproduced by permission of Boosey & Hawkes Music Publishers Ltd.*)

To the left hand side of this you see the letters 'pc.' – this is the percussion part. The bottom line, 'v.', is the cello. We're only interested in the middle, bracketed lines, marked 'pno' (piano). The pianist starts off with conventionally-notated music, which then gradually becomes covered by the black triangle. Here the pianist has the freedom to move away from the printed notes as they become obscured, leading to a violent breakdown in the music as the violin breaks apart. You'll be able to hear this in the next section.

Parody

One of the prevailing interests on the part of some of the musicians working in the Sixties was in 'old' music, music from an earlier period, as you will discover in Section 4. As well as containing a strong theatrical element, Max's works at this time also tended to draw quite heavily on earlier music, either using passages borrowed from other composers or deploying techniques used by earlier composers – and in 1972 he used the Early Music Consort (a group you will hear in Section 4) as a stage band in his opera *Taverner.*

In *Eight Songs for a Mad King* Max takes a well-known piece of music and subverts it to suit his needs, just as Hendrix subverted the US National Anthem to suit his needs. Some of you may have recognized the piece already, or may have thought that something about it sounded familiar. The piece that Max uses is an extract from Handel's *Messiah*, written in 1741, when George II was on the throne.

CASSETTE 12, SIDE 1, ITEM 9

Listen now to Item 9, the passage from *Messiah* used by Max, 'Comfort ye', bearing in mind that you've heard corrupted fragments of this already.

CASSETTE 12, SIDE 1, ITEM 10

What I'm now going to do is talk you through the ways in which Max 'parodies' Handel's music, by warping and distorting it. Turn to the cassette, Item 10, for a discussion of this.

CASSETTE 12, SIDE 1, ITEM 6

Finish your work on this piece by rewinding the cassette to Item 6, the complete work. Listen to it again. This time summarize what you have understood the main features of the song to be, and how they relate to movements in the Sixties.

DISCUSSION

The main features of the song are those already discussed under subheadings – Theatre, Exploitation, Notation and Parody. The irreverent distortion of Handel's music has some parallels with Hendrix's distortion of 'The Star Spangled Banner', a musical icon shattered. Equally, the light-hearted foxtrots poke fun, while Max's own music also uses distortion, with the voice stretched to its limits. It is very much a piece of its time, deliberately provocative, with physical involvement (players in cages and the king smashing a violin) adding to the effect.

What is Max doing now?

Eight Songs for a Mad King was one of the last pieces that Max wrote while living in London, and one of the last of his overtly theatrical, shocking works. Shortly after this he moved to Hoy, Orkney, departing from London as the dominant cultural centre. He has stayed on Hoy ever since, the influence of the Orcadian landscape stimulating a new, more reflective style, very different from the bold, shrieking sounds of the Sixties. Although Max has moved away from his earlier theatrical, violent music he has retained his interest in early music, continuing to use musical structures dating from the fourteenth to the seventeenth century.

EXERCISE

Now turn to *Resource Book 4*, D4, and read the description of aspects of Max's career since his move to Orkney. ■

4 THE EARLY MUSIC REVIVAL

In Sections 2 and 3 of this unit you looked at some of the changes and continuities in pop music and modern classical music in the 1960s. I now want to look at the new focus and importance that was given to old music at this time by what became known as the Early Music Revival. This 'revival' took place between the late 1950s and the mid-1970s and was centred primarily on London, although some other European centres and New York were important too. It had far-reaching and important effects for the way that people listen to classical music and the way it is taught, performed, sponsored and sold. Few people involved in the classical music industry today would not acknowledge the breadth and depth of the impact that this movement has had. As much as any other force in the period, the protagonists of the Early Music Revival were opponents of cultural values that, in the late 1950s, seemed virtually unquestionable. The revival of interest in music from earlier periods didn't just affect the classical music scene, but also infiltrated other areas, such as folk and popular music.

What was the Early Music Revival and why was it important?

The Early Music Revival was important for two reasons. It changed the listening habits of classical music audiences by introducing them to a range of music which most of them had not encountered before. And in the long term, the performance methods and values of the early music revivalists, particularly what became known as the quest for 'authenticity', had a permanent effect not only on performers of early music but on performers of much later music too. We are going to look at both these aspects as they are at the heart of what the Early Music Revival was about.

Let's start by defining 'early music'. At first, in the 1960s, the term was used to denote a period in the history of Western classical music which was before, or *earlier* than, the eighteenth century. Most interest was centred on the medieval and renaissance periods, and to a certain extent, the first part of the **baroque** period. However, it could be misleading to think of this revival simply in chronological terms, because early music performers soon extended their interests to later periods. As I explain below, the Early Music Revival wasn't just about a period of music – it was about the way music was performed. It wasn't just *what* you performed, but the *way* you performed it.

The term Early Music *Revival* refers to the widespread and popular interest in this type of music which occurred from the late 1950s. At this time established pioneers of early music such as the English counter-tenor Alfred Deller were joined by a new wave of specialist groups such as Musica Reservata and the Early Music Consort. The music they played, and the way it was performed, appeared new in comparison to the sounds that most people were used to from classical music – it seemed fresh and almost exotic.

But it would be wrong to draw the conclusion that all this older music was newly discovered, or that it was only in the 1950s that people started performing it. Early music had been performed for a long time before this. There were societies of 'ancient music' in the eighteenth century. These were groups of aristocratic gentlemen who met to perform, listen to and exchange views on 'ancient' music. However, from what we know of their activities, the description 'ancient' was sometimes applied to composers who had died no more than twenty or thirty years earlier.

In the late nineteenth and early twentieth centuries there was a serious and more concerted interest in genuinely 'old' music. Comparatively few people were involved and most of them were amateur antiquarians of music, but the work of these late Victorians and Edwardians was special. Their curiosity about the music of the more distant past was distinguished by two important features. First, they saw the music as part of a broad social activity, and they believed that understanding the nature of the social activities for which musicians were engaged would cast light on what music was performed and how people performed it. Second, they believed in the *systematic* investigation of music history. They believed that painstaking scrutiny of historical documents and artefacts connected with music held the key to a clear understanding of the musical past – both the music itself and the way that it was performed – and that ideas about music and its performance which were not drawn from such evidence were spurious.

The Victorian and Edwardian music antiquarians, and the enthusiasts who followed them, created the bedrock on which the Early Music Revival of the 1960s was based. But, though there were some outstanding individual researchers who also performed – such as the lute and recorder player Arnold Dolmetsch – most discussions about, and performances of, early music, took place in the confines of small groups of like-minded people, often in formally constituted societies such as The Musical Association (later called the Royal Musical Association). Most members of these societies were not professional musicians but dilettantes (several were Anglican clergymen). Their work did not capture the public imagination because popularizing early music was not one of their priorities. Most people who were interested in classical music went to the large concert halls and opera houses to hear the music of favourite composers such as Beethoven, Verdi, Handel and Mozart performed on a grand scale. Up to the 1960s early music was of interest to only a small number of enthusiasts and academics, but in the 1960s this changed.

Summary points

1   The Early Music Revival started between the late 1950s and the mid-1970s.

2   Though there are lots of definitions of what 'early music' originally was, a good working definition is that it is music which originated before 1700. However, many performers also specialized in eighteenth-century music.

Understanding the music of the 1960s – a challenge to the canon

To get a good understanding of the music of any period, it is best to see it not just in its own terms, but also in respect of what came before it and what its lasting impact was. In order to understand the context for the music of the 1960s, it is important to understand what the word '**canon**' means when it is applied to music. (Note: nothing is ever simple. In music the word 'canon' also describes a particular form of counterpoint. Here we are using the word in respect to its non-specialist, more general meaning.)

In classical music (and also with regard to works of art and literature) we use the word canon to describe a body of works – symphonies, **concertos**, operas, songs and so on – that are indisputably accepted as 'masterpieces' by the most influential commentator, such as critics, performers, certain types of audience, academics and so on. This is not a precisely defined list of pieces, but rather an assumed understanding that certain types of music – the works of particular composers – have a status which makes them a sort of benchmark for most other creative musical output. Handel's *Messiah*, the **cantatas** of J.S. Bach, the operas of Mozart and the symphonies of Beethoven fit into this category, for example. Associated with this canon are people, institutions and performing organizations. So, for example, names like the Vienna

Philharmonic Orchestra, the Royal Opera House, Covent Garden, the Royal Festival Hall, the Royal College of Music, the Third Programme (now BBC Radio 3) and Pavarotti evoke thoughts of standards and approaches to performance which seem unquestionable and of a superior quality.

FIGURE 29.17   *Royal Festival Hall. (Photograph: London Metropolitan Archives)*

However, there is not just one canon, but several. It could be argued that there is a canon of nineteenth-century piano music, of string quartets and so on. Equally there are canons in other types of music. Names like Louis 'Satchmo' Armstrong, Charlie 'Bird' Parker, Bessie Smith and Fats Waller would undoubtedly figure in thoughts of a jazz canon. If we were to think of a canon of pop groups it would be impossible to ignore The Beatles, The Who and The Rolling Stones.

How then do we know when a work is canonical? The simple answer is that we do not. There is no formal list of canonical music and furthermore the canon changes. It changes slowly, but it does change none the less – the piece of music by Hildegard of Bingen that you heard in Study Week 3 was for many years neglected. Now, however, Hildegard's music has become part of the canon. We can gain an impression of this process of change by looking at some covers of sheet music produced in the late nineteenth and early twentieth centuries.

EXERCISE

Look at the pictures which constitute Figures 29.18–20 (opposite). These are covers from three publications of works by Handel, by Novello and Co., a leading publisher of classical music. How do the covers show evidence of the existence and changing nature of the canon?

DISCUSSION

I think these covers are revealing. The answer lies in the decorative borders that surround the title of the work and the name of the composer (Handel). The names of the composers mentioned in the borders of the first two covers are the same, but on the third – which is the latest – the names of Spohr and Weber have gone and those of Brahms, Purcell and Elgar have been added. Bach, Beethoven, Mozart, Handel, Haydn and Mendelssohn remain. Three of the composers on the later cover – Purcell, Handel and Bach – interested the early music movement, but this does not reflect its influence. These composers were popular before the 1960s (Handel's *Messiah*, for example, has always had a high canonical status), but the way in which their works were performed was to change radically in the 1960s.

Summary points

1   A canon is a body of works that influential opinion formers regard as the most important. Such works are often serious and complex pieces of classical music. But this canon is not fixed; it changes.

2   The classical music that most people listened to in the 1950s was related to this canon. This music was performed in a large-scale, glossy, romantic style derived from the nineteenth century.

A method: the search for authenticity

As I have said, performers of early music were not just interested in rediscovering what they regarded as a lost repertory: they were also anxious to unveil this music in its original colours. In order to do this they had to disregard what they considered the large-scale, glossy, romanticized performing style of the symphony orchestra and opera houses, in favour of music practices that were 'authentic'. An authentic performance of a piece of music was one which adhered to the values and conventions that applied at the time when that music was written. Furthermore, the performers had to be able to show, by recourse to historical evidence, that the practices being used in such performances were 'authentic'. So it was necessary for them to approach the music in a scholarly and experimental way – experimental because historical

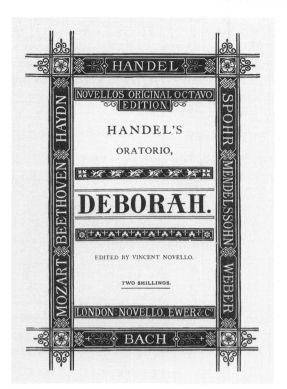

FIGURE 29.18

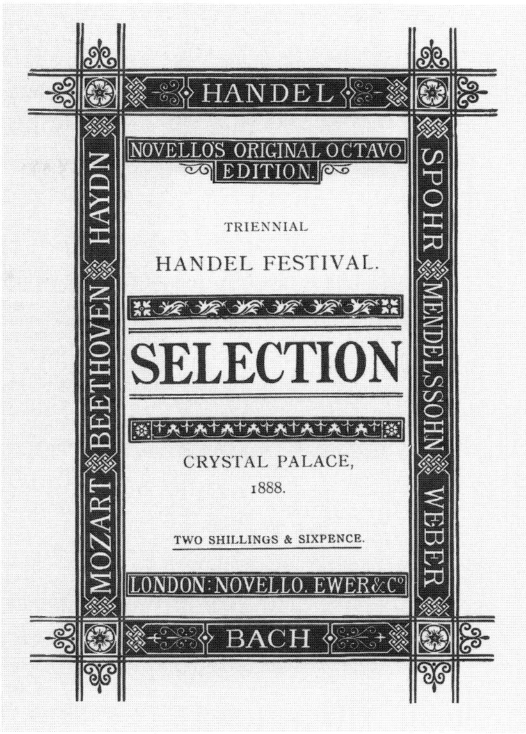

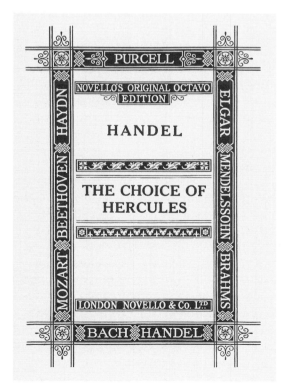

FIGURE 29.20

FIGURE 29.19

sources did not provide conclusive evidence about all performance conventions of the past. This meant paying attention to a number of details about the way that the music was performed, or to use the phrase that the early music revivalists used and which has now become standard, the **performance practices** of the time.

The text (by 'text', I mean the written notes and words)

The early music revivalists insisted that the notes and words should be those that genuinely originated when the music was first composed or heard. Thus it was important to trace the primary source for the music. Many of the published editions of old music contained changes that catered for twentieth-century tastes. Some old music was never written down – it was improvised. But descriptions of improvisations survived to the extent that it was possible to find out about and mimic those practices.

The instruments

Not all pieces of music written before 1700 indicate for what instruments the music was intended. There are several reasons for this. The two most important are that composers were usually present when their music was performed, so did not need to write too much detail into the parts, and in any case they often wished to give performers the choice about what instrument their music should be played on. The early music revivalists of the 1960s argued long and hard about what was the right way to perform early music, but they were in total agreement about what was wrong. It was wrong to perform the music on instruments that were not invented when the music was written. The right type of instruments had to be used. Many of the instruments used before 1700 were obsolete by the twentieth century, so surviving specimens were restored or copied. The timbre of old instruments was very different from the sound that modern ones make, so the values that were taught in music conservatories and practised in the music profession did not always hold in early music. The skills that a soloist learned from romantic music (such as the piece of piano music by Liszt that you heard in Study Week 3) might often be redundant in performing early music.

The sound of the voice

A lot of early music was for a voice or voices. How did singers sing before 1700? Think of the different types and styles of singing that are used today – by opera singers, folk singers, ballad singers, pop singers and the chanting of orthodox priests, for example. Early music performers asked why they should assume that the style used by concert singers in the 1950s was closer to the style used in the renaissance than that used by, for example, folk singers. Many early music singers made a name for themselves precisely because they *didn't* sound like well-trained singers of Italian opera.

The place and function of music

There were no public concerts before 1700, but by the 1950s most serious music was performed in concert halls and opera houses. **Masses**, originally intended as acts of worship in great churches and cathedrals, were performed in front of hundreds of people sitting in plush seats, by performers wearing formal evening dress. How could listeners and performers touch the real sentiments contained in the music of the past when the cultural setting in which the music was performed was so fundamentally distant from the original? Early music performers tried to understand the place of music in earlier societies, its function as music that was to be danced to, or used as part of religious devotion.

How fast, how slow? How loud, how soft?

For the same reasons that early composers did not specify which instruments had to play each part, they often did not indicate dynamics and tempo either. So in authentic performances of old music, what I have called 'the place and function' of the music had to provide the clues. A love song would be quiet, a dance would be louder, a piece of ceremonial music probably slower than a fast dance.

Summary points

1   Early music revivalists wished to perform early music in the way that it had been performed at the time it originated.

2   This led to a new interest in research into old instruments and performing conventions and practices of the past. Early music performers rejected many of the values and styles that were current in the 1960s.

The clash of values: early music v. current practices

One of the features of the Early Music Revival was the extent to which it captured the popular imagination. This was helped by a more general interest in earlier periods of history which manifested itself in BBC TV series such as *The Six Wives of Henry VIII* and *Elizabeth R* (both of which used 'authentic' music) and films such as *Anne of the Thousand Days*, *Mary Queen of Scots* and *A Man for All Seasons*. By 1970 concerts of early music were attracting very large audiences. A correspondent of the London *Evening Standard* on 7 September 1970 wondered about the dwindling audiences for symphony orchestra concerts:

> As an all-the-year round concertgoer, I have often wondered where the young promenaders go during the winter time. Do they hibernate? Very few of them seem to attend concerts on the South Bank.
>
> *(T. Cordell, Highgate)*

This drew a speedy response from Cyril Taylor, manager of Musica Reservata, one of the most important early music groups:

> Mr Cordell's letter [Monday] asks what happens to young Promenaders in winter time. If they are not to be seen in such great numbers on the South Bank this is no doubt because they cannot afford the prices. However, if he would like to see the Queen Elizabeth Hall full of them he should come to the next concert to be given by Musica Reservata.
>
> *(Cyril Taylor, Crayford, Kent)*

Early music performers believed – with some justification – that they were explorers of a lost sound world. As they found new repertory and rediscovered what they believed to be the authentic performance styles, they clashed with a musical establishment that was entrenched in a different set of values. This conflict was evident even in the 1950s.

High-brow yodellers

In April 1951, the BBC Third Programme transmitted a performance of music found in an important medieval manuscript which has become known as the **Old Hall Manuscript**. *The Listener*, a magazine founded by the BBC to cater for the more intellectual segment of its radio audience, asked Martin Cooper to review it. Cooper was educated at Winchester College, one of the most exclusive of public schools, and Oxford, and had a distinguished reputation as a writer on music. He was not impressed by what he heard:

> On Wednesday when reception was excellent [BBC transmissions had variable reception in the 1950s] I was attracted by the names of Pycard, Byttering, Queldryk, Leonel, Swynford and Typp – six fifteenth-century Englishmen whose music is preserved in The Old Hall MS. Their three and four part **Glorias** and **Credos**, sung by the Bodley Singers, provided a most abstruse and unrewarding entertainment ... This is surely a parody of the third programme. How many listeners in the British Isles can be interested in **isorhythmic** patterns in fifteenth-century masses? Surely, less than one hundred: and to the rest, as to me these naive melodies in triple time, so un-naively put together, amounted to little more than a form of high-brow yodelling.
>
> *(The Listener, April 1951, pp.683–4)*

Such derision was not unusual, though it was usually more subtle. In December 1958 a critic known as 'S.B.' from *The Musical Times*, the longest-established, monthly, classical music journal, attended a concert which was sponsored by the Arts Council and which, the reviewer admitted, drew a full house. The programme, performed by a group calling itself Musicas Antica E Nuova [*sic*] was drawn from the baroque period.

> The programme was entirely 'antica', the 'nuova' being conspicuous by its absence. Seventeenth- and eighteenth-century music seems very much to the taste of the London musical public today, but I cannot help wondering whether it is beneficial for such a young player as Carl Pini (who is also a member of Philomusica of London) to be so exclusively occupied with old music ... Young musicians of today need greater demands on their technique than Tunder, Schütz and Couperin [all seventeenth-century composers] give them.
>
> (The Musical Times, *January 1958, p.30)*

I have chosen these reviews from several similar ones. They are good examples of their type. Both of the reviewers were respected critics and were commissioned by well-known magazines that catered for the interests of classical music enthusiasts who expected to hear the music of 'great' composers performed in a way that they were used to.

CASSETTE 12, SIDE 1, ITEM 11

This exercise is based on the two reviews, but as a background to the first of them I would like you to listen to Item 11, which is a performance of Pycard's *Credo,* a piece that was probably heard at the April 1951 concert to which Martin Cooper took such exception. When you have done this, read the two reviews again. Obviously I cannot ask you to comment on their fairness in respect of the performances to which they refer, but I would like you to give a little thought to the values that these establishment critics reveal. Make a list of the points that seem to spring at you from the paper. In particular, ask whether the reviewers are commenting on the quality of the performance or on something else – the quality of the music itself.

DISCUSSION

1   Clearly Martin Cooper didn't like what he heard, but he doesn't seem to have been willing to like it either. He does not regard the music as worthy of the Third Programme. The music is naive: it lacks substance. It is not the *way* the music is performed that he criticizes, but the music itself. He makes no attempt to comment on whether it was performed well or badly: the term 'high-brow yodellers' derides the *type* of music that was performed, rather than the way it was done. Having listened to the recording of Pycard's *Credo* on your cassette, you may be inclined to agree with Cooper. I can certainly imagine what inspired the use of the word 'yodelling'. For my own part I think the performers have tried, successfully, to understand this medieval music in its own terms – in the terms of its own sound world. Cooper's terms of reference were taken from a different era

and a different set of values: those that prevailed in the classical music establishment of the 1950s.

2   I felt that the *Musical Times* reviewer, though less strident in his criticism, was not at home with this music either. The most interesting point here though, is his assertion that it is bad for aspiring musicians to get too involved with this type of music. He suggests that the demands – musical and technical – are too light. This reflects the point I made earlier about the training that musicians received at this time, and the values to which they were trained. It might also suggest that the level of musical expression of any given piece is in some way related to its technical complexity.

Such attitudes were, as I've said, widespread. So why was old music, performed in a manner that was true to its own time, so controversial? Why, within the world of classical music, and its most prestigious institutions such as the Third Programme, did early music have nuances of a counter-culture? The reason is that, for perhaps the first time ever, the early music movement questioned the classical music canon.

Summary points

1   Early music concerts became very popular in the late 1960s/early 1970s and attracted large audiences. TV period dramas such as *The Six Wives of Henry VIII* helped to popularize early music.

2   Many critics seemed to regard early music as being of lesser artistic value than later music.

3   The performance style employed by early music performers was different from and in many cases in conflict with the styles and techniques which were used for later music.

Performing music of the past

In this part of the unit I want you to listen to and compare different performances of what, on the face of it, is the same piece. The work I have chosen is a **pavane** (a pavane was a type of dance that was very popular in the sixteenth century).

CASSETTE 12, SIDE 2, ITEMS 12–14

Find Items 12–14 on the cassette. Listen to each of these items and then answer the following questions:

1   What qualities, features or elements are the same in each piece?

2   What are the differences?

3   Which sounds the most 'modern' and which sounds the 'oldest'?

Do not hesitate to write down the most obvious point: it may turn out to be the most important. Be led by your ears – by the *sound* of the music. When you make notes, try to describe the music using the terms you learned in Study Week 3 – rhythm, melody, timbre and so on (Block 1, pp.100–2).

DISCUSSION

Here is my answer:

1   The pieces are similar because they have more or less the same tune, harmonies and rhythm. The melody and harmonies are found in primary source manuscripts in England and France dating from the sixteenth century. There is also a famous printed source for the piece which dates from 1588. This is a dance tutor, a sort of renaissance 'Teach Yourself Dancing' book called *Orchesography* by Thoinot Arbeau (the name is an anagram of the author's real name – Jehan Tabourot).

2   The pieces differ in a number of important respects. Here are the ones I feel are most important:

   (a) The timbres of each piece are different. One version is sung, the others are played by different collections of instruments.

   (b) The notes are more or less the same, but some of the versions have extra notes which decorate the melody. This is particularly noticeable in Item 13.

3   I think Item 14 sounds the most modern. And indeed it is, coming from an arrangement of the pieces contained in Arbeau's book made by the English composer Peter Warlock in 1920. The original book is in the form of a dialogue between the dance teacher and Capriol, a lawyer who wishes to learn to dance. Warlock called his suite of pieces *The Capriol Suite*, but it was an arrangement rather than a realization of the original pieces. Although the extract you listened to in Item 14 is the closest that Warlock comes to the original piece, the orchestral string sounds reveal it as being the most modern of the extracts. None of the instruments used in this version existed in their present form when the Pavane was originally written.

   I think the most antique-sounding version is Item 12, the one which is sung. This is a performance by Musica Reservata (the group mentioned above), which was probably the most radical, iconoclastic and experimental group of the Early Music Revival. The directors of the group, Michael Morrow and John Becket, believed that the styles used by modern singers trained to perform nineteenth-century opera were not appropriate for early music. For this type of music they encouraged their singers to nurture their voices towards a sound closer to that used by folk singers. Also, they commissioned scholars of pronunciation to advise them on the way that French words were pronounced in the sixteenth century.

Item 13, the other purely instrumental version of the piece, is played by the Early Music Consort, directed by David Munrow. Munrow started as a member of Musica Reservata, but left to start his own group, the Early Music Consort of London. It became one of the most famous early music ensembles and was certainly the most successful in popularizing early music. This particular recording was used in the TV series *Elizabeth R.* Munrow tended to be less scholarly in his approach than Morrow and

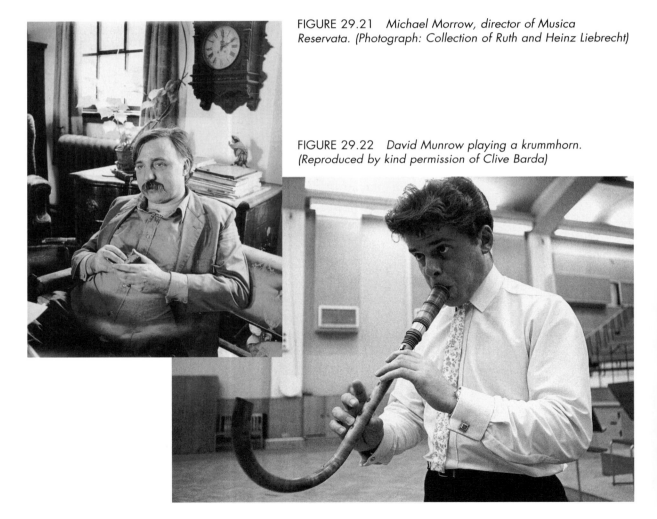

FIGURE 29.21   *Michael Morrow, director of Musica Reservata. (Photograph: Collection of Ruth and Heinz Liebrecht)*

FIGURE 29.22   *David Munrow playing a krummhorn. (Reproduced by kind permission of Clive Barda)*

Becket. His performances were often attacked for being too cute, for pandering to the public appetite for sounds that were unusual and 'olde worlde'. He deliberately chose instruments that were exotic, even though the evidence for their use in a particular piece might be slight. Becket and Morrow were less compromising. These two 'authentic' versions provide a good comparison.

The early music legacy

There was never open, acrimonious conflict between the classical music establishment and the key figures in the Early Music Revival. But there was a tension, and the resolution of this tension led to a new definition of the canon and to a new perspective on the relationship between performers and composers. By the 1980s the quest for authenticity was being applied to much later music. Even twentieth-century Broadway musicals such as *Show Boat* (first staged in 1927) were getting the authentic approach. In other ways too the effect of the Early Music Revival was considerable. By the 1990s virtually all of the standard repertory of pieces that made up the now expanded canon was rerecorded on original instruments, using historical techniques and the appropriate forces. Music colleges ran specialist early music departments, and 'authentic' performance techniques became one of the main features of university research. A number of important specialist groups were established: Gothic Voices, the Taverner Consort and Players, the Orchestra of the Age of Enlightenment, the Academy of Ancient Music, the Consort of Music, the Sixteen and the Tallis Scholars are just some of the groups that have become established in London, which has been the most important centre for this type of performance approach. In fact, you have already heard a number of 'authentic' performances in this course:

- In Study Week 3 – Hildegard of Bingen, sung by Gothic Voices; Mozart, performed by Arnold Östman and the Drottingholm Court Theatre Orchestra.

- In Study Week 13 – music by Haydn, Dibdin, Schumann, and Fortescue Harrison accompanied on keyboards appropriate to their periods of composition (in TV13).

- In Study Week 22 – Beethoven, performed by John Eliot Gardiner and the Orchestre Révolutionnaire et Romantique.

TV29 will explore some of these issues further by looking specifically at trumpets. In this programme you will see how the Early Music Revival revolutionized the way that instruments for historic performances are made, and how they are taught and played.

5 CONCLUSION

During the course of Unit 29 you've focused on music as a cultural product, concentrating on the ways in which the notion of a mainstream culture and a counter-culture can be seen to be reflected both in the stylistic features of the music being composed and in the choice and manner of music being performed. The main points you should take away from this unit are the following:

1   Music is a cultural product, and the three types of music considered in this unit, popular music, modern classical music and the Early Music Revival, need to be considered in the context of the Sixties in which they were produced.

2   These three types of music can be considered in terms of an established culture and a counter-culture.

3   In the Sixties, the Early Music Revival questioned and often contradicted the values that were most widespread in the world of classical music.

GLOSSARY

arpeggios sounding of the notes of a chord in succession (one after the other) rather than simultaneously (all together).

art music alternative term for 'classical music': music which is not, for example, jazz or folk or pop music.

avant-garde new and experimental.

ballad lyric, narrative song.

baroque in Western music the 'baroque period' begins early in the seventeenth century, and lasts until roughly the middle of the eighteenth century.

biwa type of Japanese lute.

canon body of works which the most influential opinion-formers regard as being important and having the highest status.

cantata type of choral work, usually with orchestral accompaniment.

concerto work which contrasts solo instrument(s) with orchestra.

conservatory or **conservatoire** school or college specializing in the study of music.

counter-melody a melody which moves 'counter' to the main melody, for example, in counterpoint.

Credo part of the **mass**.

dilruba stringed fiddle-like instrument.

falsetto treble range which can be produced by the adult male voice.

foxtrot dance in two-time which originated in the USA in about 1910.

Gloria part of the **mass**.

harpsichord type of keyboard instrument with plucked strings (as opposed to the piano, in which the strings are struck).

interval distance in pitch between two notes is called an interval.

isorhythmic word used to describe some forms of early vocal music.

mass main rite of the Roman Catholic church. Many composers have set the words of the mass to music.

medieval 'of the middle ages'. In music, the medieval period precedes the renaissance. Many regard the fifteenth century as signalling the end of the medieval period.

Old Hall Manuscript manuscript containing an important collection of English sacred music from the late fourteenth and early fifteenth centuries. Until 1973 the manuscript was kept at the College of St Edmund, Old Hall, near Ware, before it was acquired by the British Library.

pavane slow, stately dance in duple (rather than triple) time. It was particularly popular in England and France in the sixteenth century.

performance practice study of how music is performed. In particular, and in the context of this unit, it means the study of *historical* performance with the aim of discovering how a piece of music might have sounded when it was first heard – or during the lifetime of its composer.

phasing compositional procedure in which rhythmic patterns gradually move out of sync, or out of 'phase' to create shifting patterns.

renaissance in music, the period between the mid fifteenth century and the early seventeenth century. The baroque period followed the renaissance period.

rhythm and blues ensemble music consisting of a melody, a rhythm section and filler.

shakuhachi Japanese end-blown flute.

sitar long-necked Asian lute.

swordmandel zither-like plucked instrument.

tabla pair of single-headed Indian drums.

tambura long-necked Indian lute used as a drone accompaniment.

zither plucked stringed instrument laid on the knees or table.

REFERENCES

DAVIES, R. (1994) *X-Ray*, Harmondsworth, Penguin.

MOORE, A.F. (1993), *Rock: The Primary Text*, Buckingham, Open University Press.

Note

Words of Simon and Garfunkel, 'The Dangling Conversation' from *Parsley, Sage, Rosemary and Thyme*, Columbia COL 03 2031-2 Track 7.

Words of The Beatles, 'Within You, Without You' from *Sergeant Pepper's Lonely Hearts Club Band* EMI CDP 746442-2, Track 8.

Words of The Kinks, 'Waterloo Sunset' from *The Kinks – The Complete Collection*, Castle Classics CCSCD 300 Track 11.

Words of Peter Maxwell Davies, No.7 'Country Dance' from *Eight Songs for a Mad King*, Unicorn Kanchana Records, London DKP(CD) 9052 Track 2.

Acknowledgements

Grateful acknowledgement is made to the following sources for permission to reproduce material in this unit:

Text

p.170: Lyrics from *The Dangling Conversation* by Simon and Garfunkel, courtesy of Paul Simon Music; *p.171*: Lyrics from *Within You, Without You*, courtesy of Sony Music Ltd; *p.176*: *Waterloo Sunset* words and music by Ray Davies, reproduced by kind permission of Davray Music Ltd and Carlin Music Corp; *p.185*: Lyrics from 'Country Dance', *Eight Songs for A Mad King* by Peter Maxwell Davies, © Copyright 1971 by Boosey and Hawkes Music Publishers Ltd. Reproduced by permission of Boosey and Hawkes Music Publishers Ltd.

Figures

Figures 29.5, 29.6: Hulton Getty; *Figure 29.12*: Clive Barda/P.A.L.; *Figure 29.14*: Chris Davis; *Figure 29.16*: A section of the notation of *Eight Songs for a Mad King*, © Copyright 1971 by Boosey and Hawkes Music Publishers Ltd. Reproduced by permission of Boosey and Hawkes Music Publishers Ltd; *Figure 29.17*: London Metropolitan Archives; *Figure 29.21*: Collection of Ruth and Heinz Liebrecht; *Figure 29.22*: Reproduced by kind permission of Clive Barda.

UNIT 30 ROTHKO AND WARHOL

Written for the course team by Charles Harrison

Contents

STUDY COMPONENTS				
Weeks of study	Texts	TV	AC	Set books
1	*Illustration Book* *Resource Book 4*	TV30	–	–

Aims and objectives

The aims of this unit are to:

1 build on your interest in painting and introduce you to some significant modern examples of the art;

2 provide further practice in relevant forms of comparison;

3 introduce some of the typical concerns of modern art from the 1950s and 1960s;

4 explore the relationship between biographical and critical studies of artistic work;

5 encourage further thought about the relationship between artistic concerns and historical conditions;

6 explore the relevance and usefulness of artists' statements for an understanding of their art;

7 consider the conflict between economic considerations and artistic values in the light of a single case study;

8 explore the relationship between 'mainstream' and 'counter-cultural' interests as these are revealed through study of the work of Rothko and Warhol;

9 raise the question of periodization with regard to the development of modernism in pictorial art.

By the end of this unit you should be able to:

1 make relevant observations and discriminations when faced with two or more paintings from the modern period;

2 approach modern and abstract works of art with some sense of where to begin in the process of understanding;

3 provide a simple argument in support of the claim that meaning and emotion may be expressed through abstract forms;

4   outline some of the problems liable to occur when artistic priorities have to be reconciled with economic and utilitarian considerations;

5   visit a picture gallery or museum of art with enhanced understanding and enjoyment of any modern works on display;

6   communicate some part of that understanding and enjoyment to others.

1   INTRODUCTION

In this unit we return to the study of painting. You have come a long way from the opening of Block 1, in which we looked at a series of pictures by artists from the fifteenth to the mid-twentieth centuries. At that point the objective was to learn about technique and composition in painting and to consider the kinds of effect that are associated with the art. In Block 3 you considered two individual artists working in the late eighteenth and early nineteenth centuries, and there the emphasis was upon the historical context within which each artist was operating.

In this last unit on art history we shall try to bring these two approaches together. That's to say we shall concentrate upon the composition and effects of the works we study, but we shall also consider these as works of a particular period: the period of 'the long Sixties', extending from the late 1950s to the early 1970s. We shall consider how information about the period and about the artists' careers and working circumstances helps us to understand the art in question; but we shall also ask what the art might have to tell us about the nature of the times. In particular, we shall consider what is to be learned from the art of the late 1950s and the 1960s about the relationship between 'mainstream' and 'counter-cultural' values.

2   TWO AMERICAN PAINTINGS

Our principal focus will be on the art of the painter Mark Rothko. Rothko was born Marcus Rothkowitz in Dvinsk in Russia in 1903 to a Lithuanian Jewish father and a Prussian Jewish mother. He travelled to the United States as an immigrant in 1913, came to prominence as an artist in New York in the 1950s, and died by his own hand in 1970. He belonged to a generation of American artists known as the Abstract Expressionists. Another of the Abstract Expressionists was Jackson Pollock, whose *Summertime* (Colour Plate 13) we looked at in detail in TV1. When the mainly abstract work of these artists was shown in London in the later 1950s, it was seen by many people as demonstrating that the main initiative for the development of modern art had passed from Europe to

America. In his works of the early 1940s, Rothko had made frequent references to classical culture and mythology (you will see an example in TV30, 'Rothko at the Tate'), but the works we shall be principally concerned with are abstract paintings executed towards the beginning of our long decade, in the years 1958–9. Towards the end of that decade, in 1969, the artist gave a group of works to the Tate Gallery in London (Colour Plates 71–80). These paintings will be discussed in TV30.

During the 1960s a younger generation of artists rose to prominence in America, the so-called 'Pop' artists, with Andy Warhol notorious among them. Warhol was born Andrew Warhola in Pittsburgh in 1928 to parents who were immigrants from Czechoslovakia. He left Pittsburgh for New York in 1949 and worked as an illustrator and designer before attracting considerable attention with paintings made between 1960 and 1965. He began making films in 1963, drawing largely unscripted performances from gays, transvestites, drug addicts and other members of the New York underworld of the time. In 1966 he acted as impresario to the Velvet Underground rock band. The band's singer/song-writer Lou Reed was later responsible for 'Walk on the Wild Side', which has been seen as a virtual anthem of the counter-culture of the time (it was released in 1972). The characters featured in this song were all members of the circle that formed around Warhol. In June 1968 Warhol was badly wounded in a shooting attack by Valerie Solanas, who had appeared briefly in one of his films. Solanas was founder and sole member of SCUM (the Society for Cutting Up Men) and author of its manifesto. Warhol died in 1987 following a gall-bladder operation.

Rothko resented the Pop artists' success and disliked and disapproved of their work. We shall look briefly at Warhol's paintings in relation to Rothko's and will consider some of the issues raised by the comparison.

In fact, I propose to start straight in at the deep end with one work from each artist. Don't be daunted if they seem strange and unfamiliar. As I hope you will remember, both from TV1 and from the previous art history units, there's a surprising amount to be learned by careful observation. Please turn now to Colour Plates 76 (Rothko, *Red on Maroon*) and 81 (Warhol, *Red Race Riot*). By this stage of the course you should not need reminding to read captions carefully, but don't forget also to exercise your imagination as best you can to conjure up the actual painting to which the reproduction and caption refer. Bear in mind the size of each work and the effect it would be likely to have as a physical surface facing you on a gallery wall.

You may not be familiar with the term 'silkscreen' in the caption to the painting by Warhol. A silkscreen is a form of fine stencil on which an image taken from a photograph or some other source is captured so that it can be transferred onto another surface, such as a canvas. The fabric is first coated with light-sensitive emulsion and a transparency is projected onto it. Next the fabric is developed with hot water so that the exposed areas dissolve. A brush or roller can then be used to force ink or paint through the resulting spaces in the areas of weave. The images in Warhol's painting have been 'printed' in this manner by pressing black paint through a silkscreen laid over a red-painted canvas.

EXERCISE

Briefly note down what you think these paintings have in common; then describe what you see as the principal differences. Bear in mind that I am *not* for the moment asking you to say how you feel about them or what you take them to mean. With any work of art you approach, it's best to avoid jumping to conclusions about its meaning before you're in a position to back those conclusions up with an adequate description. Try to recall the technical vocabulary introduced in Unit 1 and apply it where relevant.

DISCUSSION

Besides the obvious points that they were both made by artists working in America and that they are close in date, you should certainly have noted that both paintings are very large (although as paintings in oil on canvas they are both made to be movable) and that both are painted principally in reddish colours. The size of the actual paintings will clearly be crucial to the way they appear, although, of course, the effect of their size will not be obvious in reproduction. You may also have described them both as 'modern' paintings, since each in its own fashion avoids traditional ways of picture-making. Despite my caution, you may have been tempted to make some comment about their imagined effect on you – such as that both convey a sense of oppression or that both of them leave you cold. If you did so, I hope it occurred to you that such comments would only really be relevant to the exercise if you could say what it is about the paintings that *produces* these effects, for in trying to answer that question you would have had to return to the task of observing and describing their characteristics.

The differences probably seem obvious enough. However, when you tried to put them into words you may have found it more demanding than you expected. You might just have said that one was interesting and the other was not, but if so I hope you tried to give reasons. In any case, I would not expect your notes to be as extensive as this discussion will need to be.

For my own part, I certainly have to think hard in order to express the differences I observe. There's a need to find precise words for different *qualities* – qualities of colour and of effect. This is always a problem. But I also keep having to revise or moderate my first impressions. On first sight I might be tempted to say that the Rothko is just a flat pattern, but then I find myself describing its background as having a degree of 'depth'. It's painted in a darker and browner red than the Warhol, with a brighter red apparently laid over the ground in a squared 'O' shape; but then as I look the orangey-red comes to seem like the background, and the central rectangle appears as if projecting outward towards me. The painting won't stay flat. (Think back to the remarks on figure–ground relations in Unit 1, pp.15–18.) There's a continual sense of push and pull between its different 'levels'. The Warhol does at least present scenes to look into, but its background is painted in a pinkish-red that looks flat; or rather the *picture plane* looks flat, although the actual surface is slightly variegated by the uneven mixing of two reds, one closer to purple than the other.

Of course, the most obvious difference is that the Rothko is non-figurative or abstract (it is not a *picture* of anything), whereas the Warhol clearly contains a picture – or several pictures – of a race riot, complete with white baton-wielding policemen setting dogs onto a black man. (The events recorded took place in Birmingham, Alabama.) But then again, I've just remarked that the Rothko sets up the kinds of figure–ground effect we've learned to associate with pictures that have objects or landscape features or people in them, while I've said that the Warhol looks flat, as one might expect an abstract painting to be. And the Rothko certainly appears the more atmospheric of the two – *as if* it had the kind of mood we associate with landscape, or even the kind of psychological effect we associate with portraiture. And now I come to notice it, the combination of flatness with matter-of-fact repetition of the images does seem to render the 'content' of Warhol's painting strangely inanimate and unreal, despite the presence of the men and the dogs. In fact, it is this dead-pan quality in the painting that I tend to experience first. You presumably noticed that the Warhol had an image of some sort printed on its surface, but did you feel a kind of shock when you looked closely 'into' the painting and saw what its grainy texture revealed? (Think back to TV4 in which boxing is shown – and to the effect of the two brief black-and-white clips from film of actual street violence.)

Having raised this last question, I now feel the need to go back and add to my list of similarities between the two paintings, for what I have come to notice about *both* of them is that they seem to change and come to life as I concentrate my attention upon them. In Rothko's I sense a slow oscillation or pulsation as its two principal levels seem to switch back and forth, in and out, so that I see the squared 'O' now as a kind of doorway through which I might pass into the space of the central rectangle, now as a background plane against which that rectangle projects like a free-standing pillar. In Warhol's painting I find myself now looking *at* a large flat surface of variegated black and red, now looking *into* scenes of violent racial conflict and oppression. In each case it is very hard to hold on to both states or aspects simultaneously.

One of the things we have learned here, then, is that although the two paintings are indeed very different in the ways in which they relate to the world around them (perhaps amounting, in Rothko's case, to a failure or refusal to relate in the traditional way – by depicting), the very fact that they *are* paintings means that they share certain important characteristics. Each must somehow hold the viewer's attention, not so much by virtue of what it shows, but rather through what *happens* when the appropriate faculties are concentrated upon it: not simply vision, but a manner of looking that is both responsive and thoughtful.

We can perhaps go further. We could say that each painting in its own way claims a considerable *amount* of attention, if only by virtue of its sheer size. All things being equal, we would expect to encounter such paintings in public rather than private spaces. On the other hand, we have already noted that each painting leaves the individual viewer in a state of uncertainty. We may know clearly enough that what we're looking at is a work of modern art, but there is a continual uncertainty about just what it is that is being looked at and seen *in* the work. This is not a condition it is easy to describe or to communicate, nor is it quite the state of mind we normally associate with public spectacles, which are more often designed to celebrate shared values and to produce a sense of certainty. The vexed relationship between public context and private uncertainty is an issue we shall explore further with regard to Rothko's work. Before we look in more detail at that work, however, I would like to inquire more closely into the figurative content of Warhol's painting.

3 PICTURING THE AGE

The next two-part exercise will help you to check the thoroughness of your reading of the detail in *Red Race Riot*, although please note that I wouldn't expect you to have gone to such lengths in responding to the initial comparison.

EXERCISE

1   How many original photographs do you think the artist used to make the seven-and-a-half frames of his painting?

2   Assuming that those photographs document the same sequence of events, can you reconstruct the order in which they were taken?

DISCUSSION

1   Warhol used three separate photographs. If we number the images A, B and C and the frames 1–8, reading from top to bottom and from left to right, then image A is used in frames 1 and 5, image B in

frames 2 and 6, and image C in frames 3, 4, 7 and 8, although only the right-hand portion of image C appears in frame 3.

2   The order in which the photographs were taken is much harder to work out. My own conclusion is that image C shows the earliest moment, when the black man in the hat in the centre of the picture with his back to the camera is being attacked by two dogs, one from each side. In this image he is deeper into the picture space than in the other two images – which means that the photographer was further away from him. The handler of the white-faced dog at the right seems to be turning as if about to join the attack. In image B the white-faced dog has been launched at the black man and has a hold on the seat of his pants. The photographer has stepped in closer to the action. In image A, which I take to be the last in the sequence, the black man's trousers have been torn, and the photographer has moved round to the left.

This analysis of Warhol's images reminds me of two illustrations from the opening unit of Block 1. The connections may seem a bit improbable at first, so don't worry if they hadn't occurred to you.

First, the combination of different but related episodes within one picture surface reminds me – of all things – of Giovanni di Paolo's painting of *St John the Baptist going into the Wilderness* (Colour Plate 4).

Second, the way in which the three images used by Warhol vary according to the position recorded by the camera reminds me of the background drawing for Walt Disney's cartoon film *Clock-Cleaners* (Plate 7). In Unit 1 that illustration was used as an example of a picture with an unusual vanishing point, and to demonstrate the connection between the organization of pictorial space and the work of the film animator. One way artists have of bringing a picture space to life, I suggested, is by making spectators feel that their own viewpoint is one that might change. In his *Red Race Riot* Warhol has used changes in the original photographer's viewpoint to vary the depth of his own picture space as we perceive it. Notice, for instance, how much 'shallower' frames 1, 2 and 6 seem than frames 4, 7 and 8.

On the basis of these two connections, there are two general points we can make about the character of Warhol's work.

On the one hand, for all that Warhol's work seems shaped by the moment of its production, it also furnishes evidence that there are aspects of the art of painting which have remained relatively constant over centuries: certain ways of representing the passage of time, certain techniques for engaging the spectator's attention, and, crucially, certain ways of *changing* under that attention as mere flat surfaces never do. Presumably the pictorial arts have remained constant in these respects because there are basic triggers of human interest which have remained constant over the same period.

On the other hand, there are certain thoroughly up-to-date characteristics that serve to identify Warhol's work firmly with its specific historical moment. The most obvious of these, clearly, relate to its figurative content (that is, to its function as a picture *of* something). The subject-matter of racial protest and violence was highly topical in the 1960s, as you will know from your reading of the history units. It is not only through its figurative subject-matter that Warhol's work relates to the world of the Sixties, however. His use of specific *techniques* also serves to evoke the means by which such images were gathered, transmitted and packaged at the time: the newspaper snapshot, the documentary film and, increasingly, the television news programme.

In fact, the images used in his paintings turn out in general to be inseparable from the original processes of their transmission into the public sphere. He drew upon press photographs of Jackie Kennedy for a series of works produced in the wake of President Kennedy's assassination (Colour Plate 82, *Sixteen Jackies*; Plate 177, *Jackie III*). After Marilyn Monroe's suicide he based a series of paintings upon a publicity still of the star (Colour Plate 83, *Gold Marilyn Monroe*), and he used police photographs for a series of *Disasters* based on images of actual car crashes (Plate 178, *White Burning Car II*). There are paintings featuring multiple images of a mushroom cloud (Plate 179, *Atomic Bomb*), and others with single or multiple images of the electric chair (Colour Plate 84, *Orange Disaster*). In each case it is clear from Warhol's use of the silkscreen process that the image has been taken ready-made from another source.

In the modern world his work represents to us, it seems that *everything* is already pictured. Under such conditions, he appears to be saying, the role of the artist is not to create original images, but rather to steep himself in the culture and to make revealing selections among the countless images with which we are already surrounded. Even here, he suggests, the artist's role is a passive one; all he need do is act as a responsive medium and the characteristic motifs of the age will inevitably assert themselves on the surfaces of his pictures. 'The reason I'm painting this way', he said in 1963, 'is that I want to be a machine, and I feel that whatever I do and do machine-like is what I want to do' ('What is Pop Art? Interviews with eight painters (Part 1)', *Art News*, November 1963; reprinted in Harrison and Wood, 1992, p.732).

The studio in which Warhol's silkscreen paintings were made was known as the Factory. Although he was generally responsible for the selection of images and for decisions about placing and design, much of the work issuing in his name was manufactured by assistants, among them some of the same 'underground' characters that featured in his films. Although certain basic triggers of human attention remain constant, there are continual changes in forms of human production, in the information that is available to us, and in the means and media by which that information is distributed. In taking account of such changes, the artist may transform our understanding of the nature and potential of pictorial art. In Warhol's case, we may come to wonder whether his art should be considered 'painting' at all.

4 THE ARTIST IN ART HISTORY

Unlike Warhol, Rothko showed no significant interest in any form of popular culture. He seems to have been as committed as Jacques-Louis David had been to the idea of painting as a form of high art. His *Red on Maroon* was produced as one of an ambitious series. He embarked on this series in 1958 in response to a commission to decorate the Four Seasons restaurant in the Seagram Building on Park Avenue in New York. At a certain point he withdrew from the commission and returned the money that had been advanced to him. During the period of some eighteen months while he worked with this commission in mind, Rothko produced far more paintings than could actually have been hung in the restaurant – around forty altogether. He seems to have envisaged a final group of seven or eight individual works, and he produced at least three separate sets as his ideas developed. The paintings acquired by the Tate Gallery in 1969 were all done in connection with the Four Seasons commission, and they were selected with Rothko's cooperation to hang as a group in one room of the gallery, but there was probably never a point at which these specific paintings were envisaged by Rothko as the ones that might decorate the restaurant.

For more information about the commission and about Rothko, I shall ask you in due course to read two very different texts. Before you do so, however, and to help you distinguish between the aims and merits of these texts, I want you to give some thought to the different kinds of publication in which the work and career of the individual artist are normally represented.

Most serious forms of study can be included in one of the three following categories.

1   Biography.

2   Critical study or review or monograph (you might like to compare the historian's use of the latter term, as discussed in Unit 26).

3   Catalogue (sometimes described as '*oeuvre* catalogue', meaning a catalogue of the artist's output, or 'catalogue *raisonné*', meaning a catalogue with details given on each entry).

EXERCISE

Make brief notes on each of these types of publication, distinguishing one from the other in terms of what you understand to be their different functions.

DISCUSSION

My own answer would read something like this.

1   A *biography* is the narrative of a person's *life*. In the case of an artist, he or she may well have been chosen as a subject because the writer was interested by his or her work, but a biography is not primarily a study of that work. It is the study of a person. An important event in the artist's life would be of interest to a biographer even if it had had no evident effect on that artist's work.

2   An art-historical or art-critical *monograph*, on the other hand, is primarily a study of the artist's *work*. It could be an enthusiastic celebration of that work, it might be highly critical, or it might be written to advance a new interpretation. It might be arranged chronologically and might well contain much biographical information, but in all cases the primary focus would be on the nature and development of the art.

3   Finally, a *catalogue* is first and foremost a kind of list of works. In the study of the development of an individual artist a catalogue of some sort is an essential starting point, for without some established body of work there is no way of being sure just what it is one is supposed to be studying. The normal convention is for a catalogue to be arranged chronologically. The most useful catalogue will be one that is fully illustrated, so that the user can readily identify each work cited. A catalogue might be partial and selective, such as an illustrated publication of all Rembrandt's self-portraits, or it might be intended to provide reference to the artist's complete output, often including lost works and works formerly attributed to the artist but now thought to be by pupils, by other contemporary artists or even by forgers. An illustrated catalogue – although not usually a complete one – will normally be published on the occasion of an important exhibition of an artist's work.

If you had some difficulty in distinguishing between the biography and the monograph, that is entirely understandable. The distinction is generally one of emphasis. There are highly informative biographical studies that have little of value to say specifically about the artist's work, and there are monographic essays that contain little or no biographical information; but equally there are many excellent studies of individual artists in which 'life' and 'work' are treated as inseparable. Nowadays the plates and list of works in an exhibition catalogue will often be accompanied both by a brief biography and by at least one monograph essay on the artist's work, thus combining all three forms of study within one publication.

As I write this, a complete catalogue of Rothko's work is in course of preparation in Washington. The author expects it to contain details of 833 works on canvas or panel and some 2000 on paper. By way of comparison, some 2000 works in Warhol's name issued from his Factory in the years 1962–4 alone. With an output as large and diverse as this, there would clearly be considerable problems in compiling a complete catalogue.

At this point I would like you to read 'Parnassus on 53rd Street' by James Breslin (*Resource Book 4*, E1). This is the opening chapter of a book on Rothko published in 1993. There are a few details it may help you to know. The Seagram Building is a skyscraper constructed in the late 1950s in the International Style – which is to say that it was built to a self-consciously modern design with an emphasis on clean lines, right-angles and unmodulated surfaces (Plate 62). The Museum of Modern Art, New York, is one of the wealthiest and most prestigious modern art museums in the world. In the 1960s it was almost certainly *the* wealthiest and most prestigious, with an authority second to none in collecting, displaying and defining the mainstream of modern art. Clyfford Still and Barnett Newman were two of the other members of the generation of American painters that came to be known as the Abstract Expressionists. You may remember Newman's early work known as *The Void* from Unit 1 and Plate 3. Don't worry if you fail to recognize any of the names of the guests invited to Rothko's exhibition opening. All you need to know is that it was attended by a host of notable artists, critics, dealers and collectors.

EXERCISE

Read the text now, and when you have finished make brief notes in response to the following questions.

1   Into which of the three categories – biography, monograph, catalogue – would you place the text you have just read?

2   Look again at Breslin's final paragraph. Bearing in mind that this concludes the opening chapter of a book (in fact, a 700-page book), what does it tell you about his way of understanding Rothko's art?

3   How much do you trust Breslin as a guide to Rothko's character and motives? Try to give brief reasons for your judgement.

4   When looking at the painting *Red on Maroon*, you probably formed a specific image of the artist who painted it. Were you surprised by the picture of Rothko that emerged from Breslin's account? If so, try to

identify the elements of that account that seemed not to match with your expectations.

DISCUSSION

1   This is clearly biography. We learn very little about what Rothko's work looks like, or about its development, but a great deal about the circumstances of his life, his feelings, his personality, his acquaintances and so on.

2   What Breslin is doing in this introductory chapter is throwing out a lure to his readers. He creates a vivid picture of a complex and somewhat tormented individual at the height of his career, then asserts that the way to understand him is to trace him back to his origins – which of course is just what the writer himself is about to do. Put in the form of a generalization, his suggestion is that the artist is what his origins make him. If and when he comes to interpret Rothko's painting, we can expect him to see it as expressing just those *biographical* themes and tensions that he has himself uncovered.

3   I would expect a wide range of answers to this question. There are some strong reasons for scepticism. Breslin's Rothko makes such a good protagonist – almost like a character from a novel. Clearly the author has collected some attention-grabbing quotations with which to engage his reader from the outset. We might ask just who it was that Rothko was speaking to in the conversation recorded in the first two paragraphs, how and when his words were recorded, and how reliable a witness it was that recorded them. (In fact, it was the writer John Hurt Fischer, to whom Rothko unburdened himself in the course of a transatlantic voyage.) At least on present showing it is the artist's personality and psychology that Breslin finds principally engaging. In his discussion of the paintings his tendency is to look for confirmation of Rothko's psychology as he understands it. Yet for a painter such as Rothko the pursuit of his art must have been a decisive issue. In Breslin's account this *professional* aspect of his motivation seems to be overshadowed by the dramatic image of the tortured individual, and by the emphasis on his malice.

On the positive side, however, this is no idle piece of journalism. Breslin *is* clearly engaged by Rothko, and he allows him to appear as a fully rounded character, with contradictory attitudes. The fact that the painter is in a sense the hero of the book doesn't prevent Breslin from showing just how difficult a character he must have been. Although he does tend to seize on a good quote when he can, there are plenty of signs that he has based his account on wide consultation among those who knew Rothko. (We have not reprinted his notes and appendices but you can take it on trust that he is scrupulous about identifying his sources.) In fact, the limited character of his discussion of the paintings might be taken as a kind of virtue: a recognition on the part of a *writer*, who is neither an art critic nor an art historian, that this is not where his strongest competences lie. (In general, I would say, the occasional passages of interpretative writing about Rothko's paintings are the weakest parts of Breslin's long book.)

4   Here, you are on your own. I ask this question not because there is any correct way to answer it, but to encourage you to reflect on the value of the two different kinds of evidence you have had to consider. What I would say is that, if you found Breslin's Rothko to be totally at odds with the Rothko you had imagined as the author of the painting, you should not be too ready to surrender that first impression. For in the end it is the painting we are primarily faced with, not the painter.

---

5 'MAKING A PLACE'

Breslin quotes a claim Rothko made to a friend, the writer Dore Ashton: 'I have made a place.' The possibility of 'making a place' seems to have been an overriding reason for Rothko's initial enthusiasm over the commission for the Seagram murals. He apparently saw this commission as an opportunity to have a group of his works shown permanently together under the kind of conditions he believed that work required. And yet when he claimed to have 'made a place', he was speaking not in the restaurant, but in his studio. What kind of a 'place' was it, then, that he thought he had made, and how was it established? To answer this we need to know more about the form of relationship between painting and viewer that Rothko aimed to set up, and about the kind of experience that he intended his work to provide. (These issues will also be explored in TV30.)

Rothko was not one of those artists who produce large amounts of theory in support of their work. When he did write or speak about his art, however, what he said was usually interesting and to the point. His beliefs about art were largely formulated in the 1940s, and he wrote comparatively little about his work after 1950. He did make one public statement at the time when he was working on the Seagram commission, speaking at the Pratt Institute in New York in October 1958, but his talk on that occasion was largely composed from material he had published earlier. In order to gain some understanding of his aims and ideas, it will therefore help if we look briefly at the wider development of his work from the 1940s onward. What follows is a selection of statements he made over the course of fifteen years.

[A] No possible set of notes can explain our paintings. Their explanation must come out of a consummated experience between picture and onlooker.

(From a letter written with assistance from Newman and signed jointly by Rothko and another painter, Adolph Gottlieb, New York Times, *13 June 1943, reprinted in Harrison and Wood, 1992, p.562)*

[B] A picture lives by companionship, expanding and quickening in the eyes of the sensitive observer. It dies by the same token. It is therefore a risky and unfeeling act to send it out into the world. How often it must be permanently impaired by the eyes of the vulgar and the cruelty of the impotent who would extend their affliction universally!

(Statement in Tiger's Eye, *December 1947, reprinted in Harrison and Wood, 1992, p.565)*

[C] For me the great achievements of the centuries in which the artist accepted the probable and familiar as his subjects were the pictures of the single human figure – alone in a moment of utter immobility.

('The Romantics were prompted ...', Possibilities I, *1947, reprinted in Harrison and Wood, 1992, pp.563–4)*

[D] I do not believe that there was ever a question of being abstract or representational. It is really a matter of ending this silence and solitude, of breathing and stretching one's arms again.

('The Romantics were prompted ...', Possibilities I, *1947, reprinted in Harrison and Wood, 1992, pp.563–4)*

[E] I paint very large pictures. I realize that historically the function of painting large pictures is something very grandiose and pompous. The reason I paint them however ... is precisely because I want to be very intimate and human. To paint a small picture is to place yourself outside your experience, to look upon an experience as a stereopticon view or with a reducing glass. However you paint the larger picture, you are in it. It isn't something you command.

(Contribution to a symposium, Interiors, *10 May 1951, reprinted in* Mark Rothko, *1987, p.85. A stereopticon is a kind of double magic lantern used to create an illusion of three-dimensionality by projecting paired images onto the same surface)*

[F] If I must place my trust somewhere, I would invest it in the psyche of sensitive observers who are free of the conventions of understanding. I would have no apprehensions about the use they would make of the pictures for the needs of their own spirit. For if there is both need and spirit, there is bound to be a real transaction.

(Letter to Katharine Kuh, 1954, printed in Mark Rothko, *1987, p.58)*

[G] I belong to a generation that was preoccupied with the human figure and I studied it. It was with the utmost reluctance that I found that it did not meet my needs. Whoever used it mutilated it. No one could paint the figure as it was and feel that he could produce something that could express the world. I refuse to mutilate and had to find another way of expression.

(Lecture at the Pratt Institute, New York, 1958, quoted in Breslin, 1993, pp.394–5)

[H] I paint large pictures because I want to create a state of intimacy. A large picture is an immediate transaction; it takes you into it.

(Lecture at the Pratt Institute, New York, 1958, reprinted in Mark Rothko, *1987, p.87)*

Look now at Colour Plates 85–89 and 73 (*Subway Scene, c.1938; Slow Swirl by the Edge of the Sea, 1944; Number 18, c.1947–8; Number 12, 1951; Untitled, 1954; Black on Maroon, 1958*), which will give you some idea of the development of Rothko's work between 1938 and 1958. The *Subway Scene* belongs to a series of pictures of figures in urban settings painted before the time when the 'mutilation' of the figure came to seem unavoidable to Rothko and his contemporaries. I include this to give you some idea of the kind of painting that he moved away from. As you can see, with the exception of this early work, the paintings can be matched approximately against the dates of the quotations.

EXERCISE

The following questions are designed to focus attention on Rothko's ideas about the nature and purpose of his work, as these are revealed in the quotations. Make some notes in response, keeping the pictures in view as you do so.

1   What were Rothko's views about the art of the past? From what you have seen in the course so far, could you identify examples of the kinds of painting he might or might not have preferred?

2   What kind of a thing was a painting for Rothko, and what were his attitudes towards it?

3   How did Rothko regard the potential viewer of his painting?

4   How did Rothko imagine the relationship between painting and viewer?

5   How would you describe the experience Rothko saw his work as offering?

DISCUSSION

In my specimen answers to these questions I will try to include the form of response I believe to be appropriate, but I shall also use my answers to advance our discussion of Rothko in general. In the process I shall be drawing on some new information that I would not expect you to possess.

1   It is clear, I think, that Rothko was interested in the kinds of picture that convey an emotional experience and that do so through their

human content. He was not interested in the kind of small picture where one is as it were 'outside' the world of the subject looking in, as with the still lifes by Nicholson (Plate 2), Moillon (Colour Plate 8) or Steenwyck (Colour Plate 10), or even the landscape by Constable (Plate 12). On the other hand, he was unsympathetic to large pictures that are 'grandiose and pompous' – a category that might well include the history paintings of David that you studied in Block 3 (see, for example, Colour Plate 41, *The Lictors Returning to Brutus the Bodies of his Sons*). Of the works we have already looked at, the one that would seem most clearly to satisfy Rothko's idea of a 'great achievement' – despite its small size – is Rembrandt's painting *The Artist in his Studio* (Colour Plate 1), which we looked at in Block 1. The same artist's *Portrait of Agatha Bas* might count as well (Plate 9). Or we might think of works by Caspar David Friedrich, discussed in Block 3, whose paintings seem so often to evoke a state of solitary contemplation, even when they contain more than one figure (*Two Men Contemplating the Moon*, Colour Plate 63). And that thought leads me to consider some further works from Block 1 which, although they don't *show* solitary human figures, seem to suggest that what they do show is what a solitary person is seeing. The paintings I have in mind are Courbet's *Still Life* (Colour Plate 9) and Church's *Twilight in the Wilderness* (Colour Plate 2).

Before we leave this question, there is a further point to be made with regard to Rothko's preferences. It is not a point that is raised directly by the question I asked, nor is it easy to grasp, but it is nevertheless important in understanding the artist's motives for developing his painting as he did. On the one hand, he sets the painting of the human figure firmly at the centre of the tradition of painting. On the other, he claims that after a certain point artists were unable to use the human figure to 'express the world' unless they mutilated it – a course he refuses to pursue. This statement raises two possible questions. The first and most obvious is: Why was it that artists found themselves driven to mutilate the human figure? The second is: What was wrong with using the human figure *and* mutilating it?

This latter may seem a perverse question, but it is exactly what many European artists did. Look for instance at Plate 180, Pablo Picasso's *Charnel House* of 1944–5, and at Plate 181, *Three Studies for Figures at the Base of a Crucifixion*, painted at about the same time by the English artist Francis Bacon. In fact, paintings such as these in which the human figure *is* evidently 'mutilated' suggest an answer to *why* the mutilation must have seemed inescapable. Given the date at which they were painted, these images inevitably appear as shaped by the horrors of World War II and the Holocaust. The implication is that in any painting in which the human figure was painted at the time, those horrors were bound somehow to make themselves felt;

that is, unless the artists retreated into mere escapism, turning their backs on the evidence as to what being human actually *meant*. A similar point was made by the philosopher Theodor Adorno with respect to literature, when he wrote in 1962 that 'to write lyric poetry after Auschwitz is barbaric' (see Harrison and Wood, 1992, p.761).

Rothko seems to be acknowledging both the force of events in the recent past and the need for that force to be registered in art – the need for art to 'express the world'. We should remember that he was a Jew. Yet, as he had written in a notebook of the late 1930s, 'History is not demonstrated by pictures, nor should pictures be demonstrated by history' (quoted in Breslin, 1993, p.124). In other words, we should not assume that the truth of any historical account can be proved by a picture, nor should we assume that a given picture can be properly interpreted by the application of historical data. In a joint interview with Rothko, broadcast in New York in October 1943, Gottlieb had spoken of the power of primitive forms of expression, which reveal 'the constant awareness of powerful forces, the immediate presence of terror and fear, a recognition and acceptance of the brutality of the natural world as well as the eternal insecurity of life'. Rothko had added, 'Those who think that the world of today is more gentle and graceful than the primeval and predatory passions from which these myths spring, are either not aware of reality or do not wish to see it in art' ('The portrait and the modern artist', typescript of a broadcast on 'Art in New York', Radio WNYC, 13 October 1943; reprinted in *Mark Rothko*, 1987, pp.78–81).

He gave certain paintings of the early 1940s titles that referred to the tragedies of the ancient Greek writer Aeschylus (see Plate 182, *Omen of the Eagle*), and he was to retain an interest throughout his life in the work of Aeschylus and Sophocles in particular and in the concept of tragedy in general. And yet he also declares his desire to end 'this silence and solitude' and to establish a state of intimacy. Rather than attempting to make pictures of what we like to call 'acts of inhumanity', he wants an art that both admits and communicates its *own* complex humanity.

2   What Rothko is gradually moving towards, then, is something on the scale and with the ambition of a tragedy or a history painting (quote E) – something that can 'express the world' (G) and thus face up to the truths that history has to tell – but with the sense of close and one-to-one contact with the viewer that we associate with the intimate portrait or the self-portrait (C and E). Again, we should note the importance Rothko places on the painting of the single figure. Yet he also believes that a painting that is a picture *of* a person can never quite fulfil the function he has in mind (G). It cannot meet the spectator on equal terms. It would be just possible, I think, to see his painting of 1944 (*Slow Swirl*) as representing two highly abstracted figures standing in the space of a simplified but dreamlike landscape.

But in the work of 1947 (*Number 18*) it is as if the relations between 'figure' and 'ground' have been spread across the picture surface so that it is the entire painting, and not any identifiable figure within it, that seems to stand up and face us.

What emerges from quote B, written in the same year, is that he has come to think of a painting *as if* it were a person, endowed with feelings of its own, and thus vulnerable to the insensitive behaviour of others. He imagines it as liable to die if deprived of sympathetic companionship. On the one hand, his attitude towards the painting is intensely protective; on the other, he wants to be absorbed by it – to be taken into it. Of course, to confuse a painting with a person would be a sign of madness. Rothko's statements should be understood as metaphorical and strategic. They are attempts to get the viewer on the side of his painting. This conclusion leads us naturally to our third question.

3   It is important to realize that Rothko himself acts as the first viewer of his own painting, as any painter must do. After all, the first person upon whom the effects of a painting must be tested is the one who stands before it at the easel as it emerges. On the one hand, the artist thus *stands in* for the imagined viewer or the public (you may recall that I made this point in Unit 1 with regard to Rembrandt's *Portrait of Agatha Bas*); on the other, the position the viewer comes to occupy is one the artist has done his utmost to explore and to define. In Rothko's case, the person he imagines as the ideal viewer is someone who will approach the painting with sympathy and treat it in the manner he conceives of it himself – *as if it were another person*. As quote B makes clear, he worries on his paintings' behalf that they will be made to suffer in the company of the 'vulgar' and the 'impotent'. That anxiety is still there in the background to quote H. The observer he desires for his painting is a 'sensitive observer', someone with both 'need' and 'spirit', who is 'free of the conventions of understanding' – in other words, open-minded and imaginative.

The need for open-mindedness in response to artistic activities was a matter of some specific importance at the time. During the late 1940s the right-wing senator Joseph McCarthy was pursuing a militant and highly publicized campaign against supposedly 'un-American' activities in all aspects of American cultural life. His ally, Congressman George Dondero, was busy 'exposing' the works of modern artists as evidence of infiltration by the forces of communism.

4   As already implied, the relationship Rothko has in mind is one of mutual respect. More than that, however, quote A speaks of a 'consummated experience' – a form of exchange in which the relationship between picture and viewer is brought to physical and emotional fulfilment. Made fifteen years later, the statement in quote H similarly specifies a transaction that is both intimate and

immediate. In quote E, from 1951, Rothko represents the painting as something by which the artist or spectator becomes absorbed, surrendering 'command' over it. *Number 12* of that year (Colour Plate 88) shows Rothko's work at its most colourful and seductive.

5   As Rothko represents it, then, the experience of the work is *like* being in the presence of another person, a person endowed with strong emotions and capable of facing up to both the best and the worst of human potential. For the viewer who comes to the encounter with an open mind, and with a capacity to acknowledge spiritual needs, the painting offers an intimate relationship leading to a form of consummation, and bringing an end to 'silence and solitude'. So, finally, when we ask what kind of place it was that Rothko thought he had made with his painting, the answer is that it was a place in which experience of this kind could occur – a place, in fact, that was established and controlled by the character of the work itself.

This last conclusion receives confirmation from a further document written by Rothko, in 1954, as guidance on the hanging of his work for an exhibition in Chicago. See Colour Plate 89 (*Untitled*) for a typical example of a work painted in that year.

> Since my pictures are large, colorful and unframed, and since museum walls are usually immense and formidable, there is the danger that the pictures relate themselves as decorative areas to the walls. This would be a distortion of their meaning, since the pictures are intimate and intense, and are the opposite of what is decorative [...] I have on occasion successfully dealt with this problem by tending to crowd the show rather than making it spare. By saturating the room with the feeling of the work, the walls are defeated and the poignancy of each single work had for me become more visible.
>
> (*Letter to Katharine Kuh, printed in* Mark Rothko, *1987, pp.58–9*)

What Rothko was proposing to instal in the Four Season restaurant, then, was a series of paintings that were 'the opposite of what is decorative', that were intended to 'defeat' the walls, and that would saturate the space with their own individual poignancy. Fischer records Rothko's interest in two specific interiors that he saw as connected to the feeling he aimed for in his own work. The first was the so-called House of the Mysteries in Pompeii, the Roman town near Naples that was buried in an earthquake and subsequently excavated (Figure 30.1). In the surviving wall paintings, Rothko reportedly found 'the same feeling, the same broad expanses of somber color' (quoted in Breslin, 1993, p.399) as he sought to achieve. The second was the staircase and vestibule of the Laurentian Library (or Medicean Library) in Florence, designed by the Italian artist Michelangelo in the early sixteenth century (Figure 30.2). Rothko had seen the Library on a trip to Europe in 1950 and acknowledged the blind windows and contained space of the vestibule as an unconscious influence in his work on the Seagram murals. On Fischer's account he expressed his admiration for Michelangelo's design.

FIGURE 30.1 *House of Mysteries, Pompeii. (Photograph: Fratelli Alinari)*

FIGURE 30.2 *Laurentian Library, Florence. (Photograph: Fratelli Alinari)*

'He achieved just the kind of feeling I'm after' (quoted in Breslin, 1993, p.400) – the feeling, as repeated by Breslin in the second paragraph of the chapter you read, of being 'trapped in a room where all the doors and windows are bricked up'. This, it seems, was also a feature of the 'place' that Rothko felt he had made.

The Four Seasons restaurant finally opened in July 1959, by which time Rothko had been at work on the commission for a year. Some time after this, probably in the spring of 1960, he visited the restaurant to dine with his wife. That night he called a friend to say that he was withdrawing from the commission and returning the money advanced to him ($7000 from a total budget of $30–35,000). By the next morning, according to the testimony of his studio assistant, he had resolved that 'Anybody who will eat that kind of food for those kinds of prices will never look at a painting of mine' (quoted in Breslin, 1993, p.406). Presumably he had realized that the diners at the Four Seasons could not be counted among those who were endowed with 'both need and spirit'.

How should we regard Rothko's action? As the consequence of his own naivety and lack of realism; the petulant gesture of an egomaniac who could not have his own destructive way in the staging of his work? Or as a form of resignation on the part of someone who had tried bravely to match his work against the actual conditions of the world, but who had inevitably failed in the face of overwhelming forces ranged against him; as a measure therefore forced on him by his responsibility towards his own work?

Perhaps the answer is that it was a mixture of both. Look back at the quotations given in the two opening paragraphs of Breslin's 'Parnassus on 53rd Street'. These are from a conversation related by Fischer which took place in the June of 1959, shortly before the Four Seasons restaurant opened. (It is recorded in full in an article published by Fischer in *Harper's Magazine* in July 1970.) If Fischer's testimony is to be trusted, Rothko had *already* identified the restaurant as a place where 'the richest bastards in New York will come to feed and show off', and had declared his 'malicious intentions ... to paint something that will ruin the appetite of every son of a bitch who ever eats in that room'. We should note that Fischer's article was not published until more than ten years after the recorded conversation and long after the breakdown of the commission had become public knowledge. This means that it is likely to have been coloured by hindsight. However, his testimony does receive strong support from a letter Rothko wrote to a painter friend as early as July 1958: 'What I like about the commission is that it has steamed up enough anger in me to imbue the pictures with unbearable bite, I hope' (letter to Robert Motherwell, quoted in Breslin, 1993, pp.376–7). Could Rothko really have expected to succeed in this intention *and* get paid?

On the other hand, there is also evidence that Rothko was excited by the commission, and that he took it as an opportunity to produce a sustained body of work of the kind he had long had in mind: work that would offer an intimate exchange to 'sensitive observers who are free of the conventions of understanding'. It seems that from the start his motives were mixed, and that they varied according to the audience he had in mind. While he may indeed have aimed to antagonize 'the richest bastards in New York', he also saw himself as working on behalf of those with 'need and spirit', and therefore as justified in pursuing any opportunity that would further his art.

6 A CONFLICT OF VALUES

One way to explain the issues we are considering is in terms of a conflict of expectations and values. We can assume that those who selected Rothko as the artist to decorate the Seagram restaurant must have had particular reasons for doing so, and definite ideas as to the likely value of the end result. For his part, Rothko seems to have accepted the commission because it provided him with the finance and the practical motivation to engage in a sustained project of work. But he would certainly have had to be very naive *not* to have had doubts about the suitability of his work for its intended venue. Representing what he was doing as an act of aggression was presumably his way of coping with these doubts while he pursued the work on his own terms. We have some idea by now of just what 'his own terms' were, although we shall need to return to the matter again in due course.

First, though, we should consider why it was that Rothko was chosen. To understand this we need to know a little more both about the Seagram Building and about the image that Rothko's painting had for those who selected it. (In the following account I draw upon background information given by Breslin (1993) in his chapter on the 'The Seagram Murals'.) The building itself was intended to serve as a prestigious headquarters for the Seagram corporation, a financial empire founded on the sale of whisky and run by the Canadian Samuel Bronfman. Within its thirty-nine floors there would also be ample space to rent out, thus providing the prospect of substantial return on the capital invested. At Park Avenue between 52nd and 53rd Streets it would occupy one of New York's prime sites. An explicitly modern design would help to purvey an image of economic vitality, of business confidence and of sophistication.

Accordingly, a budget of some $43 million was placed at the disposal of Mies van der Rohe, one of the most highly regarded architects of the European modern movement, the former director of the German Bauhaus, the school of design and architecture where many of the governing principles of that movement had been developed. His brief was to make the building the 'crowning glory' of his life. The advisers responsible for his selection were the American modernist architect Philip

Johnson, who was to act as his assistant, and Bronfman's daughter, Phyllis Lambert, who had spent time practising art in Paris. The result was a bronze and glass tower in the rigorously clean-lined style with which Mies van der Rohe had been associated since the 1920s. In the epigraph to his chapter on the Seagram murals, Breslin quotes a statement by the president of Joseph E. Seagram and Sons: 'This building is our greatest piece of advertising and public relations. It establishes us once and for all, right around the world, as people who are solid and care about quality' (Breslin, 1993, p.370).

The design for the Four Seasons restaurant was Johnson's responsibility (see Figures 30.3, 30.4 and 30.5). It is reached by a short marble staircase from the foyer. It was intended both to serve the needs of the building's prestige-conscious tenants and to attract others into what was indeed a massive advertisement for the Seagram corporation. It was clearly important that the decoration of such a facility should be consonant with the sophisticated modernist image of the building as a whole. What better, then, than to arrange a major commission from among the American Abstract Expressionists, whose work was now being hailed internationally as the latest development of the modern movement in painting? Both Lambert and Johnson were admirers of Rothko's work. The director of New York's Museum of Modern Art had also confirmed that he was 'the greatest living painter for this kind of project' (quoted in Breslin, 1993, p.373). Accordingly, a contract was arranged in which Rothko undertook to provide 500–600 square feet of painting to be used as wall decoration, the design to be entirely of his own choosing.

So far so good, one might think. But those responsible for the commission were labouring under two serious misapprehensions, one concerning the nature of abstract art in general, the other concerning Rothko's abstract art in particular. The first misapprehension lay in the association of abstract art with decoration. Lambert and Johnson seem to have felt that Rothko's works would make excellent decorations. Yet since the earliest experiments in abstract art, conducted in the second decade of the twentieth century, painters had needed to ensure that the works they produced were seen *not* simply as forms of decoration, but as having the kinds of content, significance and individuality that were traditionally associated with painting.

From the statements you have read it is clear that Rothko intended his abstract work to match the achievements of the old masters both in 'expressing the world' and in engaging the attention of the spectator. In the guidance on hanging he supplied for his exhibition in Chicago, he had written of 'the *danger* that the pictures relate themselves as decorative areas to the walls' (my emphasis). 'This would be a distortion of their meaning,' he added, 'since the pictures are intimate and intense, and are the opposite of what is decorative'. So far as he was concerned, then, to allow his paintings to serve as harmonious accompaniments to the style of the building as a whole would be to defeat the entire object

FIGURES 30.3
*View of the Four
Seasons restaurant.
Rothko's paintings
were intended for the
dining room at the far
right. (Photograph:
Ezra Stoller © ESTO)*

FIGURE 30.4　*View from the Rothko dining room into the large dining room. Three of the Rothko murals would
have hung over the doorways. (Photograph: Ezra Stoller © ESTO)*

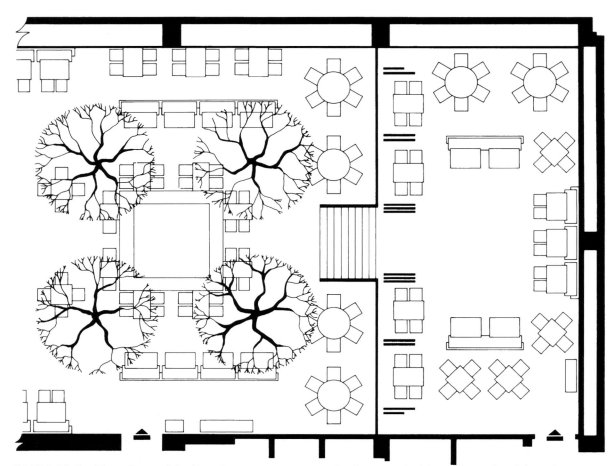

FIGURE 30.5   *Plan of part of the Four Seasons restaurant in the Seagram Building. Design by Philip Johnson, 1959. From Mark Rothko, exhibition catalogue, Tate Gallery, 1987, p.61*

of his art – which was to have his paintings assert themselves as intimate and intense *individuals*. It would be like having them treated as the visual equivalents of canned music.

The second misapprehension concerns the specific image of Rothko's work that presumably led to his selection.

EXERCISE

Look at Colour Plates 71–80 (Seagram murals) and 87–89 (*Number 18*; *Number 12*; *Untitled*), noting the dates of the works illustrated. What difference do you notice between the works painted before 1958 and those painted in 1958–9?

DISCUSSION

The answer I have in mind is that until 1958 Rothko's work was for the most part brightly coloured. In the works done in connection with the Seagram project, however, although the shapes remain broadly similar, the tones and colours are generally darker and more muted and the contrasts between different areas are on the whole less marked.

Rightly or wrongly, and all other things being equal, we tend to see brighter colours as more cheerful, and deeper and darker colours as more sombre and serious. Those who arranged the commission for the Four Seasons restaurant may have thought that the result would be a series of expensively tasteful decorative panels, which would nevertheless be relatively colourful and 'up-beat' in effect, thus fitting in nicely with the glass and chinaware, the lighting, the uniforms, the menus and the plants, on each of which a different specialist designer was set to work. But the paintings Rothko produced in connection with the commission were designed to relate only to each other and to the 'sensitive observer'. The 'place' he was working for was one that would be saturated with the 'feeling' of these paintings. And the 'feeling' in question was apparently one intended to ruin the appetites of the wealthy diners.

It is here that we need to consider further the implications of Rothko's working 'on his own terms'. The point at issue is how we regard his motivation. Of course, we cannot know what was in his mind. But we can form a considered assessment of the factors he is likely to have had to take into account, and of the attitudes he is likely to have had towards them.

EXERCISE

So, which of the following do you think more probable?

Did he:

1   embark on a series of sombre paintings as a consequence of his 'malicious intentions', consciously aiming from the start to produce something that would have to be rejected, with the hidden agenda, perhaps, of demonstrating his independence from financial considerations and thus his 'purity' as an artist;

or, notwithstanding his bravado statement to Fischer, did he:

2   accept the commission in good faith, but find, as he worked on the project in his studio – a studio arranged to provide a form of mock-up of the restaurant, complete with high ceiling and subdued lighting – that the only way he could make the paintings work together as a group was to concentrate upon a range of warm and muted tones?

Did he, perhaps, become increasingly absorbed by the technical problems and possibilities of the project, increasingly engaged by the mood of gravity and solemnity that seemed to emerge among the paintings both individually and as a whole, until he found himself in the end so far from the spirit of the commission that there was no turning back?

DISCUSSION

What is at stake here is not *only* the way we explain Rothko's motivation, but also the more general question of how we conceive the relationship between artistic priorities and values on the one hand, and those economic or utilitarian considerations by which public life is on the whole governed on the other.

To adopt the first option as our viewpoint is to see the artist as wilfully opposed to 'financial considerations' and as directing his art accordingly. The implication is that in judging the work we place ourselves on one side or the other of an unbridgeable divide: either with the idealistic artist in his attack on materialistic values, or with realistic critics of his enterprise who testify to the inescapable nature of financial considerations. The artist becomes accordingly either the heroic or the pathetic agent of his own fate.

To adopt the second option, however, is to see the artist as working within a context shaped *both* by the economic considerations that directed the commission in the first place *and* by the technical problems and possibilities that led his art away from any suitable end result, and as not necessarily in full control of either. We thus look at a wider picture than we do from the first viewpoint. On the one hand, we can acknowledge the effect of certain broad social and economic tendencies, such as those that led to the construction of the Seagram Building as an aggressive demonstration of market power. From this perspective, we can view the commission for the murals as an early indication that the kind of cultural experimentalism we observe in the Sixties rests – however uneasily – on a firm base of economic expansion. Wealth may not define the forms of art, but it does tend to encourage their development. On the other hand, we can observe that the practice of art develops to a certain extent according to interests and demands that are internal to that practice. What satisfies those interests and demands – what 'works' from the artist's point of view – may not always be consistent with the needs or aims of those who are economically empowered to act as patrons. It may not even be consonant with the artist's own original intentions – which is one reason why we should always be very cautious about accepting the declared intentions of artists as keys to the interpretation of their works.

We can derive an important generalization from this specific case. The practice of art is an activity pursued in the face of the changing conditions of social and economic life. These conditions have a powerful influence in deciding the nature of opportunity and demand for the artist's work. They may also play a part in defining its subject-matter. But to call a practice a practice of *art* is also to imply that other demands are made of it, or are made, as it were, *within* it: the demand, for instance, that it should invite comparison – in the eyes of its maker first and foremost – with other works of art produced under other conditions, by other people, even in other cultures. This is what is meant by saying that the value of works of art is an autonomous value – literally, conforming to the laws and standards of art itself, and not, for instance, to criteria of use value, of topical relevance, of political correctness or of moral rectitude.

This is not, however, to say that artists are people who are somehow detached from their own time and place. Rothko himself put the matter succinctly in response to a questioner at the Pratt Institute who had asked him whether he was a Zen Buddhist: 'I am not. I am not interested in any civilization except this one. The whole problem in art is how to establish human values in this specific civilization' (transcript in the Mark Rothko Archive, quoted in Breslin, 1993, p.394). What he did not say on this occasion, but clearly believed, is that while the typical artist is committed to 'this specific civilization' as a *place of work*, 'human values' may sometimes have to be discovered or rediscovered by looking *outside* the immediate confines of that civilization and its 'conventions of understanding' – whether it be to Greek tragedy, to Roman wall painting, to Italian Renaissance architecture or to Rembrandt's portraits.

7 HIGH ART AND ABSTRACT ART

Given our interest in the idea of counter-cultures and their growth in 'the long Sixties', we are faced with an interesting problem by Rothko's work, and by his 'malicious intentions'. There could hardly be a more clearly 'mainstream' form of culture or a higher 'high art' than one that grounds its values in Greek tragedy, in Roman painting, in Renaissance architecture and in the painting of Rembrandt. I would like you, though, to turn back now to the list of characteristics of the 'counter-culture' given in Section 2 of Unit 28 (p.123).

EXERCISE

How many of these characteristics could you associate with Rothko and his work?

DISCUSSION

I would say all or any of them. The lesson seems to be that what we have so far taken as the identifying components of counter-cultures are clearly present in the work of at least one artist whose ambition it was to measure up to the most prestigious art of the past.

We need to be careful, it seems, both about the values by which we define 'culture' and about those we identify as 'counter'. Rothko may have felt himself to be in some ways an outsider, and his art may be difficult and 'modern' in comparison with the kind of traditional academic art that might be shown in a Royal Academy Summer Exhibition, but modern art itself can claim a strong tradition stretching back well into the nineteenth century. It would be quite uncontroversial nowadays to describe Rothko's art as a late contribution to the modern mainstream.

I would like now to consider David Sylvester's short essay 'Rothko' (*Resource Book 4*, E2), in which the painter's work is set in relation both to the work of other modern artists and to other major artefacts from the broad sphere of Western culture. It is one of the few essays on his work that we know the painter himself was happy with. It was first published in 1961, not long after all work on the Seagram project had been abandoned, and it was occasioned by the first substantial British showing of Rothko's work, staged at the Whitechapel Gallery in East London. Remember the three types of publication listed in Section 4. In contrast to the text you read by Breslin, Sylvester's short essay makes no attempt to provide any biographical information about Rothko. This is a brief critical monograph.

EXERCISE

I would like you to read the essay straight through once. As you do so, compare the style of writing with Breslin's. In particular, you might like to compare the ways in which the two texts open and close. When you have completed your reading of Sylvester's essay, note briefly what you think he is trying to achieve by it. Following a brief discussion, I shall provide a commentary on some of the references and will then ask you to read the essay again.

DISCUSSION

The style of the two texts is clearly very different. Breslin aims to engage us immediately with an image of the artist at work. His manner is that of the practised story-teller, treating his subject with a kind of half-fascinated, half-detached curiosity. As we observed earlier, he uses dramatic quotation from the outset to interest us in Rothko's personal motivation, and he creates a vivid setting in the dark and cavernous studio. As we have also noted, the conclusion to this opening chapter acts as a kind of trailer for what is to be a lengthy biographical narrative.

Sylvester, on the other hand, places his reader squarely before the actual paintings. He is concerned above all to explore and to describe the experience they produce, and he uses some relatively high-flown language in which to do so. In his conclusion he returns to the works, noting how sensitive they are to the conditions of their display, in the process apparently confirming Rothko's own views on the matter.

There are two points that the texts have in common. They both emphasize the tendency of Rothko's work to make the viewer feel 'hemmed-in' or 'trapped'. And they both represent the artist as a man strangely driven by the pursuit of his art. In Sylvester's one statement about the personality of the artist he refers to him as a 'monomaniac' (a person obsessed by a single interest or idea).

As to the aim of Sylvester's essay, I would say that his main concern is to communicate a sense of the seriousness and the *worth* of Rothko's art. In order to do so, he has to engage in the art critic's most demanding and most crucial task: finding words to represent an experience that takes place, by definition, at the limits of language. (The same task faces the present author in TV30.) The high-flown language is used to persuade us of the gravity of the art. Sylvester's principal tool is the use of analogy: on the one hand, with physical sensation – it is '*as if* ...' we were borne down and then carried away – on the other, with the 'awe-inspiring' Gothic cathedral of Chartres. Note, however, that he is contemptuous of attempts to find pictures in Rothko's paintings.

Sylvester mentions a number of other artists. The first is the Dutch painter Vincent Van Gogh, who wrote to his brother in 1888 that he had been working on a picture of an all-night café, in which he aimed 'to express the terrible passions of humanity by means of red and green' (Roskill, 1963, p.288). This may seem a strange notion, but Van Gogh was working at a time when many painters were interested in the idea that colour had an innate power to express emotion and mood. What he envisaged was that a painting based largely on the contrasting colours red and green might produce a sense of suppressed psychological desperation without his having actually to depict any agonized facial expressions or desperate actions. The resulting painting is shown in Colour Plate 90 (Van Gogh, *The Night Café, Arles*), which you should refer to now.

In this case there are, of course, many other features than the colour that serve to create a sense of atmosphere and mood. We might think of the scene Van Gogh has painted as like a stage set within which a certain kind of drama is to be played out. The relevant question, I think, is what kind of drama we imagine this to be, and why. Could we say that the colour *of itself* creates a sense of the imminence or even the suppression of some passionate outburst? This is not an easy question to answer. The main problem is that once we know about Van Gogh's intentions our response to his picture is already strongly conditioned, and we cannot therefore use that response as a 'blind' test of what the picture expresses. And anyway, how are we to separate the effect of the colour from the impression made on our imagination by those objects and surfaces that are shown as coloured?

Such questions came to seem particularly interesting and important to certain artists around the end of the nineteenth century and at the beginning of the twentieth. These artists were fascinated by the idea of painting as a medium that might *not* have to rely on the kinds of association that depicted objects provide, that might leave the already familiar sights and scenes behind, and that might be made to convey emotion spontaneously and directly, as music was felt to do. They began, in other words, to conceive that art might become abstract without losing its crucial function in conveying meaning and emotion – that an abstract art might even convey meaning and emotion in a somehow more direct or more 'pure' manner for being the less easy to pin down with familiar associations and names. It was a part of their thinking that a *modern* art should not have to rely upon that which was already familiar. The idea of an abstract art thus involved a critical attitude towards conservatism in culture.

The second painter Sylvester mentions, Piet Mondrian, was also Dutch, although he worked for much of his life in Paris and ended his career in New York, where he died in 1944. During the second decade of the twentieth century he was one of the pioneers of abstract art. Colour Plate 91 (*Composition in Yellow, Blue and White I*) shows a work of his from 1937. For the modern American painters of Rothko's generation such works were fully deserving of comparison with the works of the old masters. By the time Rothko himself began painting abstract pictures, around 1945, it had come to seem to many artists that the real challenge was no longer to produce convincing pictures of reality. On the contrary, it was to find the means to establish some sense of value *outside* those 'conventions of understanding' by which 'reality' was normally defined. In a statement published in 1947 Rothko wrote, 'The familiar identity of things has to be pulverized in order to destroy the finite associations with which our society increasingly enshrouds every aspect of our environment' (see Harrison and Wood, 1992, p.564). If anything that could be pictured thus became hostage to prevailing social values, then perhaps the only way to maintain the freedom of painting was to ensure that *nothing* could be seen in it.

Sylvester refers to a distinction between Apollonian and Dionysian forms of art, as employed by the German philosopher Friedrich Nietzsche. Apollo was the Greek god of music and poetry, Dionysus the god of wine. Nietzsche used the terms to distinguish two broad tendencies in the arts in general: the controlled, rational and harmonious he associated with Apollo, the expressive and frenzied with Dionysus. Sylvester suggests that the reconciliation of these two tendencies occurs in tragic art – such as he believes Rothko's to be. He is thus locating Rothko's work not simply in a distinguished modern tradition, alongside that of such figures as Van Gogh and Mondrian. He is comparing the gravity of that work to the art of tragedy, traditionally the highest of high genres among all the Western arts.

I suggest that you now reread Sylvester's essay, bearing the above points in mind. You will get the most from your reading if you manage to strike a balance between two contrasting attitudes: on the one hand, try to imagine looking at Rothko's art through Sylvester's eyes, treating it as seriously as he means that you should; on the other, try to stand back from the prose, noting the devices used to persuade you into a form of respect for the art.

Before we leave Sylvester, there is one further connection we might add to those that he makes. You may recall from your study of Block 3 that the Neoclassical art of David was seen in later eighteenth-century France as distinguished by the formal purity of its style and by the moral strenuousness of its themes. Sylvester argues for the virtues of Rothko's art in very similar terms. Criticism such as his rests on a long-standing convention by which art is esteemed according to its autonomy – the distinctness of its values from those of the everyday, the utilitarian and the economic. This sense of opposition between the values of art and those of political economy has been a characteristic feature of theories of art in the wider modern period. It is clear that Rothko saw his own art as oppositional in this sense.

But the culture of the period *since* the 1960s has been widely characterized as *post*modern. There are those who would say the insistence on art's dissident character is inappropriate to the culture of the present. Could it be said that high art such as Rothko's represents the end of a 'modernist' era, in which artistic value and monetary value were at odds, and that more than a mere generation separates his work from Warhol's? Rather than trying to answer this question, I will offer a final comparison to suggest how the divide might be understood.

Rothko's acceptance and subsequent abandonment of the Seagram commission has served to demonstrate his difficulties in reconciling economic considerations with artistic values. Look again at Colour Plate 76 to remind yourself of the works at issue. Just three years after this painting was made, Warhol produced several silkscreen paintings of dollar bills. One of these is illustrated in Plate 183 (*Eighty Two-Dollar Bills, Front and Rear*). In an early book on the Pop Art movement, it was recounted that Warhol made these works on the advice of an art dealer: 'When she asked him what was the most important thing in his life, his

answer was, "Money". "Well, then", she reputedly advised, "paint it!" '
(Amaya, 1965, p.104).

What is of interest in this story is not so much the question of whether or
not it is true, as the fact that it was cited with evident approval and
fascination by a commentator who saw Warhol as 'the new movement's
perfect exponent' (Amaya, 1965, p.103). In an interview in 1967 Warhol
himself advised those in search of interpretation, 'Just look at the surface
of my paintings and films and me, and there I am. There's nothing
behind it' (Crone, 1970, p.23). My aim in presenting this comparison is
not to disparage Warhol, but rather to make clear how wide a gap
separates these two paintings made within the same city a mere three
years apart.

8 MODERN ART AND POPULAR CULTURE

As you will have gathered from the history units, just how we establish
the limits of any historical period will depend upon the perspective we
take and the kinds of evidence we survey. With hindsight, it does seem
that the priorities of art criticism and art history changed significantly
during the 1960s. By the later 1970s, writing in the manner of Sylvester's
essay on Rothko already seemed to have a distinct period flavour.
Viewed in negative terms, the success of Pop Art could be seen as
marking the adjustment of art to the world of mass consumership, and
thus the final abandonment or defeat of the idea that art serves as an
independent repository of critical human values or as the occasion for
spiritual forms of experience. Certainly Rothko himself felt that a world in
which Warhol's work could be taken seriously was not one in which his
own painting was likely to receive the kind of attention it required. The
feeling that the tide of his culture had turned against him may even have
been a factor contributing to his suicide.

Yet there is a more positive way in which Warhol's art might be regarded.
As we have already seen, it is explicitly engaged with its moment and its
surrounding culture. And for all the apparent casualness with which the
artist selected and processed his subjects, it appears that the resulting
images do acquire a certain poignant permanence through their status as
paintings. This achievement seems all the more surprising for the fact that
the images in question are all 'unoriginal' in the sense that they are
derived from photographic or printed sources. As discussed earlier,
Warhol's world is the world of the already represented, the already
processed – the world, in fact, of 'the media'.

Therein lies both the modernity of his art and the possible basis of its
wide appeal. It would certainly be useless to argue that art such as

Rothko's is widely popular, or even that it was intended to be. Perhaps the uniqueness of Warhol's contribution lay precisely in his apparent unwillingness to discriminate, whether between high art and popular art, between élite culture and mass culture, between mainstream and counter-culture, between 'straight' people and 'bent' people, or between the aesthetic and the economic. Represented in this fashion, he might just be made to look like the avant-garde representative of a truly liberal, postmodern culture.

This is a tempting conclusion, but I cannot resist giving Rothko a last word. Warhol's art does seem eminently suited to a culture in which the attention-span is always limited. At its best it achieves considerable complexity of effect under those conditions. But there is still much to be said for an art that reminds us, as I believe Rothko's does, just how much it can mean either to be or to discover the deserving object of an *undivided* attention.

REFERENCES

AMAYA, M. (1965) *Pop as Art: A Survey of the New Super Realism*, London, Studio Vista.

BRESLIN, J.E.B. (1993) *Mark Rothko: A Biography*, University of Chicago Press.

CRONE, R. (1970) *Andy Warhol*, London, Thames & Hudson.

FISCHER, J.H. (1970) 'The Easy Chair: Mark Rothko: portrait of the artist as an angry man', *Harper's Magazine*, vol.241, no.1442, July, pp.16–23.

HARRISON, C. and WOOD, P. (eds) (1992) *Art in Theory 1900–1990: An Anthology of Changing Ideas*, Oxford, Blackwell.

ROSKILL, M. (ed.) (1963) *The Letters of Vincent Van Gogh*, London, Letter to Theo, Arles, 8 September 1888.

Mark Rothko (1987) exhibition catalogue, London, Tate Gallery.

INDEX TO BLOCK 6

This index includes references to the Colour Plates and Plates in the *Illustration Book*; these are indicated by 'CPl' for Colour Plates and 'Pl' for Plates.

AN INTRODUCTION TO THE HUMANITIES